W9-BNO-532

HOW THE QUEEN CLEANS EVERYTHING!

PLEASE NOTE: I hope these tips provide the answers to many of your household problems. However, total success cannot be guaranteed in every case. Care and caution should be exercised when using chemicals, products, and formulas presented in this book. All cleaning treatments should be tested prior to application, in an inconspicuous place. This is highly recommended and strongly encouraged. Please read and follow all information contained on product labels with care. Linda Cobb, The Win Holden Company, and Pocket Books hereby disclaim any liability and damages from the use and/or misuse of any product, formula, or application presented in this book.

You too can clean like a Queen!

ALSO BY LINDA COBB

Talking Dirty with the Queen of Clean®
Talking Dirty Laundry with the Queen of Clean®
The Royal Guide to Spot and Stain Removal
A Queen for All Seasons
The Queen of Clean® Conquers Clutter

HOW THE QUEEN CLEANS EVERYTHING!

HANDY ADVICE FOR
A CLEAN HOUSE, CLEANER LAUNDRY,
AND A YEAR OF TIMELY TIPS

LINDA COBB

ATRIA BOOKS
New York London Toronto Sydney

1230 Avenue of the Americas
New York, NY 10020

Published by arrangement with The Win Holden Company

This edition produced exclusively for Barnes & Noble by Simon & Schuster, Inc.

ISBN-13: 978-0-7432-9182-8
ISBN-10: 0-7432-9182-4

This Atria Books hardcover edition February 2006

10 9 8 7 6 5 4 3 2 1

Designed by Jaime Putorti

Manufactured in the United States of America

These titles were previously published individually by Pocket Books

For information regarding special discounts for bulk purchases,
please contact Simon & Schuster Special Sales at 1-800-456-6798
or business@simonandschuster.com

WITH THANKS

This book is dedicated to my friends and fans in Arizona where it all started. You made me the Queen of Clean and I will never forget you. My gratitude to everyone at KTVK-TV's *Good Morning Arizona,* and to Beth and Bill at KESZ 99.9 FM in Phoenix, Arizona. Because of all of you it's still good to be Queen!

Judith Curr, Publisher, Atria Books, who guided this project from its inception.

Brenda Copeland. You can't be a bestselling author without the very best editor. One who knows how to find more in you when you think you're empty, and pushes all the right buttons.

Everyone at Atria who worked so tirelessly on this book.

Marty Velasco Hames, KTVK-TV. If I had a daughter, I would hope that she would be as wonderful a person, friend, wife, and mother as Marty. You are the best, Marty, and I value your friendship.

Beth Deveny for all her assistance through the years.

Preston and Eleanor Coon. Friends beyond compare!

To the people who keep me looking like a Queen—it's not easy, you know. Karen Hall, Judy K. (Jake) Drennen, Kathy Lockwood, and Jennifer Kimbel.

To all the wonderful people we have met along the way.

To my family. With you, I know all things are possible.

Contents

Part Four: Let's Take It Outside

Part Five: And You Thought I Forgot . . .

Introduction

It's good to be Queen! I get to travel around the country meeting all sorts of fascinating people and their equally fascinating cleaning problems. It's amazing what you can find out about a country from its cleaning and laundry troubles. I've seen it all: from carpet stains to laundry pains, from messy shoes to washday blues . . . and just about everything in between. You know, sometimes, after I've been on the road for a while, it seems to me that USA actually stands for United *Stains* of America!

One way or another I've been at this Queen business a long time. I used to own a cleaning and disaster-restoration service in Michigan. And, boy, did we see some tough problems. That's where I really became a cleaning expert. When property is damaged in a flood or a fire, you really have only two ways out—restore it or ruin it. I tried to restore most everything, and I tried hard. Sometimes—many times—I fixed things. Other times, I had to throw the item out. That was tough. But I learned something each time, and each time I got a little better at figuring out what works. I earned my cleaning crown through trial and error. But you don't have to—you have me!

Now don't get the wrong idea. I may love to talk about housework, but I hate to do it. That's why my approach to cleaning is practical and easy. I like to do things the sensible way, and I like to keep things simple. I follow a no-nonsense "tips and hints" method of housekeeping that stresses convenience and results. I also try to offer something for everyone. So whether you're a cleaning diva or you failed your home economics class, whether you're a Felix Unger or an Oscar Madison, rest assured: you've come to the right place. Expediency is my goal. Get the job done so that you can get back to your life. But get the job done well.

Look around your home. You probably have manuals for all sorts of things: appliances, electronics, gardening, do-it-yourself repairs. The list could go on and on. You might even have the operating instructions for that old eight-track player! (Disco anyone?) But do you have a manual for keeping your palace sparkling clean? Well, now you do! Look no further than *How the Queen Cleans Everything* for all those miraculous cleaning tips and surprising shortcuts to solve hundreds of cleaning challenges in every room. Learn the best way to clean your kitchen and bathroom, how to clean your carpet and bare floors, how to control odor, tame dust bunnies . . . even how to keep your backyard deck safe, sound, and looking its best. And let's not forget the most important thing—have fun doing it!

How the Queen Cleans Everything is my answer to all of you who have asked for my tips in one big "everything you need to know" hardcover. So here it is, a compendium of three of my bestselling books, *Talking Dirty with the Queen of Clean®*, *Talking Dirty Laundry with the Queen of Clean®*, and *A Queen for All Seasons*—with some extra tips and other fun stuff thrown in for good measure. It's the indispensable big book for people who want a clean house and a full life, for people who don't have a great deal of time for housework, but want to see results nonetheless.

Enjoy! And if you need to clean this book, just wipe it down with a damp cloth and a little bit of your favorite soap!

Linda Cobb

Let's Clean House

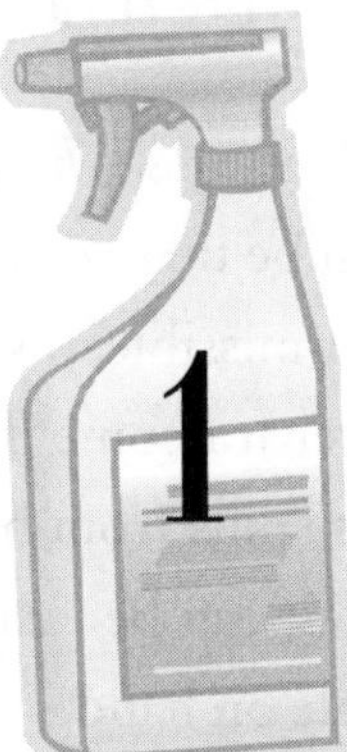

1
Stain Removers That Are Hiding in Your Cupboard

You may not know this, but some of the very best spot and stain removers are things you use every single day! Not only do these stain removers work great—they're right at your fingertips!

Alcohol: Rubbing alcohol is great for grass stains and so much more.

Ammonia: The perspiration stain fighter.

Automatic dishwasher detergent: Keep this on hand as a bleach substitute and whitener/brightener even if you *don't* have a dishwasher. Liquid, powder, and tablet form all work well. If you choose the tablet, make sure it has dissolved before you add clothes. Pour directly on stain, or soak.

Baking soda: Removes odors.

Club soda: My favorite *Oh my gosh, how did I do that?* spotter. Use it on any fabric or surface that can be treated with water. A slight dabbing on dry-clean-only fabrics is also permissible, just be sure to test first! Use club soda on any spill—ask the waiter for some if you're dining out—dab it on and blot it off. Club soda keeps spills from becoming stains and brings the offending spill to the surface so it can be easily removed. It's totally safe. I always make sure to have a bottle on hand.

Cream of tartar: I bet you have some of this in the kitchen cupboard, but how often do you use it? Well, here's your chance. Mix cream of tartar with lemon juice and you have a wonderful bleach for white clothes spotted with food or other stains. It's even effective on many rust stains.

Denture-cleaning tablets: The cure-all for white table linens with food stains and white cotton with stains. Dissolve one tablet per ½ cup water. Pour directly on stain or spot.

Dishwashing liquid: A wonderful spotter, used undiluted on tough stains.

Glycerin: You can remove tar, tree sap (think Christmas tree), juice stains, mustard, ketchup and barbecue sauce.

GOJO Crème Waterless Hand Cleaner®: Totally awesome for removing grease and oil, including shoe polish.

Hydrogen peroxide: 3 percent hydrogen peroxide is super for removing blood stains, especially if they are fairly fresh. It also is a wonderful bleaching agent for stubborn stains on white clothes. Combine ½ cup of hydrogen peroxide and 1 teaspoon of ammonia for an unbeatable stain removal combination. Make sure to use 3 percent and *not* the kind you use to bleach your hair!

Lemon juice: This is nature's bleach and disinfectant. I don't know where we'd be without it. If you have spots on white clothes, apply some lemon juice and lay them in the sun. Apply a little more lemon juice prior to laundering, or prespray and launder as usual. This is really effective on baby formula stains.

Meat tenderizer: A combo of meat tenderizer (unseasoned, please, or you'll have a whole new stain!) and cold water is just the answer to protein-based stains such as blood, milk, etc.

Salt: Sprinkling salt on spilled red wine will keep the wine from staining until you can launder it. Mixed with lemon juice, salt will remove mildew stains.

Shampoo: Any brand will do. Cheap is fine. I save the small bottles from hotel/motel stays and keep them in the laundry room. Great for treating ring-around-the-collar, mud and cosmetic stains.

Shave cream: That innocent-looking can of shave cream in your bathroom is one of the best spot and stain removers available. That's because it's really whipped soap! If you have a spill on your clothes (or even your carpet), moisten the spot, work in some shave cream, and then flush it with cool water. If the offending spot is on something you're wearing, work the shave cream in and then use a clean cloth (a washcloth works fine) to blot the shave cream and the spot away. A quick touch of the blow-dryer to prevent a ring and you're on your way. The best thing about shave cream is that even if it doesn't work it won't set the stain, so the spot can still be removed later. Keep a small sample can in your suitcase when you travel. It's saved me more than once!

WD-40® Lubricant: Check out your garage or the "fix-it" cupboard. If you don't have any, pick up a can the next time you're at the hardware store or home center. Why? Because we've all had those nasty grease stains and oil stains on clothes: salad dressing misses the salad and gets the blouse, or grease splatters when you are cooking—or crayon/lipstick/Chap Stick® gets on your clothes! WD-40® is your answer. Spray some on, wait 10 minutes, then work in undiluted liquid dishwashing soap and launder as usual. Works well on everything *except* silk!

White vinegar: A great spotter for suede—used undiluted. It's also a wonderful fabric softener. Just put ¼ cup white vinegar in the final rinse. (And no, you won't smell like a salad!)

It's worthwhile to keep these things on hand. As you can see, most are inexpensive and have other uses. They'll make you the cleaning Queen—or King!—in your home.

"God created company so that the house would get cleaned."

—Rita Emmett

2 Cleaning Products You Should Never Be Without

There are five cleaning products you should never be without, and most of them are things you already have in your home. You can purchase generous-size containers of all of them for a total of $10 and they will last for months. They can be used alone, together or in conjunction with other common household products such as salt or dishwashing liquid to help you handle most of the cleaning problems in your home. They are especially good for people with allergies and those of us who want to cut back on the chemicals in our homes.

Now we'll take them in order and talk about their many uses.

Here's Your
Shopping List

White Vinegar
Baking Soda
Lemon Juice
Club Soda
Spot Shot Instant Carpet
Stain Remover®

White Vinegar

Use white vinegar to remove heavy soap scum and mineral deposits from showers, tubs and sinks. Warm the vinegar and put in a spray bottle. Spray on showers, tubs and sinks and let soak for 10 to 15 minutes. Then use a nylon scrubbing sponge to remove scum. Respray if necessary. To remove mineral deposits from around drains, close drain and pour in enough white vinegar to cover the drain area. Let soak overnight, scrub with a nylon scrubbing sponge, drain vinegar and rinse.

To remove scum and mineral buildup from shower heads and keep them free-flowing, put undiluted white vinegar in a plastic bag. Tie around the shower head overnight. Scrub head and poke any loosened mineral deposits with a toothpick, rinse and enjoy your next shower.

To remove soap scum and mildew from plastic shower curtains and liners, fill the washing machine with warm water, 1 cup of white vinegar and your regular laundry detergent. Add the curtains, along with several old, light-colored towels. Run through complete cycle and rehang curtain immediately.

Add 2 to 3 tablespoons white vinegar to hot water along with your regular dishwashing liquid to cut grease on dishes and crystal.

Add ¼ cup of white vinegar to the washing machine during the final rinse to soften clothes and remove lint from dark clothes.

Apply, undiluted, to the skin with a cotton ball to deter bugs—they hate the way you taste, but the odor disappears immediately from your skin.

Neutralize pet urine odor with diluted white vinegar (25 percent vinegar to 75 percent water) sprayed on carpets. Always test in an inconspicuous spot before treating a large area.

Clean stainless steel sinks with a paste of baking soda and vinegar. Don't let the foaming scare you—it works great!

Make a window cleaner in a spray bottle with ¼ cup white vinegar added to 1 quart of water.

Make air freshener in a spray bottle with 1 teaspoon of baking soda, 1 tablespoon of white vinegar and 2 cups of water. After the foaming stops, put on lid. Shake before using.

Clean vinyl floors with ½ cup white vinegar to 1 gallon of warm water.

Keep drains free-flowing with ½ cup baking soda and ½ cup white vinegar poured down the drain on a monthly basis. After pouring in baking soda and vinegar, cover the drain for 15 minutes (it will foam). Then flush with cold water.

Clean mirrors with a solution of half vinegar and half water. Wet a sponge, soft cloth or paper towel, wash and then buff dry. Never spray water onto a mirror. Moisture that gets into the edges and behind mirrors ruins the silvering on the mirror, resulting in dark spots.

Spray vinegar on the underarms of clothes and let soak 15 to 30 minutes to deodorize and minimize underarm stains.

Make an excellent toilet cleaner with 1 cup borax and 1 cup vinegar. Pour the vinegar over the stained area of the toilet, then sprinkle the borax over the vinegar. Soak for 2 hours and then brush and flush.

Baking Soda

Baking soda is a great deodorizer, cleaner and mild abrasive. Use as you would a soft-scrubbing product or cleanser in tubs and sinks.

Keep food disposals fresh and free-flowing by putting the stopper in the disposal and adding 3 inches of warm water and a handful of baking soda. Turn on the disposal and let water run out.

Remove perspiration stains and odor from clothing by applying a paste of baking soda and water and letting it soak 30 minutes prior to laundering.

Mix 1 gallon of warm water and ¼ cup of baking soda. Soak freshly washed socks in this for 30 minutes. Spin out in the washer (do not rinse out the solution), dry and you will have odor-eater socks.

Clean smudges on wallpaper with baking soda and water.

Remove crayon from hard surfaces with baking soda on a damp rag.

Use on any hard surface as a mild abrasive to remove stains.

Use as a bug killer for aphids. Use 1½ teaspoons of baking soda per pint of water and apply every 7 days.

To clean grout (any color), mix 3 cups of baking soda with 1 cup of warm water. Scrub grout with a brush and rinse.

Use baking soda on a damp cloth to polish silver.

To remove burnt food in casseroles, fill dish with hot water and add 1 tablespoon of baking soda and allow to soak.

To clean up pet vomit, sprinkle on a heavy coating of baking soda. Let it absorb moisture and dry, then scoop or vacuum up. The baking soda will neutralize acids and help prevent stains. Follow with Spot Shot Instant Carpet Stain Remover®.

Remove heel marks from hard floors with a damp cloth and baking soda.

Clean screen stains and mineral deposits off windows by dipping a soft, wet cloth in baking soda and rubbing gently. Follow by washing windows as usual.

Remove streaks and greasy film from car windshields with a thin paste of baking soda and water. Rinse well.

Put in the bottom of cat litter boxes to help eliminate odor. Put in a thin layer of baking soda and then add the litter as usual. This works with clay or clumping varieties.

Lemon Juice

Lemon juice is nature's bleach and disinfectant.

Apply to clothes, undiluted, to remove fruit-based stains. Let soak 30 minutes and then launder.

Remove rust from clothes by applying undiluted lemon juice and laying the garment in the sun. It disappears like magic.

Bleach spots off Formica™ counters by using straight or mixing in a paste with baking soda.

Clean brass and copper with lemon juice and salt. Sprinkle salt on a half-lemon and rub metal, then rinse thoroughly. If you don't have fresh lemons, you can also mix bottled lemon juice and salt.

Make a cleaner in a spray bottle with 2 cups of water, 2 tablespoons of lemon juice, ½ teaspoon of liquid dish soap, 1 tablespoon of baking soda and 1 teaspoon of borax. Shake before using to clean any hard surface.

Apply lemon juice to chrome and buff to a shine.

As a bleach alternative, use ¼ cup of lemon juice and ¼ cup of white vinegar mixed in 1 gallon of warm water and soak clothes for 15 minutes prior to washing.

Remove stains from hands with lemon juice.

Bleach wooden breadboards by applying lemon juice and letting it sit overnight. Wash and rinse in the morning.

Club Soda

Club soda is the best emergency spotter there is. Keep club soda on hand to clean up spills on carpet and clothing. Remember to react as soon as possible to a spill. If you act fast, a spot shouldn't become a stain. Club soda will remove red wine, coffee, tea, pop (yes, even red pop!), Kool-Aid™ and any other spills you can think of. Lift any solids carefully off carpet or clothes and then pour on the club soda, blotting with an old rag until all the color from the spill is removed. Don't be afraid to really wet the carpet, it won't hurt it—carpet goes through countless dippings in water as it is made. Blot carpet easily by folding a rag and standing on it, turning the rag as it absorbs moisture and discoloration from the spill. The carbonation in the club soda brings the offending spill to the surface so that you can blot it up, and the salts in it will help prevent staining.

If you spill on your clothes in a restaurant, ask for a little club soda or seltzer and use your napkin to blot the stain until it is removed. At home, you can pour the club soda directly onto the spot, flushing it out.

I have found that club soda will even work on many old stains, too. Always keep several bottles on hand.

Spot Shot Instant Carpet Stain Remover®

Every home needs a good all-purpose carpet stain remover. Skip the kinds that foam, dry and you vacuum up; they leave residue in the carpet that attracts dirt. Spot Shot Instant Carpet Stain Remover® has never failed me in years of cleaning. It effectively removes water- and oil-based stains. Use it on pet stains, lipstick, makeup, hair dye, food spills, mystery spots—even old spots. Follow the label directions and you will be amazed at how well it works. It's inexpensive and available at grocery stores, Target, Wal-Mart™ and hardware stores. Make sure you have a can on hand for emergencies. It works great in conjunction with the club soda method discussed above.

3 The Smallest Room in the House

Over the years I have found that there is one room that generates question after question. That room is the bathroom.

Once, when I was eating in a wonderful little Chinese restaurant, the proprietor—an elderly gentleman—followed me into the ladies' room to see if I thought his bathrooms were clean. He was using the methods that I had recommended on television and was making his own cleanser from my recipe. Let me tell you, his bathrooms were spotless! It made me think that of all the rooms in your house, the bathroom is probably the room that most guests always see and have the most private time to observe. I have tried virtually every cleaning product on the market and developed many of my own "Queen's concoctions"—what follows are the best and easiest cleaning tips I can offer.

Cleaning Fiberglas™ Showers and Tubs

Heat white vinegar until it is hot, but not too hot to pour into a spray bottle and work with. Spray it on the shower and tub heavily. Wait 10 to 15 minutes and then moisten a scrubbing-type sponge with more of the vinegar and scrub down the shower, using additional heated vinegar as necessary. Rinse well and dry.

Removing Hard-Water Marks

Many plastic-type tubs have a dimpled slip-proof bottom that defies cleaning. I have found that using a good gel cleaner or a mild cleanser, such as the homemade types listed on page 25, and a piece of fine drywall sandpaper (looks like window screen) works the best. Cut the sandpaper into a workable size, apply the cleaner and rub. Use this only on dimples in plastic and Fiberglas™ tub and shower bottoms.

Stubborn Spot Remover for Showers

For stubborn shower spots and scum buildup, use a dry soap-filled steel wool pad on a dry shower. Do not allow water to become involved in this process, as it will cause the steel wool pad to scratch. Follow up with the vinegar process described at the beginning of this chapter.

Keeping Plastic Showers Clean

To make shower upkeep simple, apply a coat of car wax. Do not use this on the floor of the tub or shower. After showering, use a squeegee to wipe down the shower door and walls, and your shower will stay clean and you'll have fewer problems with mildew.

Cleaning Porcelain Tubs

To clean and polish a porcelain tub and remove stains, make a paste of powdered alum (available in drugstores) and water. Rub well, as if using cleanser. For stains, make a paste of powdered alum and lemon juice; apply and let dry, then moisten with more lemon juice and rub well. Rinse thoroughly.

Borax and water makes a great cleaner for porcelain. Make a paste and rub well, then rinse.

Keeping Tile and Grout Clean

You can keep ahead of grout cleaning if you use a dry typewriter eraser on dry grout to remove mildew and stains as they appear. For bigger problems, make a paste of baking soda and chlorine bleach and apply to the grout. Let dry and then rinse. Do this in a well-ventilated area, using care near carpet or fabric. Even the fumes of chlorine bleach can remove color from towels left hanging in the tub area.

Tile and Grout Cleaner

Combine 2 parts baking soda, 1 part borax and 1 part hot water, adding additional water as necessary to form a thick paste. Apply to the tile and grout and scrub with a soft brush. Rinse well.

Cleaning Soap Scum and Mildew off Plastic Shower Curtains

Put the shower curtain in the washing machine with one cup of white vinegar, ¼ to ½ cup of your favorite liquid laundry detergent, and several old, light-colored towels. Fill the washer with warm water and run through complete wash and rinse cycle. Remove from the washer and hang on the shower rod immediately.

Cleaning Mineral Deposits from the Shower Head

Fill a plastic sandwich bag with undiluted white vinegar. Tie this around the shower head and leave overnight. In the morning remove the bag, scrub the head with a brush and it's ready to use.

Cleaning Chrome Faucets

Use white vinegar on a cloth or sponge to remove water spots and soap scum. Dry and buff with a soft cloth. Rubbing alcohol is also a great spot remover. Apply, then dry and buff.

To shine chrome or any metal fixture in a hurry, use a used dryer fabric softener sheet on a dry fixture.

Put ½ cup of baking soda down the bathroom drain and follow with the vinegar in the plastic bag—great drain opener! Wait 30 minutes, then flush with water.

Removing Hair Spray Residue

You can use this formula to remove hair spray residue from any hard surface—vanities, tile, floors, walls, etc. Mix a solution of ⅓ liquid fabric softener and ⅔ water in a spray bottle. Spray on the surface to be cleaned, and wipe. Not only does it remove hair spray, it also acts as a dust repellent and shines vanities beautifully!

Removing Bathtub Decals

Lay a sheet of aluminum foil over the decals and heat with a blow-dryer on high. Work up the edge of the decal with a dull straight-edge (credit cards work great) and keep applying the heat as you pull. If the decal is stubborn, lay down the foil as necessary and heat well and peel again. To remove the residue try petroleum jelly, denatured alcohol or nail polish remover. Test these products in a small area first before applying.

> A three-tiered wire fruit basket hung on the shower rail makes a great catchall for soaps and sponges and all the other necessities you'll need for bath time.

Cleaning Shower Door Tracks

Plug the drain holes in the door track with a little bit of paper towel made into a ball. Pour in undiluted white vinegar. Let this soak for 30 minutes, unplug the holes and rinse the track with a spray bottle of water and run a rag down it. This will flush the accumulated buildup out of the track.

Toilet Tips

If you have indoor plumbing, then you have to clean the toilet once in a while, whether you like it or not. Follow these tips and it will be a breeze:

Removing Hard-Water Rings

Shut off the water at the toilet tank and flush. Spray undiluted white vinegar around the inside of the toilet, then sprinkle borax onto the vinegar. Let soak about 30 minutes and then scrub with a piece of fine drywall sandpaper (looks like window screen—available at hardware stores and home centers). If you have an old hard-water ring, you may need to repeat this several times.

Plop-Plop-Fizz-Fizz Cleaning

Drop a couple of denture-cleaning tablets into the toilet and let sit overnight. Brush under the rim with your bowl brush and flush.

Rrrrust

There are, of course, acid bowl cleaners available from grocery stores, home centers and janitorial supply stores that will remove rust from toilets, but for an inexpensive, nontoxic way to remove rust, try this: Once a month sprinkle a layer of Tang™ Breakfast Drink or lemon Kool-Aid™ on the sides of the toilet and in the water, leave for 1 hour, brush and flush. Repeat if necessary. (For those of you who are wondering, citric acid oxidizes the rust.)

To keep your toilet clean and your dog happy, put several tablespoons of Tang™ Breakfast Drink in the toilet before you leave for work or at bedtime. Let it soak, use your toilet brush to swish around under the rim, and flush. The great thing about this is you don't have to worry if the kids get into the toilet bowl cleaner.

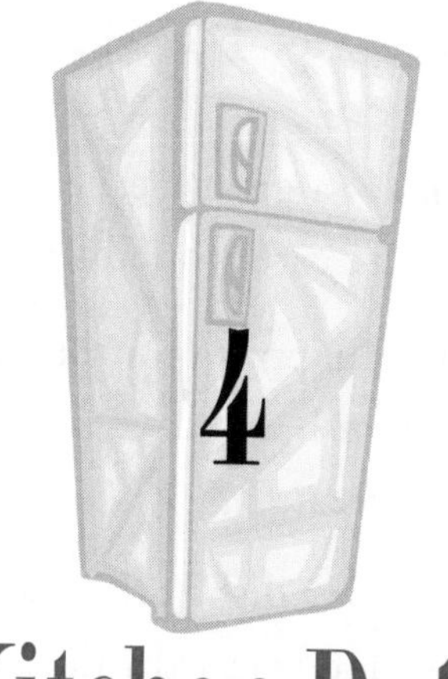

4 Kitchen Duty

I don't think there is a room in the house that gets messy faster than the kitchen. So let's clean up!

Appliance Magic

Many of us have white appliances in the kitchen. In order to keep them from yellowing, try this formula when you clean the exterior.

Combine:

8 cups of water
½ cup of chlorine bleach
½ cup baking soda
2 tablespoons borax

Wash white appliances thoroughly (using care around carpet or fabric), rinse well and dry.

* Rubbing alcohol makes a great cleaner for the exterior of all types of appliances. Use care around flames.
* Club soda is a wonderful polish for the exterior of appliances. It doesn't have to be fresh and have fizz; even if it has lost its carbonation it works great.
* Don't grab your everyday dishcloth to wipe down appliances; it will transfer grease and smear the finish.

Cutting Boards

Remove odors from breadboards by wetting and then rubbing with a little dry mustard. Let sit for a few minutes and then rinse. To disinfect breadboards, especially wood, keep a spray bottle with 1 quart water and 3 teaspoons of liquid chlorine bleach. Spray on, let sit at least 5 minutes, and then rinse with hot water.

Broiler Pan

For quick, easy, neat cleaning, put the broiler pan in a plastic garbage bag and lay some paper towels on it. Spray with ammonia, close bag and leave overnight. In the morning, open bag (away from face, remember the fumes), wipe with the towels that are in the bag, remove, wash broiler pan and throw out the rest of the mess.

To clean burned-on pans, fill the pan or casserole with hot water and throw in several used dryer fabric softener sheets. Let soak (even overnight), rinse and wash.

Automatic Coffeemakers

Depending on how often you use your coffee pot and how hard your water is, you may want to do this once a month to once every 3 months.

Fill the water reservoir with undiluted white vinegar. Place a filter in the coffee basket and turn the pot on. Allow about half of the vinegar to run through and then shut off the pot. Let it sit for about 30 minutes, then turn the coffemaker on and allow the balance of the vinegar to run through. Clean the pot out well, fill the reservoir with fresh, cold water and allow it to run through. Run the fresh water through twice.

To Clean the Glass Pot

Use lemon and salt and rub with a sponge, or use baking soda and lemon juice or water and rub with a sponge. Rinse well.

To Clean the Basket and Other Parts

For white plastic units, soak any removable parts in hot water with dishwashing liquid and about ¼ cup of chlorine bleach. Soak about 30 minutes and rinse well. This helps remove stains and oils. For dark-colored coffeemakers, use dishwashing liquid and about ¼ cup of white vinegar in the same manner as above.

Chrome Burner Rings and Guards

Remove the burner rings from the stove. Lay a single sheet of paper toweling on each pan and moisten with ammonia. Place them in a plastic bag and close the bag. Leave for several hours or overnight. Open bag (pointed away from face, please) and remove the parts. Wash, rinse and dry.

Dishwashers

To remove that milky film from glassware and clean the inside of your dishwasher, follow this procedure:

Fill the dishwasher with your glassware (no metal, please). Use no dishwasher detergent. Put a bowl in the bottom of the dishwasher and pour in 1 cup of household bleach. Run through the wash cycle, but do not dry. Fill the bowl again with 1 cup white vinegar and let the dishwasher go through the entire cycle. Now you have the film removed from your dishes and the dishwasher clean in one easy step.

Dishwasher Odor

Sprinkle borax in the bottom of the dishwasher and leave it overnight. Using a damp sponge, use the borax to wipe down the inside of the dishwasher, door and gaskets. No need to rinse, just do the next load of dishes.

Dishwasher Rust

To remove rust from the inside of the dishwasher, fill both detergent cups with Tang™ Breakfast Drink and run through the normal cycle. If rust is bad, several treatments may be required. When doing this don't put dishes or detergent in the dishwasher.

"You do the dishes, you make the beds, and six months later you have to start all over again."

—Joan Rivers

Dishwasher Spot Stopper

To keep your dishes spot-free, use this formula. Combine the following ingredients in a container with a lid:

1 cup borax

½ cup baking soda

To use: Add 1 teaspoon of the mixture to the dishwasher along with your regular dishwasher detergent.

The Pain of Drains

This is the best nontoxic drain opener you will ever use. Pour 1 cup of salt (table salt, rock salt, any kind) and 1 cup of baking soda down the drain. Follow with a kettle of boiling water. If the problem is congealed grease, it will be gone immediately. For the very best results, don't use the drain for several hours. If you need a stronger product, use 2 tablespoons of washing soda (available where laundry products are sold) dissolved in 1 quart of hot water and pour it slowly down the drain. Flush with hot water after 10 minutes.

Once a month, pour a handful of baking soda into the drain and add ½ cup of white vinegar. A small volcano will erupt. Cover the drain for several minutes and then flush with cold water after 30 minutes.

Cleaning the Disposal

Keep your garbage disposer clean and free-flowing by filling the sink with 3 inches of warm water and mixing in 1 cup of baking soda. Drain it with the disposal running.

Using the Plunger the Easy Way

Yes, there really is a special way to use a plunger to make it work more effectively. Close the overflow to the sink (usually in the front of the sink) by plugging it with an old rag. If you don't do this, the water will go down one hole and come back up the overflow. Fill the sink with 4 to 5 inches of water. Put the cup of the plunger over the drain and press down hard. Then pull the handle up, push down again and repeat 10 to 12 times.

IT'S THAT EASY . . .

Adding a little petroleum jelly around the rim of the plunger gives even better suction.

Microwave Magic

To clean your microwave quickly and simply, wet a dishcloth and place it in the center of your microwave. Turn on high and allow the cloth to sort of cook for about 30 to 40 seconds. The steam that this creates will help loosen any hardened spills and you can then use the heated cloth to wipe the inside clean. A note of caution: Don't try to use the cloth immediately; it will be very hot. This is a great way to disinfect your dishcloth, too.

Deodorizing the Microwave

To give your microwave a clean, fresh smell, place a bowl of water in it and add 3 or 4 slices of fresh lemon or 2 tablespoons of lemon juice. Cook on high for 30 to 60 seconds.

For the very worst odors, such as burned popcorn, place vanilla extract in a bowl and microwave for at least 30 seconds. Leave the door closed for 12 hours, remove the vanilla and wipe down the inside of the microwave.

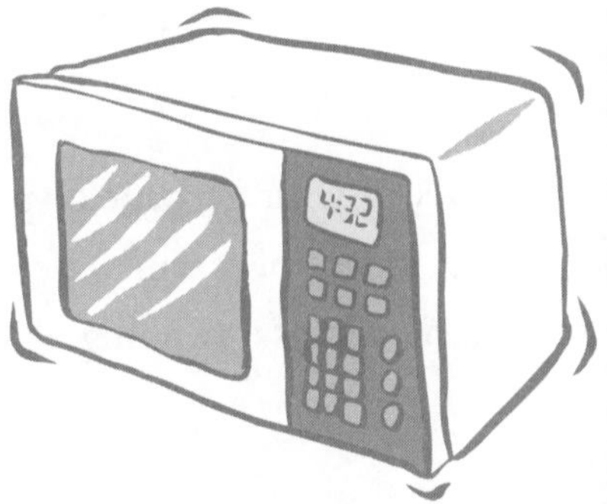

The Smoking Oven

When something runs over in the oven and starts smoking and smelling, grab the salt. Sprinkle on a heavy layer of salt and continue cooking. The smoke and odor will stop immediately. When done cooking, close the oven and wait overnight. The next day you will be able to lift out the spill with a pancake turner!

Cleaning the Oven

Preheat oven to 200 degrees and leave on for 15 minutes. Shut off and leave door closed. Fill a shallow glass dish with ammonia and place on the top shelf. On the lower shelf place a pan filled with 2 cups of boiling water. Close the oven door and leave the pans inside 2 hours or overnight. Remove ammonia and water; make a paste of ammonia, ½ cup baking soda and 1 cup white vinegar. Spread paste over surfaces and leave on for about 15 minutes. Scrub with a sponge and steel wool pad (if necessary), then rinse. This even works on heavily soiled ovens.

DID YOU KNOW?

You can clean and sanitize your sponge and dishcloth by wedging them into the dishwasher and washing them along with a load of dishes. You can also wet the sponge or dishcloth and put it in the microwave for 30 seconds.

Making Your Own Cleanser

For a great nonabrasive scouring powder for disinfecting, combine:

- 4 parts baking soda
- 1 part borax

Store in a shaker container.

For a nontoxic grease-cutting scouring powder, combine:

4 parts baking soda

1 part washing soda

Store in a shaker container.

Stick a piece of masking tape on the top of your abrasive cleanser, leaving only half the holes free—your cleanser will last twice as long!

Cleaning and Protecting Cooktops

I receive so many questions about cleaning cooktops that I decided to devote a section just to that. Actually, glass and smooth-top ceramic surfaces are fairly easy to clean if you follow a few rules when dealing with them.

Clean the surface only when it is cool, with either dishwashing liquid, a paste of baking soda and water (3 parts baking soda to 2 parts water) or a specially formulated cooktop cleaner. Apply this with a paper towel or soft cloth.

Rinse thoroughly and towel dry. Do not use a soiled dishcloth or sponge to wipe the top; it may leave a film, which can cause discoloration the next time it is heated. If this discoloration occurs, remove it with a specially formulated cooktop cleaner.

Burned-on soil can be removed with a razor-blade scraper. Avoid abrasive cleaners and pads.

If your cooktop is in really bad shape, you will have to take more drastic action before you can have cleaning ease.

You can try a product called Bon Ami®, which comes in a can, much like cleanser. This product can safely be used on mirrors, windows, windshields, etc. It has a mild pumice action. Use it very carefully with a soft, wet rag to remove heavy soiling. You can also use a mild ammonia solution along with a scrubbing-type sponge. Another product that will help remove stains and burned-on food is nongel toothpaste, applied with a soft cloth.

Follow up these cleaning procedures by washing with dishwashing liquid and water and rinsing well. Rinsing with club soda will put a nice shine on the top surface.

I have found a wonderful product called Clean Shield® Surface Treatment. Using this allows you to do what I call "preventive cleaning." You apply this, and in the future when you clean, spills and burned-on food bead up. It makes your stovetop surface react as if it were nonstick cookware—spills wipe off with nothing more than a damp cloth. You can safely use this on all surfaces except wood and paint—even glass! Call 1-800-528-3149 to find out where it is sold in your area.

To remove stains from nonstick cookware, boil 2 tablespoons of baking soda, ½ cup of white vinegar and 1 cup of water for 10 to 15 minutes. Reseason the pan with salad oil.

Refrigerator Odors and Spills

When you wipe out the refrigerator, always use a cloth or sponge moistened with white vinegar. It leaves a clean, fresh scent and helps prevent mildew.

A dab of vanilla, lemon or orange extract on a small pad of cotton will keep the refrigerator fresh-smelling without a perfume odor.

Many common refrigerator odors may be removed by placing a small tub filled with charcoal in the middle rack in the refrigerator. I use the charcoal made for fish tanks.

If you are shutting off a refrigerator, be sure to prop the door open a crack for air circulation and put a container of fresh coffee grounds inside to ward off unpleasant odors. For strong odor removal, a container or nylon stocking with coffee grounds in it works wonders.

For cleaning ease, wipe the inside of the refrigerator, including shelves, with a cloth dipped in glycerin, available in the hand cream section at the drugstore. This light coating will keep spills from sticking. Even milk or sticky substances will wipe right out.

Freezers

Try using the glycerin in freezers, too. That way spills, even though frozen, wipe right out.

Wash out the freezer with a solution of 1 gallon warm water and ¼ cup borax to clean and deodorize. Rinse and dry.

Cutlery

Stainless steel cutlery is easy to clean. Mix the following ingredients in the kitchen sink or any nonaluminum container:

¼ cup chlorine bleach
¼ cup Calgon Water Softener®
1 gallon very hot water

Immerse stainless steel cutlery in the solution for 30 minutes and wash as usual. This is not for use on real silver.

To remove stubborn spots from stainless steel, use a little nongel toothpaste or some silver polish in a separate container with a little ammonia added to it. Apply this with a soft cloth; wash, rinse and dry.

Wash silver cutlery as soon as possible after using to prevent tarnish-causing stains.

Stainless Steel Sinks

So much of my mail asks about cleaning and keeping up the appearance of stainless steel sinks. One such writer suggested using the sink as an ugly planter and using nothing but paper plates and plastic silverware! Take heart—here are ways to keep them clean and actually enjoy them.

Regular Cleaning

Clean with a paste of baking soda and water and rinse well. Drying the sink helps to prevent water marks and rust.

Polishing

Polish with flour. Put a tablespoon of flour in a dry sink and rub with a soft cloth. Then rinse and dry. Another polish method is club soda. Put the stopper in the sink, pour in some club soda and rub with a soft cloth. Again, dry to prevent water spots.

Removing Rust and Water Spots

Use white vinegar on a soft cloth or sponge. It will not only erase the spots, but will also brighten the sink. Rubbing alcohol or lighter fluid will also remove rust marks. Remember the flammability of lighter fluid and use with care.

Removing Stains

Prepare a paste of 3 parts of cream of tartar to 1 part hydrogen peroxide and apply it to the stains. Allow it to dry and then wipe with a wet cloth or sponge.

To Shine

Coat the sink with a few drops of baby oil. Wipe it off with paper towels. If it doesn't seem shiny enough, repeat the procedure.

Erasing Hairline Scratches

Using very fine steel wool, gently give the entire sink the once-over to obliterate hairline scratches. Then wash and buff with a soft cloth.

Metal Cleaners

Here are some fast, easy homemade metal cleaners. Always test in an inconspicuous spot before using.

Brass

Use a mixture of lemon juice and salt. Wipe on until clean, then rinse and dry. Not for use on brass-plated pieces.

Copper

Use ketchup or Worcestershire sauce. Wipe on, rub until clean, rinse and buff.

Gold

On small pieces, use nongel toothpaste and a soft brush, such as a toothbrush. Rinse well. Any household ammoniated cleaner mixed 50/50 with water also works well.

Chrome

Rub with aluminum foil wrapped around your finger or hand, or wipe with a dry, used dryer fabric softener sheet.

When using your double boiler, drop several marbles in with the water. If it should start to boil dry, the marbles will rattle, alerting you to the problem before the pan is ruined.

The Queen's Best Kitchen Quick Tips

To remove food odors from plastic containers, fill with warm water and add a little dry mustard—¼ teaspoon is plenty for an average-size container. Let soak for an hour or so and then wash.

- To remove stains from plastic, put the open container in the sun. For stubborn spots, brush with a little lemon juice first.
- To chase away the odor of burned foods, boil some lemon slices or 1 tablespoon of bottled lemon juice in a saucepan for a few minutes.
- To chase away the odor of fried foods, even fish, place a small bowl of white vinegar next to the stove as you are frying.

DID YOU KNOW?

If you crack an egg at an angle, you won't break the yolk!

- Clean porcelain pieces and the sink by filling the sink with warm water and adding several denture-cleaning tablets.
- Remove stains from the countertop by massaging a paste of cream of tartar and lemon juice into the stain, let it soak and then rinse.
- Clean and sanitize your sponge and dishcloth by wedging them into the dishwasher and washing them along with a load of dishes. You can also wet the sponge or dishcloth and put it in the microwave for 30 seconds.

* To remove grease from wooden cupboards, apply a very thin coat of car wax, let it dry and buff.
* Do not wash silver and stainless steel together in the dishwasher. The stainless may stain the silver.
* Remove plastic stuck to toasters with a little nail polish remover. Be sure toaster is unplugged.
* Store your steel wool pad in the freezer each time you finish with it and it will never rust. Just tuck it into a sandwich bag.
* To clean a scorched pan, fill with warm water and add several tablespoons of baking soda. Boil until the scorched parts loosen and float to the surface.

IT'S THAT EASY . . .

Remove rust from baking pans by rubbing with cleanser and a cut raw potato.

* Spray a grater with nonstick cooking spray before using and cleanup will be a breeze.
* Clean the outside of a cast-iron pan with oven cleaner. Clean the inside by boiling a solution of water and a couple of tablespoons of white vinegar in it. Re-season with cooking oil and store with a piece of wax paper in it after each use. Never wash the inside of the pan with soap.
* To clean the inside of a thermos, fill with warm water and add 1 teaspoon of chlorine bleach. Let soak 30 to 60 minutes and rinse well.

* Preserve wooden salad bowls by wiping with a paper towel soaked in cooking oil. This prevents drying and cracking. Do not immerse in water for more than just a few seconds to clean. Always dry thoroughly.

DID YOU KNOW?

A small chip on glass can be smoothed out with a few gentle strokes of an emery board.

* Remove rust from a knife or other kitchen utensil by sticking it in an onion for about an hour. Move the piece back and forth to help the onion juice do its work.
* Always put glass dishes into hot water sideways and they will never break from the expansion and contraction.

If you or someone in your family has asthma or allergies, you know the horror of opening cleaning products and having an attack. Try a new product from a company called Soapworks®. They have a line of products created by a woman in direct response to her son's asthma attacks, which occurred every time she opened cleaning products and started to clean. The product is called At Home All-Purpose Cleaner™. It can be used undiluted for heavy jobs, such as degreasing, or diluted 100/1 for light cleaning. Totally safe, user- and earth-friendly, mildly scented and it works! Check out www.soapworks.com for information on their line of fabulous products.

Kitchen Basics

Starting out in a new home and concerned that you might end up with four skillets and no pasta pot? Here's a list of the basics. You can fill in your special needs.

- 10- to 12-inch skillet with a lid
- 6- to 8-inch skillet
- Covered saucepans in various sizes
- Covered casserole dishes in various sizes
- 8-inch-square baking dish
- Mixing bowls
- Cake pans—whether you bake cakes or not they are great for things like cinnamon rolls, even when purchased from the refrigerator case
- Roasting pan with a rack
- Cookie sheets—at least two
- 13 x 9 x 2 pan
- Bread pans—one or two of these are good for cooking meatloaf and other dishes
- Muffin pan
- Large pasta-type pot, sometimes called a Dutch oven
- Toaster
- Coffeemaker—the most important to me!
- Knives—a good basic set. This should include a carving knife, serrated bread knife and several paring knives. Remember, knives are an investment, so buy the best you can afford.

* Measuring cups
* A rubber spatula or two
* Can opener and bottle opener
* Kitchen shears
* Rolling pin—if you use one
* Plastic storage bowls
* Tongs
* Garlic press—if you use garlic
* Cheese slicer
* Colander
* Cooking utensils, including a large spoon, slotted spoon, large fork, and ladle

Now, the gadget group:

* Grater
* Whisk
* Egg slicer
* Apple corer
* Steaming rack

These things you may or may not want depending on your tastes.

* Mixer—the small handheld kind work well and take up less room!
* Blender
* Toaster oven

* Microwave oven
* Food processor
* Electric grill
* Specialty cooking pans

And, of course, a couple of really good cookbooks!

Q: "So what's in the chef's surprise?"
A: "That's the surprise."

—Old Vaudeville routine

5

Floor Cleaning—Now Step on It

Once you know a few basics, you can clean your floors quickly and easily—just like the pros.

Sealing Ceramic Tile

Sealing your grout is a must. Purchase sealer from the store where you bought your tile or from a home center.

Cleaning Ceramic Tile

"My idea of housework is to sweep the room with a glance."

—Anonymous

Ceramic tile is not porous—you can clean effectively with warm water. Many cleaners leave a residue on the tile surface that looks like a smeary coating. A good neutral cleaner for tile is 1 gallon warm water, 2 tablespoons of ammonia and 1 tablespoon of borax. Never use vinegar. It is acidic and will eventually etch the grout.

Never use a sponge mop on ceramic tile. It works like a squeegee, depositing the dirty water into the grout tracks.

Sweep or vacuum floor prior to washing.

Use a rag or chamois-type mop.

Rinse mop, frequently changing the water as it becomes soiled.

If you have a gloss-finish tile, it may be necessary to dry the tile. Use a clean terry rag under your foot to do it the easy way.

Dusting Wood Floors

Use a dry dust mop to remove dust or vacuum floor, being sure not to use a vacuum with a beater bar—this can mar the floor.

Cleaning Wood Floors with Tea

Brew 1 quart of boiling water with 1 or 2 tea bags. Let it come to room temperature. Wring out a soft cloth to just damp and wash floor, keeping the rag clean. Do not overwet floor. This will clean the floor and cover many imperfections. Buff with a soft cloth if desired.

Repair Scratches in Wood Floors

To fill scratches, use a crayon or combine several to match the floor. Wax crayons for wood are available at the hardware store. Work the crayon into the scratch, then heat the repair with a blow-dryer and buff with a rag. This will work the repair into the floor so well, you'll never know it's there.

DID YOU KNOW?

Tea is a wonderful cleaner for wood because of the tannic acid.

Clean and Wax

There is a product made by Bruce Floor Care Products that is a cleaner and wax in one. It comes in two colors, light and dark. If your floors are very bad, you might consider trying this product before you spend the money to refinish the floors. Follow the directions on the can carefully, and allow plenty of time to do the job, working in one small area at a time.

Cleaning Vinyl Floors

For cleaning vinyl floors, including no-wax floors, sheet vinyl and linoleum:

Sweep or vacuum the floor well. Mix 1 gallon of warm water and 1 tablespoon of borax. Wring out mop or rag well in the solution and wash the floor, keeping the rag clean. No rinsing is necessary. Using borax preserves the shine on floors, even those that have been waxed.

Waxing Floors

When you wax a floor, it is wise to buy the wax from a janitorial store, which sells commercial products that hold up well to wear and traffic.

On a clean floor apply 2 thin coats of wax, allowing ample drying time between coats. It is imperative that the floor be clean, otherwise you will wax in the dirt.

The next time you wax, wax only the traffic area where the wax is worn off, feathering it into the other areas to blend. This eliminates wax buildup around the edges of the room.

Purchase a wax-stripping product from your local janitorial supply store. It is more efficient than ammonia and also very reasonably priced.

The Miracle of Microfiber . . . Or Is It?

Microfiber cloths and mops clean without chemicals—just water and the cloth or mop. Do these products work? Well . . . yes and no. The old adage *you get what you pay for* certainly holds true in the microfiber business. If you are purchasing these cloths dirt cheap, you are wasting your money. If they do not contain thousands of fibers, they won't clean as they should. Here's the dirty lowdown on the very best.

Euronet USA makes the ACT Natural® Mop. A dry mop/wet mop with a telescoping handle, this miracle cleans vinyl, ceramic, wood—any hard flooring—beautifully with nothing but water. Just wring the mop out in water, stick it to the velcro pad and go! Machine wash. Check out www.euronetusa.com or call 1-888-638-2882.

6

The Queen's Royal Carpet Treatment

Carpet is one of the most expensive investments you will make in your home. With proper knowledge about choosing a good-quality carpet that fits your lifestyle, and cleaning and stain removal guidelines, your carpet will give you many years of enjoyment and quality wear.

Know Your Carpet

Most residential carpet is made from one of four fibers: nylon, polyester, olefin or wool (or a combination). All of these fibers can make great carpet, although nylon is one of the most cost-effective and durable. Here are some other things to be aware of when making that important purchase.

Face weight is a common-sense measurement that you should be aware of when purchasing carpet. The key to remember: More fibers are almost always better.

Fiber density is a measurement of how closely packed carpet fibers are to each other. Carpets with high density tend to look better longer and will give carpet a soft feeling when walked upon.

Carpet fiber twist is very important to be aware of, especially with cut-pile types of carpet. Fibers that have more twists per linear inch usually make more durable carpeting.

Carpet padding is absolutely critical to good carpet performance. Too much or too little can cause premature failure in many carpets. The best pads, believe it or not, are those that are thin and firm. Avoid pads thicker than 7⁄16 inch.

The Basics

When you vacuum, make sure you have cleaned your vacuum canister or changed your disposable bag so you are getting the best possible suction. Vacuum across the nap of the carpet and then in the direction of the nap to restore it to its original appearance. Always overlap your strokes to be sure you cover all areas. How often you vacuum depends on your family size, and use of the rooms, but try for at least twice a week. Some of you may even find vacuuming every day makes sense for you. Remember, it's all about you . . . what works best for you.

"I'm not going to vacuum till Sears makes one you can ride on."

—Roseanne

Cleaning Carpet

Many people ask me how to go about hiring a firm to clean carpeting. Listed below are some general guidelines to follow. Always call more than one company, looking for comparable pricing. Ask each company the same set of questions, and remember word-of-mouth is one of your best allies. Ask your neighbors, your friends, and the people you work with which companies they have used and how satisfied they were.

Questions to Ask

Cost Per Square Foot or Room

Find out if there is a square footage limitation per room and if your room sizes fit within the limitation. Remember to ask about hallways, walk-in closets and bathrooms. They may count as a whole room when companies offer room pricing. If the cost is figured by square foot, measure the length and width of your rooms and multiply length by width to achieve the square footage. Add the total square footage of all of your rooms and multiply by the cost per square foot. This should give you an accurate price.

Find Out What Method of Cleaning Is Used

Steam cleaning or extraction is the preferable way to clean. Ask if the company uses a "truck mounted unit." A portable cleaner will not generate the same powerful extraction process that a truck unit will.

Do They Clean with Hot or Cold Water?

Cold water will not remove stubborn, greasy soil. A truck-mounted cleaning system should hook up to your cold water, usually at an outside tap, and heat the water as it flows through the truck.

Is the Company Insured?

If they damage your furniture while moving it or bang into a wall, you want to be sure they can cover the cost of the repair.

Ask About Experience

Be sure you are hiring trained professionals who do this for a living.

Remember the Investment

Again, carpet is one of your most expensive investments, so treat it with the care it deserves and it will last much longer and look better.

Before Cleaning Carpets

- Pick up all small items from carpets.
- Remove all items from furniture to be moved.
- When possible, remove dining chairs and other small, light pieces of furniture.
- Pick up all small area rugs.
- Remove things from the floor of the closet if it will be cleaned.
- Remove anything from under beds if they are to be moved.
- Open as many windows as possible, if weather permits.
- If house is not left open, turn on the air conditioner or heat, whichever is appropriate.
- If possible, set fans so they blow across the carpet.
- Wash the soles of the shoes or slippers that you will be wearing

on the damp carpet, otherwise dirt from the soles will be transferred to the carpet.

- Do not move furniture back until carpet is completely dry.

After Carpets Are Cleaned

BEWARE of slippery linoleum and other hard floors when stepping from damp carpet.

- Do not put towels or sheets or newspapers on the carpet.
- If you have had the carpet treated with carpet protector, you will need to allow extra drying time.
- Vacuum carpet thoroughly after it is dry with a clean vacuum.

Spotting Guide

The number one rule of spot removal on carpet is to always keep several bottles of club soda on hand to use on spills on any kind of carpet. If you spill, follow this advice:

Blot up as much moisture as you can—laying old towels over the spill and standing on them is a great way to start.

- Scrape up any solids.
- Pour club soda on the spill. Don't be afraid to really pour it on. The carbonation in the soda will "bubble up" the spill so that you can blot it up. Again, cover the spot with clean, light-colored towels or rags and stand on them. This will really help to absorb the spill. Continue to pour and absorb until all color from the stain has been blotted up and the towel is coming up clean.

- Follow up with a good carpet stain remover. I prefer Spot Shot Instant Carpet Stain Remover®.
- When you spot-clean carpet, never rub, as it will only spread the stain and will cause abrasion to the carpet fibers.
- This is a good general cleaning method for most spills and definitely will not cause any damage.

Red Pop, Kool-Aid™

Grab the club soda fast and follow the above method. If the stain is old, still try the club soda—it will help lighten the stain. After using your carpet spotter, if the spot is still present, saturate with hydrogen peroxide or undiluted lemon juice. Wait 15 minutes and blot. Continue to apply and check your progress, just to be sure you aren't lightening the carpet.

DID YOU KNOW?

White wine removes red wine stains! Just grab the white wine and pour it on or saturate with salt and follow with the club soda and carpet spotter.

Nail Polish

Blot up as much polish as possible with a tissue or anything handy. Then test the effect of nonoily nail polish remover on an inconspicuous part of the carpet. If there are no ill effects to the carpet pile, apply the nail polish remover with an eye dropper or a nonsilver spoon, blotting immediately after each application. Always use nonoily polish remover. If regular nail polish remover does not work, buy straight acetone at a beauty supply house, pretest again, and apply as directed above. Once you have removed as much as possible (have patience) follow with Spot Shot Instant Carpet Stain Remover®, applied according to the directions. If color staining remains, apply hydrogen peroxide to bleach or lighten the stain.

Mud

Cover wet mud with salt or baking soda and let dry thoroughly before touching. Once it is dry, vacuum it using the attachment hose to concentrate the suction on the mud. Use a good carpet spotter, following the directions, to complete the process. For red dirt or mud, use a rust remover such as Whink® or Rust Magic® to remove any color residue. Make sure you test the rust remover in a small area first.

Coffee and Tea

The best defense is a good offense when you spill coffee. First, act as quickly as possible. Hot coffee is the equivalent of brown dye. Blot up all of the spill that you can and immediately apply club soda. If you don't have club soda (shame on you), use plain cold water. Really pour it on and blot, blot, blot. Follow with a good-quality carpet spotter. If a stain remains, you can attempt to remove it by pouring on hydrogen peroxide, waiting 15 minutes and then blotting. If it is lightening the stain, continue, and as a final step, rinse with cold water or club soda.

Use Shaving Cream

The great instant spot remover! If you have a spill and have no carpet spotter available, grab the shaving cream. It is particularly effective on makeup, lipstick, coffee and tea. Work it into the spot well, and rinse with either cold water or club soda.

Guide to Special Spots

Tar and Mustard

Work glycerin (available at drugstores in the hand cream section) into the spot. Let it sit 30 to 60 minutes. Working carefully with paper towels, use a lifting motion to remove the spot. This may require multiple treatments. Follow with a good spotter, such as Spot Shot®.

Removing Indentations in Carpet

Lay ice cubes in the indentations caused by furniture. Be sure to cover all of the indented area. Leave overnight and then fluff the nap with the tines of a fork the next day.

Candle Wax

Put ice in a plastic bag and lay over the wax, allowing it to freeze. Chip off all the wax that you can. Next, lay brown paper over the wax (a grocery bag works great; use the area without the writing) and press with a medium/hot iron. Move the paper as it absorbs so that you don't redeposit the wax on the carpet. Have patience and continue as long as any wax shows up on the bag. Next, apply a good carpet stain remover.

Soot

Sprinkle with salt and wait at least 2 hours and then vacuum, using the attachment hose to concentrate the suction. Spot with a good spotter or Energine Cleaning Fluid®.

Gum

Freeze with ice in a bag and chip off all that you can. Work a little petroleum jelly into the remaining residue and roll the gum into it. Scrape up and follow with a good spotter or Energine Cleaning Fluid®.

Glue

Try saturating glue with undiluted white vinegar. Working with an upward motion, work it out of the fibers and spot with Energine Cleaning Fluid®. For rubber cement, use the method described for gum.

Ink

Spray on hair spray or blot with rubbing alcohol. For heavy spots, try denatured alcohol. Blot well and follow with a spotter.

Armed for Battle

Always keep a good carpet spotting product on hand! I have found an incredible product that removes not only fresh red stains, but also old ones. It will work effectively on such things as red wine, red pop, Kool-Aid™, cranberry juice, red food coloring and even black coffee and tea. It is called Wine Away Red Wine Stain Remover™. Don't let the name fool you, if you are a mom you need this product, if you drink red wine you need it too! It is totally nontoxic and works on carpet and upholstery, even car seats. Call 1-888-WINEAWAY for a purchase location near you.

7

Upholstery Cleaning Made Easy

This chapter will give you all the information you need to choose upholstered furniture wisely, spot-clean it, handle emergency spills and clean it thoroughly.

One of the first things everyone should know about upholstery is that there are different cleaning methods for different types of fabric. There is a simple way to check to see how the furniture you have now should be cleaned, and even more important, how a new piece should be cleaned. This will help you make good decisions on wearability and cleanability before you get the piece home.

Cleaning Codes and What They Mean

Upholstery is supposed to be marked with a code that allows the consumer to know in advance what type of cleaning the manufacturer recommends for that particular piece of furniture. These instructions, known as cleaning codes, are generally found under the seat cushions on the platform of the furniture (the part that the cushions sit on). I will discuss each cleaning code individually below. If you do not find the code under the seat cushions, check all tags for instructions and never buy any upholstered furniture without knowing how it can be cleaned. This information is essential.

W

If you find a W on your furniture, it means that it can be cleaned with water. This would mean that you could rent an extraction carpet and upholstery cleaning machine from the home center or hardware store or use one that you have purchased to clean the fabric. You can also use water in spotting spills. This is the most durable and cleanable fabric you can buy. It is ideal for dining chairs, family room furniture, anything that gets heavy use or where spills might occur frequently.

S

If you find an S on your furniture, it means that it must be cleaned with cleaning solvents (dry-clean only) and you cannot apply water to it. This would eliminate spot-cleaning with water-based products. Dry-clean-only fabrics are generally not as durable and also do not clean as well. If you have a piece with this code, do not allow it to become heavily soiled before calling in a professional cleaner or you will be disappointed with the results. If you need to spot-clean a dry-clean-only fabric, try using Energine Cleaning Fluid®, available at grocery and hardware stores. Test it first in an inconspicuous spot to be sure it doesn't damage the fabric. Apply with a clean, light-colored cloth and blot continuously. Once you have removed the spot, use a blow-dryer to dry the spot quickly so it doesn't leave a noticeable ring on the fabric.

S/W

This code means a combination of solvents and water can be used to clean the upholstery. It does not appear on many pieces. It is best left to the professionals to clean this. Use furniture with this code in low-use areas.

X

This code does not appear on furniture as much anymore, but it does appear frequently on fabric blinds and shades. It means that the item is not cleanable and is a vacuum-only piece. Beware!

Don't Undress Your Furniture

Many people have asked me about taking the covers off the foam cushions and washing them in the washing machine—DON'T DO IT! The zippers are in the backs of cushions only so that the foam cushions may be changed by a professional if necessary. If you remove the cushion covers and wash them, they may shrink and not fit back on the foam correctly; no matter what, it is virtually impossible to get them back on the foam forms evenly and correctly. Plus, they will be noticeably cleaner than the rest of the sofa and will fade and wear out more quickly.

Spot Cleaning

If you need to spot-clean a cushion, unzip the zipper and put a pad of paper towels or a folded white rag between the foam and the cushion covering. Apply your spotter, carefully following the directions. Try not to rub the area, as it causes abrasion on the fabric surface—BLOT, BLOT, BLOT. I have had great success with Spot Shot Upholstery Stain Remover®. It is easy to use and works on a wide variety of spills and soiling. It can be used on a wide variety of fabrics (always test any spotter in an inconspicuous area before using) and works well on the sofa or chair body as well as the cushions. It is great for food spills on dining chairs. Remember, whatever spotting method you choose, always first do a test area where it won't show.

"I can't have children. Because I have white couches."

—Carrie Snow

Candle Wax Meets Upholstery

If you have the unfortunate accident of having candle wax come in contact with your upholstery, don't despair. First, put a large quantity of ice in a plastic bag and lay it on the wax long enough to allow the wax to freeze. Remove the ice and immediately chip up any wax that you can.

Next, take a brown grocery bag and, using only the part without writing, lay it over the wax. Using a medium/hot iron, press over the wax, allowing it to absorb into the paper bag. Move the bag continuously to a clean area. Once you have absorbed as much of the wax as possible, use Energine Cleaning Fluid® to spot-clean the area, remembering to use a blow-dryer to dry the spot when you are done.

If any staining remains, use 3 percent hydrogen peroxide from the drugstore applied with a spoon to bleach out the wax color. Apply peroxide, wait 15 minutes and blot, continuing until the color from the wax is gone.

Slipcovers

Some slipcovers can be laundered in the washing machine. Just make sure to wash unusually large or bulky covers in a large, commercial washing machine.

Don't forget to test for colorfastness (see Chapter 39). Shake out or vacuum the slipcovers before washing and remember to follow the instructions on the care label.

Pretreat any spots or spills before laundering. Fels-Naptha Soap® worked into the arms and headrest will remove a lot of the greasy soiling. Wash in cool water and mild detergent and make sure to rinse well—twice if necessary. Do not overcrowd the slipcovers in the machine or you will be disappointed with the results.

Dry according to the care label. Heavy items such as these need room to breathe, so if you're going to hang your slipcovers to dry, make sure to spread them over several lines, spaced at least 12 inches apart. If you're using the dryer, you should check and rearrange the covers frequently.

Press slipcovers with an iron heated to the appropriate temperature for the fabric type, and fit the covers back on the furniture while they are still slightly damp. Not only will they stretch more readily when damp, but they will shrink slightly as they dry, and that will draw out wrinkles and creases. When the covers are good and dry, you may want to apply a light coating of fabric protector to help keep them soil-resistant.

Leather Furniture

Keep leather furniture out of direct sunlight, otherwise it may crack and dry out. You should use hide food once or twice a year to ensure that the leather remains supple. Make sure you rub it in well so that it does not come off on clothes. I like to apply it, rub it in well, let it sit for 12 hours and then buff again before using the piece. Dust or vacuum regularly and clean with saddle soap or wipe with a damp cloth rubbed across a wet bar of glycerin soap or moisturizing facial soap, such as Dove. If the leather piece is tufted and has buttons and piping, use a soft, bristled toothbrush or paintbrush moistened and rubbed across the soap. Always dry leather with a clean, lint-free cloth.

If you have a sealed leather table or desktop, clean, polish and seal it with paste wax once or twice a year.

Water Spots

Simply run a damp sponge over the area and allow to dry.

> To remove ink stains and spots from leather furniture, apply a little cuticle remover. Dab it on the spot and rub gently with a soft cloth, wipe and buff. You may need to allow the cuticle remover to sit for 10 minutes or so before rubbing for difficult stains. Reapply if necessary.

Dark Stains

If you have light-colored leather furniture and apparel with dark stains on it, try wiping gently with a thin paste of lemon juice and cream of tartar. Gently massage in, then finish off with a soft damp cloth. Be sure to rinse well and follow up with one of the cleaning methods above.

Removing Mildew

To remove mildew from leather furniture, apply a coat of petroleum jelly, allow to sit for 4 to 5 hours and then rub off.

Making Hide Food

Make your own "hide food" by mixing 1 part vinegar to 2 parts linseed oil in a jar with a lid. Shake well and apply with a soft cloth, changing it frequently as it soils. Buff well so oil won't transfer to clothes. Test in an inconspicuous area before using on light-colored leather.

Dry Cleaning

I am frequently asked about dry cleaning items such as drapes, bedspreads, comforters, covers on upholstered cushions, slipcovers and antique items. Here are some final thoughts.

Draperies: Dry cleaning or professional laundering can prolong the life of your draperies and valances. With proper care, draperies can be expected to last from three to five years. Unfortunately, environmental conditions such as humidity, exposure to sunlight, and water damage from rain and condensation can discolor and weaken fabric, leaving draperies vulnerable to shredding when they are agitated during the cleaning process. Age, moisture, light, heat and nicotine can also damage draperies and turn them yellow.

Shrinkage is a big concern for draperies that have not been preshrunk, especially cottons and rayons. Your dry cleaner has stretchers to help eliminate this problem.

Distortion and fabric stiffening can also occur during the cleaning process. This depends on the fiber, weave, and design of your drapes. In addition, some draperies have a reflective coating that may not make it through the dry-cleaning process.

Talk with your dry cleaner *before* you have your draperies cleaned. Examine your draperies together. Be clear in your expectations and be honest as to the age of your drapes. Otherwise . . . it's curtains!

Bedspreads and comforters: Many bedspreads and comforters should be dry-cleaned or professionally laundered. Check for care instructions at the time of purchase so you know what is recommended. Tailored and quilted pieces are best done professionally.

Be sure to include all matching pieces when you have the bedspread or comforter cleaned. That way colors will remain uniform.

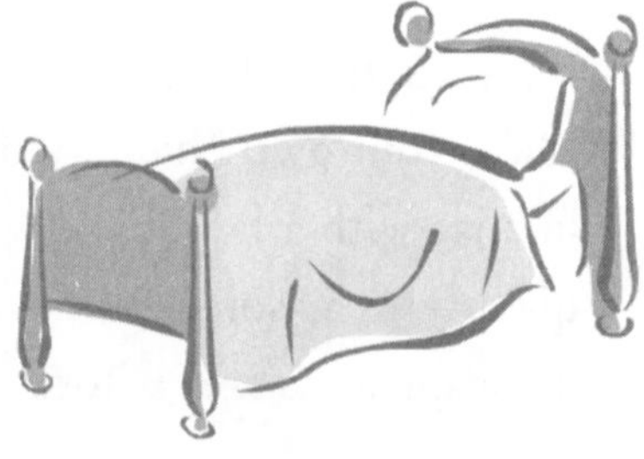

Upholstery and slipcovers: Upholstery is usually cleaned in place by professional cleaners, such as those who do carpet cleaning. These professionals will be able to maintain the color of your upholstery so that it matches the rest of your furniture.

So, why do cushion covers have zippers if we can't take them off and dry-clean or launder them? It is to allow for foam replacement, *not home cleaning.* Once you remove these covers, it is almost impossible to put them back on evenly with the seams straight. My best advice? Never remove and launder cushion covers.

If slipcovers are removed for dry cleaning or laundering, you need to be aware of whether they were preshrunk and what the shrinkage factor is. Check at the time of purchase.

It's a good idea to have slipcovers cleaned by professionals. They can ensure that the proper size machine is used and that there is no crowding, which can set in wrinkles. They also have the right equipment for touch-up pressing.

Antique fabrics: These are your treasures. They belonged to mom or grandmother or a favorite aunt. You love them, you treasure them, and now they are dirty.

Antique quilts, linens and fabrics require great care during the cleaning process. Not every cleaner is equipped for this so you may have to check around. Let your cleaner know right away that the item is very old and treasured. Proper cleaning by a careful professional might just well restore an aged and discolored piece.

Word of mouth is the best great way to find a good-quality dry cleaner. Don't be afraid to ask around. Ask, too, what the cleaner's policy is on damaged items.

Prolong the Life of Your Fabrics

- Bear in mind that closely woven fabric is more durable than loosely woven fabric.
- Consider sun exposure when selecting fabrics. If you are putting drapes at a sunny window, look at acrylic, polyester and glass fibers.
- Read all the care instructions immediately. If you don't want to be bothered with a lot of care, select another item.
- Rotate drapes at windows that are the same size to vary exposure to light.
- Be sure your cleaner knows what your care label recommends.
- Regular cleaning can prolong the life of all fabrics. Clean your household items on a regular schedule.

8

Let the Light Shine: Cleaning Lampshades

Fabric covered and stitched: I find the easiest way to wash these shades is in the bathtub! Put enough cool water in the tub to allow you to roll the shade on its side. Add some mild soap or detergent. Swirl the shade in the water/soap combination gently. Remove the soapy water and rinse the shade, using the same method—make sure the water is cool. Shake the shade gently to remove excess water and allow to dry in an upright position. Drying can be speeded up by using the blow-dryer. This works particularly well on thick and corded areas that dry more slowly.

Paper shades and shades with glue: You can't wet these shades, so your best bet is to vacuum them frequently with the duster brush on your vacuum. You can also purchase a soot-and-dirt removal sponge at the hardware store or home center. It's basically a big block eraser that you use dry to erase the dirt away. It works beautifully, just as long as you don't allow the shade to become heavily soiled. This eraser can also be used on washable shades.

Make sure the soot-and-dirt removal sponge is used dry on a dry object. You may wash the sponge, but be sure to let it dry before using it again.

ACT Natural® Microfiber Cloths also work well on lampshades. Dampen the cloth (only slightly damp, please) and wipe down the shade. It will remove dirt and hair without harming the shade.

Parchment shades: Dust or vacuum these shades regularly. You can use the soot-and-dirt removal sponge on these too. Even a slice of white bread with the crust removed will work! Rub the bread over the shade, preferably on the outside, and watch the dirt fall away with the crumbs.

Plastic shades: Wash these in warm water and mild soap. Dry them well and then restore the shine with spray furniture polish.

Scorch marks: Unfortunately, scorch marks on lampshades are not removable. The material is weakened by the heat and the damage is permanent. Take care when choosing bulbs. Scorch marks are generally caused by bulbs that are too large for the shade.

Q: How many Queens does it take to change a lightbulb?
A: There is only one Queen.

9

Today's Wood–Tomorrow's Heirlooms

Wood furniture in a home is a big investment. Properly cared for, it will last and keep its new appearance for years, eventually to be called "antique" by our grandchildren and great-grandchildren. Here are some tips to keep your furniture looking great, some tips on fixing problems that arise, plus the recipe for making your own furniture polish.

Making Your Own Furniture Polish

There are several great furniture polishes you can make at home with ease. The general rule for homemade polish is to rub it in with a soft cloth and wipe it off and buff with another clean, soft cloth.

Combine ¼ cup white vinegar and 1 cup olive oil in a clean container. Shake before each use.

Combine 1 cup of mineral oil and 3 drops of lemon extract. Shake before each use.

Grate 2 ounces of beeswax (available at drugstores) into a jar and cover it with 5 ounces of natural turpentine. Shake occasionally until dissolved, or stand in a bowl of hot water. Apply to furniture with a soft cloth (just a small amount is all that is needed) and buff with a clean, soft cloth. If it becomes hard over a period of time, set it in a bowl of hot water. This formula seems to work especially well on unvarnished furniture.

To cover scratches on wood furniture, use a crayon the color of the wood. Apply to the scratched area, heat with a blow-dryer and buff the crayon into the scratch with a soft cloth.

For darker woods, rub the meat of a pecan or walnut into the scratch and buff well.

To cover scratches on mahogany or cherry wood, use iodine.

Water Marks/Heat Scars and White Rings

Massage mayonnaise into the marks and leave it on overnight. The next morning, wipe off the mayonnaise and the marks should be gone. You can also use petroleum jelly, butter or margarine. If you have a really stubborn spot, mix cigarette ashes or rottenstone (available at the hardware store) with the mayonnaise and repeat the above procedure.

Nongel white toothpaste is also effective in removing white water rings. Dab toothpaste on a damp cloth and gently massage the ring in a circular motion until it's gone. Wipe and buff with a soft cloth. Apply furniture polish if necessary.

Remove Old Polish and Dirt

Put 2 tea bags in a pot with 1 quart of water and bring it to a boil. Cool to room temperature. Dip a soft cloth in the solution, wring it until it is just damp and wipe furniture with it. Buff dry with a soft cloth, then decide if it requires polish.

Restoring Dried-Out Furniture

Dab petroleum jelly on a soft cloth and polish to help feed and restore dry wood. You will be amazed to see the wood grain and natural luster appear.

Cleaning Very Dirty Wood Furniture

Mix a solution of 1 quart warm water and 3 or 4 drops of dishwashing liquid. Wash the furniture with a soft cloth wrung out until it is damp, rinse and buff dry.

Removing Stickers from Wood

To remove a price tag, identifying label or decal from wood, pull up as much of the sticker as possible, then dip a cloth in vegetable oil or baby oil and gently scrub the area until the sticker and adhesive are gone. Finish by buffing well with a soft cloth.

10

Taming Dust Bunnies Without a Whip

Dusting is one of those thankless jobs that we all have to do. No matter how many times we do it, we still have to do it again and again. These are things that you can do to make the job easier and faster.

Home-Treated Dust Cloths

There are many dusting products on the market that you can buy, but you can easily make your own treated dust cloths for just pennies. Here's how:

Use your favorite cleaning product to make up a bucket of hot, sudsy water. Add a couple of teaspoons of turpentine. Throw in some clean, cotton dust cloths, stir so that they get saturated, and let them soak for 8 to 10 hours (I usually leave them overnight). After they have soaked, wring them out and air-dry them. As soon as they are dry, they are ready to use.

Mix together two cups of hot water and one cup of lemon oil. Dip lint-less cloths into the solution. Squeeze thoroughly and air-dry. Store in a covered metal can—an old coffee can works great.

Lambswool Dusters

For dusting hard-to-reach and high areas, use a good lambswool duster. Do not use a feather duster; it simply shifts the dust around. A lambswool duster attracts dust, is easily washed and can be used for years. Look for these at janitorial supply stores and home centers, in mail-order catalogs and on websites that sell cleaning supplies.

Use cornstarch to remove extra furniture polish and wipe off fingerprints on wood furniture. Shake a little on the surface and polish with a soft cloth.

Dust Repellent

To keep dust off blinds, refrigerators and glass-top tables, mix a solution of 1 part liquid fabric softener to 4 parts water. Spray on or apply with a soft cloth and dry with a soft cloth. This will repel the dust.

11

Off the Walls—Wash Them Like the Pros

Wall-washing can actually be easy if you have the right equipment and do it the right way. Here are some tips for spotting, removing marks and washing walls.

Have All the Right Stuff

When you are ready to wash walls, be sure you gather up the right things to do the job quickly and easily. Get things together before you start and have the furniture moved away from the walls so that the washing process will flow smoothly. Do it like a professional. Here is a list of the things you should have:

2 buckets

Natural sponge (not one of those awful nylon ones)

Baking soda and a soft rag

Art gum eraser

Dropcloths

Ladder

Ingredients for cleaning solution of your choice

2 strips of washcloth or terry rags and 2 rubber bands

Use a dropcloth on the floor around the area you will be washing—it will save you time and mess in the long run. A fabric dropcloth is preferable to plastic, as it absorbs and isn't slippery when wet. Before you start to wash, wrap a strip of washcloth or turkish toweling around your wrist several times and secure with rubber bands. This will keep drips from running up your arms when you are working with your arms above your head.

Removing Marks

The first thing you want to try to do is erase the marks on the wall away. Use an art gum eraser that you keep on hand for this purpose and erase just the mark. This works on many types of marks. If you still have some stubborn spots, use a little baking soda on the corner of a white rag and rub gently, doing just the mark. Nongel toothpaste also is a good spot remover; use it on a cloth over the tip of your finger.

Crayon Marks

If you have kids, you have probably had crayon on the wall. To remove crayon easily, spray with WD-40® Lubricant and wipe crayon away with a paper towel. Follow up with a soft cloth and a solution of hot water and a little dishwashing liquid, washing in a circular motion.

Ink and Marker Marks

To remove ink or Magic Marker®, use hair spray (the cheaper the better), rubbing alcohol, or for really tough spots, denatured alcohol from the hardware store. Always spot carefully, trying to do just the spot.

Great Wall-Washing Solutions

Try one of these wall-washing solutions:

- 1 gallon warm water, ½ cup ammonia, ¼ cup white vinegar and ¼ cup washing soda
- 1 gallon warm water, 1 cup ammonia and 1 teaspoon mild dishwashing liquid

For really professional results, rinse the walls with clear water after washing with either of these solutions. If you choose not to rinse, then be sure to change the cleaning solution frequently as it becomes soiled.

Where to Start

You have the wall free of marks, your dropcloths are in place, your wrists are wrapped for drips and you have your washing solution ready. Now wet your natural sponge (available at janitorial supply stores, home centers and hardware stores). Don't skimp and use a nylon sponge or a rag; it will drag as you wash and take you twice as long. A natural sponge has thousands of "scrubbing fingers" and will get the job done fast, easy and right. Begin washing at the bottom of the wall and work up, doing the ceiling last. Drips of water are much easier to wipe off a clean wall and won't leave marks like they do on a soiled wall.

Don't Stop!

Once you start on a wall, don't stop in the middle. Complete one full wall or the full ceiling before you take a break. If you stop in the middle of a wall or ceiling, you will have "tide marks" where you stop and start again.

Keeping Walls Clean

You can make your own brushing tool to use between washing, to dust down the walls. Tie a clean dust cloth loosely around a broom head and use to dust ceiling thoroughly from time to time and to dust down walls. Give the broom a shake now and then as you are working to remove dust.

Grease Spots on Wallpaper

Make a paste of cornstarch and water and apply to the grease spot. Allow it to dry, then brush or vacuum it off.

Apply a double fold of brown paper (a grocery bag works well, but don't use the part with the writing on it) and press over the grease spot with a warm iron. This may require several efforts. This method also works well on candle wax. Follow up with a little hair spray or alcohol.

> To remove crayon from wallpaper, rub lightly with a dry soap-filled steel wool pad. Do this very gently. You can also try rubbing with baking soda on a damp cloth. On vinyl paper, try using a little silver polish.

Smudges, Marks and Mystery Stains on Wallpaper

Erase with an art gum eraser.

To remove marks from nonwashable paper: Rub a scrunched-up piece of white bread over the marks. Rub very gently. You may need to repeat this a few times before you make progress.

Washing Wallpaper

Wash vinyl and washable papers with one of the mild wall-washing solutions in this chapter.

Cloth Wall Coverings

To clean grasscloth, burlap or cloth wall covering, vacuum with the soft duster brush on the vacuum. Do this regularly to maintain the appearance.

Wood Paneling

Clean wood paneling following the suggestions in the chapter on wood floor cleaning.

12

The Nose Knows—Odor Control

One thing I have found is that most people associate clean with what they smell. We want everything to smell clean. Here are some ideas that will perk your nose right up.

Product Corner

For those of you looking for a foolproof product you can purchase to use in eliminating all odors with success, I highly recommend ODORZOUT™, a 100 percent natural product that stops many odors almost on contact—odors such as urine, mold, mildew, smoke, foot odor, skunk, paint and virtually every odor you can smell. It is made of blended natural zeolite minerals, contains no perfumes and is 100 percent safe for use around children and pets. You can even use it in the cat litterbox. In my testing, I have found no odor it didn't work on. Call 1-800-88STINK for more information or to order, or visit the website: www.88stink.com.

Burned Food

Boil a few slices of lemon in a saucepan to clear the air of the smell of burned food.

Fried Food

This works on any fried food odor, but the next time you fry fish, be sure to try it. Place a small bowl of white vinegar next to the stove when you fry foods. The odor seems to disappear.

Refrigerators

To deodorize refrigerators, leave a bowl filled with clean clay cat litter or charcoal on the shelf to absorb odors. This is particularly helpful in refrigerators that are going to be shut off or moved. Make sure you leave the door partially open at all times to allow air circulation, and put some litter or charcoal in an old nylon stocking and tie the top shut. Lay this in the refrigerator and it will control odors. For strong odors, nothing works better than dry, fresh coffee grounds. Put them in a bowl and leave in the refrigerator until odor disappears. This can be used in conjunction with the cat litter or charcoal very effectively.

Cars

If you smoke in the car, put a layer of baking soda in the bottom of the ashtray to absorb smoke odor. Empty it frequently. Dryer fabric softener sheets placed under the seats also help to keep the smoke smell under control. For musty smells, put cat litter in a nylon stocking, tie the top shut and place several under the seats or in the trunk.

Wood Trunks, Dressers and Chests

Many times old wood trunks and dressers will have a musty mildew or old odor. To eliminate this, take a slice of white bread (yes, it has to be white), put it in a bowl and cover with white vinegar. Leave enclosed in the trunk or drawers for 24 hours. If odor remains, repeat the process. If mildew odor persists in dresser drawers, shellac or varnish the inside of them and odor will be sealed in and eliminated.

Wintergreen oil is a wonderful household deodorant. Purchase some at a health food store and put a few drops on cotton balls and stash in plants, decorative pieces, etc., around the house.

Make Your Own Air Freshener

In a gallon jug, combine 1 cup baking soda, ¼ cup clear ammonia and 1 tablespoon scent (use your imagination—any scented oils or extracts work). Slowly add 16 cups of warm water, label and store. To use, pour well-shaken solution into a spray container and mist air as needed.

Laundry Odors

Odor can be a big laundry problem. There are a number of perfumed products that claim to remove odor and leave fabric fresh-smelling. It's been my experience, however, that most of these products just mask smells. I don't know about you, but I'd rather not have lilac-scented perspiration.

Putting white vinegar in the final rinse will remove some odors. But for difficult odors, such as smoke, urine, pet, garlic, gasoline, etc., you need a much stronger product. Again, I highly recommend ODORZOUT™. Use it dry or wet. It doesn't cover up odors—it actually absorbs them! And it's safe for people with asthma or allergies too!

To use dry, sprinkle directly on clothes that have an offensive odor, and allow them to sit for several hours. Intense odors, such as gasoline, can be treated for several days with no harm to the fabric. Just make sure you allow air to circulate—the product won't work in an enclosed space.

To use wet, simply fill the washing machine and add 1 to 2 teaspoons of ODORZOUT™. Agitate for a minute and then add the clothes and your detergent. Launder as usual.

ODORZOUT™ is great when sprinkled on pet bedding several hours before laundering. You can also use it to control odor in hampers and diaper pails. It is safe and nontoxic for use around kids and pets, which is a big plus.

Try the ODORZOUT™ Pouch as well. You can put them in empty shoes to eliminate smells, and in cupboards and drawers to keep odors at bay. I love the convenience.

Another good general odor remover for laundry is 20 Mule Team® Borax Laundry Additive. Add this to any odorous load of laundry. Just follow the directions on the box. This product is safe for all washables.

Remember, if it stinks, it's best to treat it immediately, before the odor can be passed on to other items.

13

Kids' Corner

Kids are life's reward and add great joy to our lives. They also test all of our patience and cleaning skills. If you have children, large or small, or you have grandchildren, you need to memorize this chapter, or at least know where this book is at all times!

Baby Shoes

To make baby shoes easy to polish, rub them with the cut side of a raw potato or some rubbing alcohol prior to polishing. After polishing, spray with hair spray to keep the polish from rubbing off so easily. Put a little clear nail polish on the areas that are always scuffed and the shoes won't wear as much in those areas.

Bath Helpers

Put small slivers of mild soap into the open end of a small sock and tie shut, or make a small slit in a small sponge and insert soap. These won't slip out of small hands (or yours when washing the baby).

For a great safe way to bathe a toddler, put a plastic laundry basket with mesh openings in the tub and put the child in it. It's a safe answer to bathing in the tub. But remember: Never leave a child alone in the bathtub.

Diaper Pins

If you are using cloth diapers, you know the misery of a dull diaper pin. To keep pins safely in one place where you can easily grab them, and to make them slide through fabric easily, store them stuck into a bar of soap.

Meal Mess Helper

To avoid those messy spills under baby's high chair, put a plastic tablecloth under it at mealtime. Cleanup will be a breeze and you can even put the tablecloth in the washing machine with an old towel, detergent and warm

Dear Queen of Clean:
My twin babies have stains on their clothes from zinc oxide ointment. How can I remove the stains without ruining the clothes?
Have Twins in Topeka

Dear Twins:
For zinc oxide stains, use hot water and detergent, rubbing the fabric against itself to remove the oil. Then soak the garments in white vinegar for 30 minutes after treating, then launder as usual. Your twins' clothes will be good as new . . . times two!

water. Hang to dry. This is a great tip when your toddler eats in Grandma's dining room!

Cleaning Stuffed Animals

Dust heavily with baking soda or cornstarch and work in well with your fingers. Roll the toys in towels or place in a plastic bag and leave overnight. The next day, use a clean brush to brush the toys thoroughly after removing from the bag. Doing this outdoors saves cleanup.

Formula Stains

On white clothes, apply undiluted lemon juice and lay the garment in the sun.

On colored clothes, make a paste of unseasoned meat tenderizer and cool water or an enzyme product from the laundry section at the grocery store. Apply and let sit for at least 30 minutes prior to laundering. Rubbing with a bar of wet Fels-Naptha Soap® will also help.

Cleaning Training Pants

To keep training pants white and odor-free, soak in a solution of 2 tablespoons of borax (available in the laundry section at the grocery store) and 1 gallon of hot water. Soak 1 hour prior to laundering.

DID YOU KNOW?

The easiest way to clean your baby's teething rings is in the dishwasher! Tie the teething rings in the top basket and wash them with the dishes. This works well for rattles too!

To Remove Gum from Hair

Rub cold cream or petroleum jelly into the gum. Use a dry Turkish towel-type rag to pull down on the hair strands and petroleum jelly. Work until all is out, then double shampoo.

That old reliable peanut butter also works great. Massage the gum and peanut butter together between your fingers until the gum is loosened and can be removed. Freeze the area with ice cubes in a plastic bag and then pick out the gum.

Crayon

For crayon marks on fabric, place the stained surface down on a pad of paper towels and spray with WD-40® Lubricant, let stand a few minutes, turn over and spray the other side.

Again, let sit a few minutes. Apply dishwashing detergent and work into the stained area, replacing the toweling as it absorbs the stain. Wash in the hottest water for the fabric you are working with, using your regular laundry detergent and all-fabric bleach.

To remove crayon from walls, spray with WD-40® Lubricant. Wipe off with a paper towel. Wash with hot water and liquid dishwashing detergent, working in a circular motion. Rinse well.

Watercolor Paint

Watercolors can be removed from fabric. Don't fret. Brush and rinse as much of the watercolor from the surface as possible. Apply a soft-scrubbing product with a damp sponge and rub in a circular motion, working toward the center of the spot. Rinse and dry. If any stain remains, apply nail polish remover to a cotton ball, blot the stain and rinse. Repeat as needed.

To remove watercolor paint from carpet, apply rubbing alcohol with a sponge, blotting the stained area lightly. Turn the sponge as the stain is absorbed. Repeat until no more stain is being removed. Most of the remaining stain can be removed with a damp sponge and soft-scrubbing product. Rinse carpet well.

Magic Marker®

To get rid of marks on appliances, wood or hard plastic, first try wiping with a damp sponge. If any stain remains, apply a soft-scrubbing product with a damp sponge, working in a circular motion, and rinse. If the stain remains, saturate a cotton ball with nail polish remover, blot the remaining stain and rinse well. This works on paneling, painted wood, tile and no-wax vinyl floors.

For marker stains on carpet, dampen a sponge with rubbing alcohol and use a blotting motion to absorb the marker, changing the sponge as needed. Apply a good carpet spotter, such as Spot Shot Carpet Stain Remover®, as directed on the can.

Marker stains on clothing should be rinsed with cold water until no more color can be removed. Place the fabric on paper towels and saturate with rubbing alcohol, using a cotton ball or small cloth to blot the stain. Replace the paper towels as often as needed to prevent restaining the fabric. Treat the stain with a lather from a bar of Fels-Naptha Soap® and launder as usual.

Chalk

To remove chalk from masonry, painted surfaces, vinyl flooring, tile, plastic and glass, brush and rinse as much of the chalk from the surface as possible. Remove the remaining stain with a damp sponge or cloth dipped in a soft-scrubbing product. Rinse surface well.

Chalk on carpet can usually be removed with a good vacuuming. Vacuum the area well, using the attachment hose to concentrate the suction over the chalk. If stain remains, use a good carpet-spotting product.

For chalk marks on fabric, place the stained area on a pad of paper towels and blot the spot with rubbing alcohol. Work in a lather of Fels-Naptha Soap® and launder as usual.

Glue on Carpet and Fabric

For water-based glue such as Elmer's™ School Glue, fold a paper towel to overlap the glue spot and saturate to almost dripping with warm water. Place this on the glue spot and leave on for about 45 minutes to an hour to allow the glue to soften. Rub the glue spot with a wet rag in a circular motion to remove all the glue you can. Repeat this procedure until glue is removed. Follow with a good carpet spotter.

Silly Putty™ Clay and Similar Products on Carpet and Fabric

Scrape off what you can with the dull edge of a knife. Spray with WD-40® Lubricant and let stand about 10 to 15 minutes. Scrape again. Respray as required, wiping up the stain with an old rag. Once you have removed the residue of the product, apply rubbing alcohol to the stain and blot, blot, blot. Reapply as necessary.

To remove from hard surfaces, spray with WD-40® Lubricant and wipe with a paper towel or old rag. Wipe any remaining stain with a cloth saturated with rubbing alcohol. Wash with a solution of dishwashing liquid and hot water, working in a circular motion. Rinse well.

Writing on Plastic Toys and Doll Faces

Ink and marker are very difficult to remove from plastic surfaces. Try applying a cotton ball saturated with rubbing alcohol. Let sit for 15 minutes and then rub. Sometimes using the pressure of a cotton swab dipped in alcohol helps. You can also try rubbing with a little cuticle remover on a soft cloth. Apply the cuticle remover, wait 10 minutes and then rub gently with the cloth.

14

Are Pets Turning Your Home into a Barnyard?

Do your pets have accidents in the house? Did you have a pet-sitter while you were on a trip and the cat didn't use the litterbox and the dog didn't go outside? Do you know what to do when the cat leaves you a hairball surprise on the carpet or the spaghetti didn't agree with the dog? Help is on the way! Here's all the information you need to clean up pet accidents and keep them from happening again.

Pet Odor

Pet odor caused from urine or feces is one of the toughest deodorizing problems you will face. The stain from the problem is only a small part of the dilemma. Unless you completely deodorize the area where the pet accident occurred, the animal, especially cats, will return to the spot and resoil it.

Pet odor is a protein-based problem and cannot be eliminated by normal spotting procedures. In order to remove odor, you must use an enzyme product to digest the protein, particularly in urine. If you do not use the correct cleaning procedure, the cat or dog will locate the smell and re-use the area, since animals operate primarily on a sense of smell.

Enzyme products may be purchased at pet supply stores, veterinary clinics and janitorial supply stores. There are many enzyme products available. Two that I particularly like that are available nationwide are Outright Pet Odor Eliminator® made by the Bramton Company, and Nature's Miracle®.

I have had experience with both products and find that they both work well. I tend to favor Outright because I successfully used it in my former business and personally (thanks to Zack, my 17-pound Bengal cat) for 15 years.

Do not be fooled into believing that you can spray on a deodorizer and the odor will magically disappear. It won't happen, and you will have wasted time and money on a product that doesn't work. Now let's get to the basics of pet odor removal.

First, Remove and Blot

You must remove any solid waste from the area and blot up any liquid residue using a heavy pad, paper towels or old, disposable rags. Lay this pad on the carpet and stand on it to absorb as much liquid as possible.

Step Two, Treat

Now you are ready to treat the accident with the enzyme product of your choice. Read the directions on the product carefully, following them exactly. Do not be afraid to really saturate the carpet. Generally, pet accidents soak through the carpet back and into the pad, so the enzyme treatment needs to soak in just as deeply. Water will not hurt your carpet; it is dipped in water numerous times during the dyeing process. Not putting the enzyme in deeply enough will not eliminate the odor. This is the most important step, so be sure to saturate the entire area, covering the circumference of the stain thoroughly, too. Remember, the urine goes into the carpet deeply and spreads.

The Secret

Cover the treated area with a plastic garbage bag or a dry cleaner's bag. If there is any lettering on the bag, do not let it touch the carpet or it will transfer to the carpet. Weight the plastic down with something heavy—the idea is to keep the enzyme from drying out until it can do its job, which is digesting the protein in the urine or feces. Leave the plastic in place at least 24 hours, preferably 48 hours—resist temptation, don't peek!

Step Three

Uncover the area and allow it to dry thoroughly. This may require as much as 10 days, depending on how deeply you treated the spot. To speed drying, let a fan blow across the area.

Step Four

Once the area is completely dry (and only then), check for odor. If there is still odor, retreat as directed above. If the odor is gone, clean the area with a good-quality carpet spotter that specializes in pet stains. I like Spot Shot Instant Carpet Stain Remover®. I have used it for years; and it works quickly and efficiently and won't leave residue in the carpet to encourage resoiling.

If you have pets, keep some enzyme cleaner and carpet spotter on hand for pet accident emergencies.

Don't Panic If You Have No Enzyme or Carpet Spotter!

There is hope even if you don't have an enzyme product on hand. First, soak up as much liquid as possible from the carpet and remove any solids. If you have club soda on hand, pour that on and blot by standing on paper towels or rags (if you have no club soda, then use cold water). Do this repeatedly to remove as much urine as possible. Mix a mild solution of white vinegar and water (⅓ cup vinegar in a 1-quart bottle filled with cool water) in a spray bottle and spray onto pet stains to help remove the smell. Rinse with clear water and blot. Now go to the store at the earliest possible moment and buy the enzyme product and spotter and use as discussed previously.

Oops! The Carpet Changed Color

Urine spots may change the carpet color. The carpet may be lightened or bleached. Many times this is not obvious until the carpet is cleaned the first time after the accident. It is more common when the stain has not been treated in an appropriate manner. If this happens, try sponging the area with a mild ammonia solution. This will sometimes return the carpet to its original color, or at least make the stain less noticeable.

Pet Accidents on Upholstered Furniture

When pets have accidents on upholstered furniture, you must first be sure that the fabric can be cleaned and treated with water. Check the platform of the sofa or chair under the cushion to determine the cleaning code. It should be listed on a tag. W indicates that the piece can be cleaned with water, so it can be treated as described on page 51. Clean the area using a good-quality upholstery spotting product. If the code is an S, this means solvent must be used in the cleaning process and this must be done by a professional. Do not apply an enzyme product or spotter. Call a professional. In this instance, the foam in the cushion may require replacing after cleaning.

Removing Pet Hair from Fabric

Sometimes the vacuum cleaner isn't enough to remove pet hair from upholstered furniture. If this is true in your case, try one of the following methods:

- Dampen a sponge and wipe over the furniture, rinsing the sponge as necessary.
- Wipe down with your hands while wearing rubber gloves.
- Wrap tape around hands and wipe, changing as needed.
- Wipe with dampened body-washing puff.
- Wipe with a used dryer fabric softener sheet.

If a pet urinates on a mattress, treat it as described on pages 82–83, but when done treating with the enzyme, cover the spot with plastic and stand the mattress on edge to expedite drying. If possible, leave the enzyme on for 12 hours. Remove the plastic and sprinkle the area with borax. Let dry thoroughly and vacuum well. If necessary, follow by cleaning with a good-quality carpet spotter.

When the Cat Leaves You a Hairball or the Spaghetti Doesn't Agree with the Dog

If you have pets, you know what it's like when your cat or dog suffers a digestive upset. You hear the problem begin and run to move the dog or cat off the carpet (which seems to be their favorite place to leave "gifts"), but you're too late and faced with a mess to clean up.

First, resist the temptation to wipe up the mess. If there are solids that can be picked up with a paper towel, do so, but do not smear the accident into the carpet. Trying to wipe it up immediately will only make the mess worse. Instead, sprinkle a heavy coating of baking soda on the area and allow it to dry. The baking soda will absorb moisture and digestive acids. Once the area is dry, remove with paper towels or vacuum the area, removing all of the mess that will come up. Vacuum very thoroughly to remove the baking soda. Then, and only then, you should grab the rag and the cleaner. Use your favorite carpet spotter, following the directions carefully. Remember to blot rather than rub.

If any discoloration remains after cleaning, try applying either undiluted lemon juice or hydrogen peroxide from the drugstore. Let it soak on the stain for 15 minutes and then blot. If the spot is still visible, apply again, watching carefully to be sure that there are no changes in carpet color. If you need a more aggressive treatment, mix lemon juice and cream of tartar into a thin paste. Apply to the spot, let dry and then vacuum up. When done with any of these procedures, rinse the carpet with cool water.

Keeping Cats from Digging in Your House Plants

To keep your cat from digging in indoor flower pots, place a cotton ball dipped in oil of cloves just below the soil line.

If your pet is eating your house plants, here's a great product to try. It's called Bitter Apple and is simply sprayed on the plant leaves. It won't hurt the plant or your pet. Its bitter

Help your pet get through those hot summer days by putting a few ice cubes into his water bowl.

taste will immediately stop the pet from chewing on the plants. Try your local pet store.

If Your Pet Meets the Wrong End of a Skunk . . .

If your pet meets the wrong end of a skunk, apply Massengill™ douche, mixed as directed on the box. Do this outside and do not rinse. To help avoid eyes, apply a little petroleum jelly around the eye area.

A Sticky Situation

You don't need expensive products to remove gum from pet hair. Believe it or not, peanut butter works great, as does petroleum jelly and cold cream. Massage the gum and peanut butter together between your fingers until the gum is loosened and can be removed. Freeze the area with ice cubes in a plastic bag and then pick out the gum. Your dog might not like the ice cubes, so if you'd rather, you can try cold cream or petroleum jelly instead of peanut butter. Just rub cold cream into the gum. Then use a dry Turkish towel-type rag to pull down on the hair strands and petroleum jelly. Work until all is out, then double shampoo.

To deter fleas, sprinkle salt in the crevices of the dog house.

15

Leave No Stone Unturned: Meticulous Marble

Bathroom and kitchen countertops are usually synthetic (cultured marble). However, marble used in living room and other furniture is usually the genuine article, as is marble flooring. Seal it with a stone sealer when it is new because it is very susceptible to stains, and wipe up spills quickly because marble absorbs moisture. It also can be easily scratched by grit. Be realistic about your expectations when you have real marble flooring or furniture. It will probably not maintain its showroom shine and some scratching cannot be avoided.

Clean marble regularly by sweeping it first and then using a soft cloth or sponge with a solution of mild liquid soap and warm water to wash it. Do not overwet the marble, instead use a damp cloth or sponge and keep the cloth or sponge clean as you work. It is a good idea to rinse marble and dry it with a soft cloth after washing. Do not use acidic products, such as vinegar or lemon juice, as they will etch the marble. Other things to avoid are scourers and solvent-based cleaners.

As you are washing if you find spots that are not responding to the washing solution, sprinkle on a little 20 Mule Team® Borax or baking powder and rub with the damp cloth or sponge. You can also use a commercial marble polish available at hardware stores and home centers.

When you are spotting marble remember that warming it first with a blow-dryer will open the pores and make it easier to remove the stain.

Bathroom and kitchen marble can be cleaned with 1 part liquid fabric softener to 2 parts warm water. Clean thoroughly and polish with a soft cloth.

If you have old marble that you are trying to clean and restore, there is an old-fashioned recipe that has been around for years, but it still works. It is effective on heavily soiled surfaces and for stains:

Cut up three or four bars of Ivory Soap and dissolve them in hot water until you have a thick gelatin-like syrup (you can grate them if you want). Paint this on the marble and let it sit for about a week. If the thick syrup starts to dry, simply add some additional water to the mix or add more of the solution. At the end of the week, rinse off the Ivory Soap solution, rinsing several times, and dry with a soft cloth.

Now let's talk about other stains.

To restore the shine to marble, rub with a cloth dampened with turpentine and then buff well. Dispose of the cloths outside in the trash when you are done.

Grease Stains

Grease stains usually are circular in shape and often dark in the center where the initial grease landed and then spread. Wash the circular area with clear ammonia and rinse extremely well. If this does not work, try saturating the stained area with 3 percent hydrogen peroxide and then working in powdered whiting (available at hardware and home centers in the paint department). Cover the area with plastic wrap and tape it down with masking tape. Let sit for 15 minutes, then rinse well. Repeat as necessary. Buff and then polish and reseal the area.

Rust Stains

Use a mixture of commercial rust remover and powdered whiting to remove rust. Follow the directions for grease stains. Once the rust is removed, rinse well and rub with a dry cloth. This method also works for tea and coffee stains.

Water Stains

A wet glass will leave a ring on marble. To remove it, apply 3 percent hydrogen peroxide with an eye-dropper or spoon and then add a drop or two of clear ammonia. After 30 minutes, wipe the area with a paper towel, rinse and dry.

For fine scratches on marble, you can use a paste of baking soda and water and the buffing wheel on your electric drill. Large areas are best left to the professionals.

Wine

For white wine stains, saturate the area with 3 percent hydrogen peroxide. Let sit 15 minutes or so and then rinse and dry. For red wine, use Wine Away Red Wine Stain Remover™ as directed on the container.

Mystery Stains

Many times you will find a stain on marble and have no idea what it is. For those stains, combine 3 percent hydrogen peroxide and some cream of tartar and rub with a soft cloth until the stain is removed. For tougher stains, massage with some nongel toothpaste and a soft cloth, then follow with the hydrogen peroxide and cream of tartar treatment again.

16

Company's Coming!

A Quick Tidy

I get lots of letters from people wanting to know how to tidy a messy house in a hurry. We're all busy these days, but we still want to take time to entertain, to kick back at home and enjoy the company of friends, whether it be with a delicious home-cooked meal or a double supreme pizza with extra cheese! But often we're dashing from here to there, with only a short time to ready the house for our guests. So what to do for a quick tidy?

Well, the first thing to remember is not to panic. Your house doesn't need to be perfect, it just needs to be welcoming. Okay, a toy truck and a dirty pair of sneakers in the entry hall aren't exactly welcoming. But you can take care of that without much fuss.

First thing I suggest is to take a pan of boiling water and sprinkle some cinnamon in it. Now, don't worry. I'm going to keep this simple. I'm not trying to add to your worries. And I'm not going to suggest that you make little place cards out of pinecones or anything, but if you sprinkle some cinnamon in some boiling water and let it simmer, then the house will have a beautiful, homey aroma. You'll start to relax and your house will be welcoming for your guests. It's a warm fuzzy. And it's very easy.

Once you've got the water simmering, grab a laundry basket, and go from room to room and pick up all those misplaced items. And if you have kids who suffer from dropsy, as I call it, then you'll have some picking up to do. Just pick up the toys and the Walkmans and the Game Boys and the sports jackets, put them in the laundry basket and place the basket in an out of the way place such as a closet. Done.

> Do your kids suffer from dropsy? You know, they drop things here, they drop things there . . .

Next thing is to close the doors to the kids' rooms. That's another problem easily solved.

And last, go into the bathroom that your guests will be using. Take a cloth—I recommend Euronet USA's ACT Natural® Microfiber Cloths. They clean and disinfect without chemicals, using only water—just dampen the cloth and wipe it around all surfaces: sinks, mirrors, and taps. . . . Presto that's that!

Now, put on some music, dim the lights a tad and relax. Enjoy your guests and enjoy your home.

One Night Stands . . .

Are you one of those people who say, "Be sure you come and stay with us when you're in town"? Well now is the time to pay up, because, guess what, they're here!

If you're expecting out-of-town guests, you'll want everything to look its best, especially the room where your guests will be sleeping. Try to look at the room as if you were a guest—better still, get a feeling by spending a night in the guest room itself.

First, you'll want the bed to be as comfortable as possible. That means the best mattress you can provide covered with a good mattress pad for comfort and protection. If you use a zip-on plastic mattress cover with a good cotton, quilted pad on top, you'll know the mattress is clean. Just store the mattress covers right on the bed.

Freshly washed linens and several choices of pillows are a great welcome. Provide extra pillows for those who read in bed. When I wash my linens after company leaves, I make sure they are good and dry, and then I store them in an old pillowcase to keep them fresh and clean and ready for use without rewashing. Covering your pillows with zippered pillow protectors will also allow you to keep the pillows clean and sanitary. Wash the protectors with the sheets and then put back on the pillows.

Make the bed up with blankets appropriate for the season and be sure your guests have easy access to an extra blanket or comforter, should they require it.

Let your friends know they are welcome by giving them plenty of open hanging space in the closet, even if you have to remove some of your stored clothing. Put plenty of hangers within reach, and make sure to include some for hanging trousers, skirts, etc. Putting in some cedar chips for fragrance is a nice touch.

If you have several pillows stacked on the closet shelf, tie them together like a gift package with ribbon or string. This gives them stability and they will sit on the shelf better and not tumble out every time you open the closet door.

You're ahead of the game if you have a guest bathroom. When I have guests, I always set out a pretty basket filled with containers of shampoo, conditioner, and mouthwash that I have collected at hotels in my travels. I add a couple of inexpensive toothbrushes, travel-size toothpaste, deodorant, hair spray, shave cream, hand cream, a sewing kit, a disposable razor, anything that I think a guest might need. Be sure to provide plenty of fresh towels and hooks to hang them on and hooks for robes when showering. It is nice to add both soap and shower gel to the shower for your guests. If you have room, a shelf or area to put personal grooming things during the visit is always welcome.

If your family bath doubles as a guest bath, the things I talked about above still apply. If you can clear out a small area in one of your storage areas for your guests' grooming needs to be stored and designate a towel area for them too, it will make everyone more comfortable. A good lock on the door is a must for everyone's peace of mind.

Look for unusual ways to display towels, such as rolling them and sliding them into a decorative wine rack that you hang on the wall or set on the floor or vanity.

Sometimes we use our spare rooms as junk rooms or storage rooms. If this is the case, a quick pickup will go a long way to making your friends feel welcome. Who wants to spend a night in a room that resembles a U-Store-It locker? Clear off surfaces as much as you can—a spare laundry basket or an empty box will hold clutter just fine. You don't have to empty the room, though. Family photos are always welcoming, as are knickknacks and memorabilia. If you really want to be *the hostess with the mostest,* you might put out a nice bunch of fresh flowers. Once you've done this, put your feet up. Your friends have come to visit you—not inspect the wallpaper. So relax. Have fun. And remember . . . next time it's your turn to visit them!

Part 2

The Year Ahead

17

What Does Clean Mean to You?

I've been at this cleaning business a long time, and still I'm surprised by the number of people who get hung up on what to clean and when. Seems that for some people, cleaning is a dirty word. They want to know how often to clean this, when to put away that—as if there's going to be a big test at the end of the cleaning semester. But life's not like that. Sometimes you win. Sometimes you lose. Sometimes your house is clean. Sometimes . . . well, let's just leave it at that, shall we?

I don't believe in keeping to someone else's schedule and someone else's rules. I believe in making my schedule work for me, and I have only one rule: IF IT'S NOT DIRTY, DON'T CLEAN IT. We're all busy, and we all have better things to do than clean house. No one but the Marines wears white gloves these days, so we don't have to be concerned with the white glove test. That said, few of us are happy living in a home that's dirty or unkempt. It's hard to relax when the dust bunnies are having a rodeo in the corner of your living room.

Sit back and think for a moment. What does clean mean for you? How organized do you want to be? Are you the type of person who's just dying to rearrange the magazines at the dentist's office, the one your office mate runs to when she spills cola on her keyboard? Or are you the person whose idea of cleaning is to put the dirty dishes in the oven, whose laundry schedule is determined by *Can I get away with this another day?*

Chances are, you won't have to think too much about this. You already know who you are. You know what makes you comfortable and how you like to live. I suspect that despite our natural tendencies, most of us flit between one group and another. There are times when we feel that things are ordered and under control, just as there are times when chaos rules. I'm not trying to get you to change teams, to convert you or give you a cleaning citation. I want you to find your comfort, to do the things that will get you there, and help you stay there.

And that's where this section comes in. I've started off with a list of things to think about, from everyday household tasks that you'd never overlook (like washing dishes) to those uncommon tasks and easy oversights, such as flipping your mattress and cleaning the gutters. I'd like to encourage you to find out what's right for you. Some people, for example, may like to change their sheets every week. Others may find every two weeks often enough for them. A schedule only works if it's flexible and realistic. Start with that in mind and you can't go wrong.

That's part of what this section is about. Establishing a routine that works for you. The other part? Fun stuff. Each month brings its own particular signature. February, for example, can be a time of high heating bills, but it's also a time for Valentine's Day and romance, and that can mean flowers, champagne and chocolates (for starters . . .). I'll let you in on the best ways to care for flowers, how to help keep the bubble in that bottle of champers, and what to do when the chocolate strays on to the furniture and bed linen. (Oh, don't tell me you've never eaten chocolate in bed!) Turn to April, and you'll find some fun, natural ways to color your Easter eggs, as well as how to get ready for allergy season. October contains some Halloween fun, and December, as you might imagine, rounds out the year with lots of holiday advice.

But that's not all. I've included a few recipes throughout the book (well . . . you *have* been asking), and I'm also including some recommendations from my four-legged co-writer: Zack The Palace Pussycat. Zack helped me with my last two books (mainly by sitting on the manuscript), and this time he wanted to contribute further. Look for his suggestions, marked with a paw print. They provide advice from the feline point of view—and of course remind us that behind every successful woman there's usually a rather talented cat.

This is not your typical cleaning book. But then again, I'm not your typical Queen!

It's About Time

Daily Duties

Personally, there are only two things that I do *every* day: kiss the King and feed the cat. I make the bed most days (it's so much nicer to come home to), and I do try to see that the dishes are done, but sometimes I'm just so busy or distracted that even the simplest tasks fall by the wayside. We're all very busy. We all have too much to do. That's why I've kept this list of daily chores short. Carry out these few tasks on most days and you'll find your life running smoother than you could imagine. Miss a day . . . well, the dishes will still be there tomorrow.

- Make beds.
- Put dirty clothes in the hamper.
- Hang up clothes.
- Clean up spills.

* Wash dishes.
* Wipe counters and stovetop.

Twice Weekly

I've kept this list gloriously short—only one item:

* Vacuum carpets!

"The early bird gets the worm. I'd rather sleep in and have toaster muffins."
—Shirley Lipner

You can get away with vacuuming carpets just once a week (six days is the average gestation period for dust bunnies), but vacuuming twice weekly will prevent the dirt from getting ground into the fibers, and will therefore prolong the life of the carpet.

Weekly

Weekends were made for more than housework, so try spreading these tasks out through the week if you can.

* Sweep hardwood floors.
* Dust hard furniture.
* Dust knickknacks.
* Do the laundry.
* Change sheets.
* Clean sinks.
* Clean showers and tubs.
* Clean the toilet.
* Clean bathroom mirrors.

* Empty trash cans, put out garbage. (Clean the trash can if odors remain.)
* Sweep porch, patio and doormats.

Biweekly

* Vacuum stairs.
* Dust TV/VCR/stereos, etc.

Monthly

* Replace the bag on your vacuum.
* Vacuum upholstery.
* Clean makeup brushes and sponges.
* Clean hairbrushes and combs.
* Vacuum drapes.
* Clean mirrors.
* Vacuum or dust blinds and shutters.
* Dust ceiling fans.
* Dust woodwork and dust down any cobwebs.
* Wash kitchen and bathroom area rugs.
* Vacuum carpet edges.
* Check hard floors and rewax heavy-traffic areas if needed.
* Clean out the refrigerator.
* Spot clean the kitchen cabinet fronts.

* Clean the fronts of stove, refrigerator, dishwasher, etc.
* Check the furnace filter: change or clean if needed.
* Hose off entry mats.
* Sweep out the garage.

Quarterly

* Sweep or wash the walkways and driveways.
* Change or clean the furnace filter.
* Wipe off lightbulbs as you dust (be sure they are cool).
* Look over knickknacks and wash or thoroughly clean any that require more than dusting.
* Flip the cushions on chairs and sofas for even wear.
* Clean humidifiers and dehumidifiers.

Twice a Year

* It's got to be done: clean the oven.
* Clean stove hood and/or exhaust fan.
* Check the contents of freezer for things that are past their freshness. Clean freezer.
* Turn the mattresses on beds.
* Wash any plastic, vinyl or leather furniture.
* Clean scatter rugs.
* Dust books on shelves, making sure to dust shelves under the books.

* Vacuum the heat registers and cold air returns.
* Vacuum under furniture.
* Check silverware and clean if necessary.
* Replace that little box of baking soda in the refrigerator.
* Dust all the things you haven't been able to reach all year long.
* Clean bedspreads and slipcovers.
* Clean closets as you change seasonal clothes.

Annually

* Wash blankets and comforters.
* Dust down walls.
* Wash walls (every two years).
* Strip any waxed floors and rewax.
* Wash all windows and screens.
* Wash or dry-clean drapery.
* Move and clean under and behind large items.
* Wash blinds.
* Clean carpet and upholstery.
* Clean any areas you have avoided all year long.
* Have the air conditioner checked and cleaned.
* Have the furnace checked and cleaned.
* Sort through the medicine cabinet, clean it, and organize and discard old medicine.

* Clean out kitchen cupboards, wash and reorganize.
* Replace the batteries in smoke detectors and other safety devices.
* Check the batteries in flashlights.
* Clean rain gutters.
* Wash all exterior windows.
* If you have a chimney, clean it.

So there you have it. Your annual checklist. Now for the fun stuff.

"There's always room for improvement. It's the biggest room in the house."

—Louise Heath Leber

18

January

It's January, a time of good intentions and new beginnings. We've made our resolutions and, with any luck, have recovered from our seasonal indulgences. We're ready for a fresh start. But first we have to clean up from last year. That means putting away the Christmas decorations, taking down the tree, and storing the lights and all that half-price wrapping paper that seemed like such a good idea at the time. So let's get to it. If we start now, we'll still have time to enjoy that Super Bowl party!

Let's Un-Deck the Halls

Putting up decorations can be a lot of fun, what with all the excitement of the holidays to look forward to. But there are few surprises after Christmas—unless, of course, you're talking about that mystery stain you've just discovered on the hall carpet. The best way to clean up after the holidays is to take a deep breath, roll up your sleeves, and get down to it.

The sooner you start, the sooner you'll be finished. And isn't that what it's all about?

Lights

If you just whip the lights off the house and tree and toss them in a box, you'll hate yourself come next December when you find them twisted, tangled and broken. Wrap them around an empty paper roll instead. Take a large paper roll—one from wrapping paper will do fine—and cut a notch at one end. Tuck one end of the lights in the notch and start rolling them around the tube. When you get to the end of the tube, make another notch to fasten that end of the lights. Do this to each strand, clearly labeling the tubes as you go—indoor or outdoor lights, tree lights or decorative strands, etc. Make sure you separate any lights that aren't functioning properly and mark those too, either for repair or scavenging.

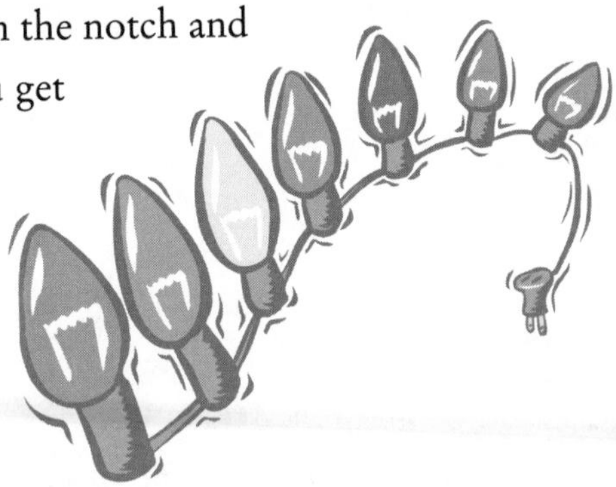

Large lights or extra long lengths can be rolled in a circle, like a cowboy loops a rope. Delicate, expensive or special light strands can be stored in the type of inexpensive plastic food bowls that come with covers. The lights won't get crushed or broken, and they can be stacked for storage without damage.

Christmas Trees

Taking down the tree is really a two-person job, so try to enlist some help. A tree bag is your best bet, as it will prevent pine needles from being trailed through the house. Just make sure to buy a bag large enough to cover the base of the tree, and long enough to cover the height. The first step is to siphon off all the water that you can—a turkey baster works great. Next, lay a large covering, such as a plastic shower curtain, on the floor. Take a good look around to ensure that breakables are safe, and make sure you're well out of range of any hanging light fixtures. Loosen the tree stand, and gently tip the tree onto the covering, being careful not to shed too many needles or spill any remaining water left in the reservoir. (Remember the first rule of cleaning: If you don't make a mess, you won't have to clean it up!) Don't pull the bag up haphazardly, and don't tug. Be gentle and gradually unroll the bag up the length of the tree, something like putting on a pair of panty hose. (If you wear panty hose, that is . . .) Once you've got the tree into the bag, tie it tightly and drag it outside. You can, of course, carry the tree, but there's always the chance that you'll drop it, and that may cause damage.

Artificial trees can be stored fully assembled in Christmas tree storage bags. Simply open the bag, "fold" up the limbs on the tree as directed (You did keep the booklet that came with the tree, didn't you?), place the tree carefully into the bag and zip it up! Lack of storage space may dictate that you dismantle the tree and keep it in a box. If that's the case, just make sure to identify the branches, base and stem—unless, of course, you like jigsaw puzzles.

Ornaments

First, make sure to dust the ornaments before you store them. Used fabric softener sheets are great for this job, but you will need rather a lot. Wipe the ornament with the used dryer sheet, then cover it so that the *other* side of the sheet touches the ornament. The fabric softener sheet will protect the

DID YOU KNOW?

Decorative candles can be cleaned quite easily with a cotton ball moistened with rubbing alcohol.

ornament during storage, and the residue of softener will help to repel static electricity—and, therefore, dust—when you hang it on the tree next year! Once you've wrapped the ornament, place it gently in a storage container, such as a shoe box or plastic storage carton. Those large metal canisters that once held popcorn are great, too.

Whatever container you use, make sure not to overcrowd it or force the lid down, and try not to use tape to secure the box. Tape can ruin the box for future use and, if stored in an attic, can get sticky and gummy during the hot summer months. That can cause a real mess. A bungee cord hooked around the ends of the container will keep the lid firmly closed. Try that instead.

Once again, make sure to mark the storage container, and make sure to separate ornaments that are expensive or have sentimental value. Delicate elongated ornaments can be stored inside a toilet paper tube, and smaller items can be placed safely in egg cartons. Save silk balls that are starting to unravel by giving them a spritz with some hair spray or spray starch.

Wrapping Paper

The most important thing about storing Christmas paper is to actually remember that you have it so you don't go out and buy more next year! Either put the paper in an obvious spot so that it's the first thing you see as you start to take out the decorations, or make a note that you have *x* number of rolls on hand. It's not a bargain if you buy it twice!

I store my wrapping paper under the bed. Long plastic storage containers meant for this purpose work exceptionally well, and can be found quite inexpensively in dollar and discount stores. If you don't have a storage container, lay the rolls of paper on the floor and tie them together with some string or an elastic band. A bungee cord hooked into the ends of the rolls will hold the paper in a neat bundle. Just make sure to slip them into a large garbage bag to keep them clean during storage. Some people like to store their wrapping paper and ribbons in an old suitcase. That can work well, just as long as you remember which one you've used. You don't want to end up in the Bahamas with nothing to wear but Santa Claus wrapping paper and a big red bow! As I've said, labeling is important.

I HATE IT WHEN THAT HAPPENS . . .

You've just found the perfect color bow at the bottom of the bag and, darn, if it isn't crushed! Not to worry. Crushed bows can be brought back to life by putting them in the dryer on air fluff (no heat) for a few short minutes. Presto! Good as new.

Ribbons and Bows

- Store premade bows in a plastic storage or shoe box to prevent them from getting scrunched up. If you've bought an assortment of bows, tip them out of the bag and into the box. Those bags always seem to be too small to hold the bows, and so many of them wind up flattened and bent.
- Keep rolls of ribbon tidy by putting a rubber band or ponytail holder around the roll. You'll prevent unraveling that way.

Baubles, Bangles and Beads—In Other Words, *Miscellaneous!*

- Garland is usually too lush to be wrapped around just one paper roll, so fasten a few tubes together with a rubber band and wind the garland around that. Make sure you wrap the garland around the roll like a candy cane, side-to-side, and secure it in notches that you've cut in each end. Don't draw the garland from top to bottom—the strand could stretch or break.

* Dust silk flowers before storing them with a blow-dryer, set on cool.

Save those empty baby wipe boxes. They come in handy for storing gift tags and those slivers of ribbon that are so handy for decorating small packages.

* If you store Christmas dishes in plastic wrap or stacked in Ziploc™ bags, you won't have to wash them before using next year.
* Make sure to launder Christmas tablecloths and napkins prior to storing. Old spills will oxidize during storage and can be difficult, if not impossible, to remove.
* Take care when storing the Nativity scene. Wrap each figure separately, either in tissue paper or a used fabric softener sheet. Paper towels don't work well for this job because their fibers can catch on any rough edges. If you do scratch a figurine, try touching it up with a child's colored pencil.
* Artificial wreaths can be stored year-to-year in a large pillowcase (depending on the size of the wreath) or in a large plastic bag. Wrap some tissue paper around the wreath first, but be gentle when removing it—you don't want to damage any of the branches. If the ribbon on the wreath is flattened, just plump it up with a curling iron.

Delicate Christmas knickknacks can be stored in egg cartons.

* Many charities make good use of discarded Christmas cards.

St. Jude's Ranch, for example, is a nonprofit youth home that teaches kids a trade and a way to earn money by cutting off the verse and making the fronts into new cards. Entire cards are welcome, as are cards with the backs cut off. For more information call 1-800-492-3562, or visit St. Jude's website at www.stjudesranch.org.

Making a List, Checking It Twice

Make a note of what seasonal items you've stored, and *where* you've put them. If you make a list of what you think you'll need next year—wrapping paper, Christmas cards, extension cords, larger-sized pants—you'll be in a good position to pick up bargains. More important, you'll save yourself that last-minute flurry of panic when you realize that your tree lights don't reach the outlet. Remember: Excitement is good. Panic is bad.

It's Time for That Super Bowl Party!

I love Super Bowl parties. Everybody seems to be in such great spirits. Good friends, good food, and good fun. What could be better?

Touch-Ups after Touchdowns

You wouldn't cry over spilt milk, so why shed a tear over beer? First thing to do for a beer spill on the carpet is to blot up all the liquid you can, then flush the area with club soda and blot, blot, blot again. Now turn to a great carpet spotter like Spot Shot Instant Carpet Stain Remover® and follow the directions carefully. Try to avoid carpet cleaners that contain stain repellents. If the beer doesn't come out during the first try, the repellent could lock in the stain and you could be left with a permanent mark.

Salsa—the sauce, not the dance—tastes so good and stains so bad. For salsa spills, blot with club soda as soon as possible, then treat with Wine Away Red Wine Stain Remover™ or Red Erase®. Both are fabulous at removing red stains from carpets, upholstery *and* clothes.

Guacamole is my favorite, but what a cleaning disaster it is! Think about it: It's oily *and* green. Clean up guacamole spills on carpets and upholstery by scraping with a dull, straight edge, such as a credit card. (The one you used to pay for the party should do nicely.) Remove as much *gunk* as possible, then flush with club soda and blot, blot, blot! Let sit 10 minutes, then flush with cool, clear water. Once the surface is dry, apply a good carpet and upholstery cleaner according to the directions on the container. If you still have a green reminder, mix up a solution of ½ cup of hydrogen peroxide and 1 teaspoon of ammonia, spray on liberally, let sit 15 minutes, then blot. Continue until the stain is removed and then flush with club soda and blot until you have removed all the moisture possible.

> Beer stains on clothes? Flush with cool water, work in a few drops of liquid dishwashing soap and launder as usual.

If you happen to be wearing the guacamole stain, treat with Zout® Stain Remover or rubbing alcohol. Gently dab the alcohol on the stain and let sit for 15 minutes before pretreating and laundering as usual.

If your house has that smoky, day-after smell, bring some white vinegar to a boil, then reduce to a simmer for about 30 minutes, being careful not to let the pan boil dry. Let the vinegar stand, and after a few hours unwanted odors will be absorbed.

If the upholstery smells like smoke, lay a clean sheet on the furniture and sprinkle it with ODORZOUT™. Let sit overnight, then remove the sheet and shake outside. ODORZOUT™ is all natural and won't hurt anything. For carpet odors, sprinkle directly, then vacuum in the morning.

Spilled ashtray? Don't reach for the vacuum—at least not right away. You could have a nasty vacuum fire on your hands, at which point you'll be wishing that a spilled ashtray was your only problem! Pick up any butts and dispose of them in an empty can until you are sure they are cool. Ash on hard floors should be cleaned with a broom and dustpan; ash on carpet should be vacuumed using only the hose—no beater bar, which could grind the ash into the carpet. If you're sensitive to cigarette odors, you may want to dispose of the vacuum bag or empty the canister. Never apply water to an ashtray spill. You'll have a black, gooey mess on your hands that's far worse than anything you started with.

DID YOU KNOW?

Simmering orange or lemon peels can give your home a fresh, natural scent.

Somebody break a glass? It's bound to happen. Pick up the large shards first, then use a cut potato to pick up the slivers. (Yes, a potato.) Just cut the potato in half and press down on the glass with the damp side. Vacuum the remaining small pieces, using the attachment hose to concentrate the suction, then vacuum the carpet thoroughly. Never use a vacuum with a beater bar to vacuum glass until you've picked up all you can with the potato and the attachment hose. The beater bar will only flip the glass around, making it harder to clean up the debris.

Let's Dish!

Guacamole is such a wonderful Super Bowl tradition. And now that you know how to clean it up, you can serve it with flair! Here's my favorite recipe:

CHI CHI'S SUPER BOWL GUACAMOLE

4 ripe avocados, mashed or pureed (can do in food processor)
½ cup canned diced green chilies
¼ cup minced onion
1 tablespoon salt
¼ cup lemon juice

Combine all ingredients, cover and chill. Serve with corn chips. Makes about 3 cups.

19

February

This is the month of cold weather and high heating bills. Thank goodness it's also the month of love. Offset the winter cold by snuggling with your honey. Let those Valentine's flowers remind you of spring, and brighten those long winter nights with some sparkling jewelry. And if Cupid does leave his mark, well, look no further for some quick cleanup tips.

Conservation for the Nation

Cuddling is an energy-efficient way to keep warm. Want to save water? Bathe with a friend! Of course there are other ways to save on your energy bill.

- Why heat an empty house? Lower the thermostat when your family is out during the day—try 65 degrees or so—and bring the heat back up in the evening. If you lower the temperature when everybody is toasty warm in bed, you'll cut your bill even further. A double setback thermostat can adjust the temperature according to your needs. It's well worth the money.

* Moist air retains heat, so invest in a humidifier (or adapt your existing heating system) and you could lower your thermostat by another 3 or 4 degrees. That can save you up to 12 percent on your heating bill!

* A gas-fired heating system should be professionally cleaned and serviced at least once a year to keep it working at maximum efficiency. Oil-fired systems should be cleaned and serviced twice a year. Those of you who have had the misfortune of a furnace backup *know* I'm giving you good advice. Cleaner is better.

* Shut the dishwasher off at the dry cycle and allow dishes to air-dry with the door partially open.

* Just cooked a nice roast dinner? Leave the door open a crack (once you've turned off the oven, that is), and let the heat warm the room as the oven cools. Don't do this if you have young children—nothing is worth a potential burn.

* Keep radiators, registers and ducts clean. Vacuum with the duster brush attachment; for hard to reach spots use a telescoping duster. Make sure they're clear of debris and free from obstructions, such as furniture and draperies.

* Replace furnace filters frequently. A clean filter will distribute heat more efficiently. Check filters monthly, say the first of every month. Vacuum to remove dust, and replace filters when vacuuming alone won't get the filter clean. Disposable filters should be replaced at least every three months.

* Heat can escape through air conditioners, so store yours if you can. If that's not possible, do your best to winterize the

unit. Cover the outside of the a/c with cardboard cut to size, and then wrap it in a heavy-duty plastic. Drop cloths and plastic tablecloths are ideal. Secure the covering with a bungee cord, making sure to avoid corner flaps that might tear in the wind.

* Conserve energy in winter *and* summer by adjusting the rotation on your ceiling fan. A counterclockwise rotation will push the hot air from the ceiling down into the room—perfect for winter. A clockwise rotation will pull up warm summer air and replace it with a nice, cool flow.
* Conserve water by taking showers instead of baths. The average bath uses 25 gallons of water, whereas the average shower uses just 10 gallons.

> That "small load" setting may save water, but the washing machine still goes through the same number of rotations. Avoid washing small loads if you can.

* Don't leave water running while you brush your teeth. Turn it off until you're ready to rinse.
* Whenever possible, use cold or warm water for washing clothes. Always use cold water to rinse.
* Clean the lint filter on your clothes dryer each time you dry a load. Clothes will dry faster and more efficiently.
* That little black dress may be a hot number, but there's no reason to keep it warm. Keep closet doors closed.

Happy Valentine's Day!

Flowers, jewelry, candy? I'd love Valentine's Day even if it *wasn't* the day the King proposed!

Petal Pushers

- Do your best to select the freshest flowers available. Look for healthy stems with unblemished leaves and petals. Flowers that are just beginning to bud will last longer than those in full bloom.
- Be sure to remove leaves that fall below the waterline. They can contaminate the water.
- Cut stems on an angle while holding them under running water, then immerse in fresh water. It's best to do this in the early morning when it's coolest.
- Coarse, heavy stems (you'll find them on flowers such as gladiolus, mums, pussy willows, forsythia, and even roses) should be split with a sharp knife before placing in water. This will encourage the stem to drink up the water. Pounding the base of the stem with a wooden spoon works well, too.
- Change the water every day. And for a longer life, add one of the following mixtures:

  A teaspoon of sugar and about ¼ teaspoon of lemon juice

  Several aspirin tablets that have been dissolved in a little warm water

A tablespoon of liquid bleach. That will stop the water from clouding; particularly useful when using a clear vase.

* Prolong the life of flowers by keeping them cool and displaying them out of direct sunlight.
* Remove anthers from lilies. Those long, pollen-bearing shoots can rub off on clothes, carpeting and walls and can be extremely difficult to remove.

Clean pollen stains from clothing by sponging with rubbing alcohol. Don't use anything with ammonia. That will set the stain.

Artful Arrangements

* Flowers too short for the vase? Place stems in plastic drinking straws before arranging.
* Vase too deep? Fill it with marbles prior to adding water and flowers.
* Wilted flowers? Snip about an inch off the ends and stand them in hot water for about 20 to 30 minutes before returning to a vase of clean, cool water.
* Make sure floral foam is saturated with water before adding flowers.
* Arrange large flowers first, then follow with smaller blossoms and greenery.
* Coffeepots, teapots and milk bottles make lovely imaginative vases.

DID YOU KNOW?

Tulips are the only flowers that continue to grow after they've been cut!

- Plastic hair rollers are great for arranging flowers. Stand them upright in the bottom of the vase and place stems in the cylinders to keep them in position.
- Try to match the flowers to the vase. Hourglass shapes are good for single-bloom flowers like tulips, and urns are great for flowers that droop easily. Slim, cylindrical vases are best for tall flowers like gladiolus.
- Placing your arrangement in front of a mirror will double the impact of your flowers.

Diamonds Are a Girl's Best Friend

Who doesn't love to get a gift of jewelry? Who doesn't know how to care for it?

- Rubbing alcohol is great for cleaning costume jewelry. Pour a little rubbing alcohol over the piece—place the jewelry in a shallow dish or small container first—and gently brush with a soft toothbrush. A word of caution: Many costume pieces are glued, and soaking can loosen the glue. Try not to saturate. Finish with a quick rinse in cool water and wipe dry.
- Costume jewelry that doesn't contain glue can be cleaned with denture-cleaning tablets. Drop a few tablets in a cup of warm water and allow the jewelry to soak for 5 minutes or so. Rinse and dry well. For intricate pieces, dry with a blow-dryer.
- Remove dirt from intricate pieces by brushing with a soft-bristle toothbrush and some white, nongel toothpaste. Rinse by brushing with a clean toothbrush and just water, and dry well.

* Clean diamonds by placing in a tea strainer and dipping them in a pot of boiling water into which you have added several drops of ammonia and a drop or two of dishwashing liquid. Immerse for a few short seconds and then rinse in cold water. For extra sparkle, dip the diamonds in a little bit of undiluted vodka or alcohol for a minute or two, then rinse and pat dry. This may be used for hard stones such as diamonds, rubies and sapphires. *Do not* use this method on emeralds.

Restore the luster to pearls by buffing gently with a soft cloth moistened with olive oil.

* Emeralds are extremely soft. They can crack easily and absorb water, so buff them with a soft toothbrush or an ACT Natural® Microfiber Cloth. Don't soak them or immerse them in water, and if you want a thorough cleaning, take them to a professional.
* Remove tarnish from silver with a paste of lemon juice and baking soda. Apply the mixture with a soft toothbrush, then allow to dry. Remove with a clean, dry toothbrush and polish with a clean, soft cloth.
* Jade can be washed in mild, soapy water. Dry immediately.
* Opals and turquoise are porous stones that should not be washed. Brush settings with a dry, soft toothbrush and shine with chamois-type leather or an ACT Natural® Microfiber Cloth.
* Wash gold in a bowl of soapy water. A soft, gentle stroke with a soft toothbrush will help clean crevices, details and links.

Dry with a soft, lint-free towel and then buff with a chamois or microfiber cloth.

* Always fasten a chain-link necklace before storing to prevent tangles. Chains that tangle easily can be slipped through a drinking straw. Cut the straw to half the length of the chain, drop the chain through and fasten the clasp on the outside of the straw. No more tangles.

I HATE IT WHEN THAT HAPPENS . . .

Tangled chains got you in knots? Place a drop of baby oil on the chain, then gently untangle by pulling the links apart with two sewing needles.

The Valentine's Day Stain Chain

Love should last forever, not that chocolate stain.

* Chocolate on clothes requires special treatment. Scrape off all you can with a dull straight edge, taking care not to force the chocolate more deeply into the fabric. Gently apply some Zout® Stain Remover, allow it to sit on the fabric 5 minutes or so (don't let it dry), and then flush under a forceful stream of warm water. If a grease mark is still visible, sponge with any good dry-cleaning solution such as Energine Cleaning Fluid®. For really tough stains, soak in Brilliant Bleach® by Soapworks®. Follow package directions carefully.
* Chocolate on carpets should be treated immediately with your favorite carpet cleaner. Try Spot Shot Instant Carpet Stain Remover®. For really stubborn stains, saturate the area

with ½ cup of hydrogen peroxide, to which you have added 1 teaspoon of ammonia. Allow to sit for 20 minutes, then blot. You may need to repeat this process. Once the stain is gone, flush the area with club soda and blot by standing on old, heavy towels. This should remove the moisture. Allow to fully dry before walking on the area.

* Champagne spills should be sponged immediately with club soda. The salt in the soda will help to prevent permanent stains and the carbonation will draw the spill from the fibers. Two remedies for the price of one!
* Dried alcohol stains will turn brown as they age, so quick removal is important.
* Champagne spills on clothes should first be blotted with club soda, then pretreated with a good laundry stain remover.
* Champagne spills on carpets should be treated with Spot Shot Instant Carpet Stain Remover®. Just make sure to blot well with club soda first. Treat spills on upholstery the same way, drying with a hair dryer to prevent a ring from forming.
* Stains from pink champagne can be removed with Wine Away Red Wine Stain Remover®.
* Perfume stains can be avoided if you apply your fragrance before you get dressed. Make sure it's dry before putting on your clothes.
* Perfume is a combination of alcohol and oil—deadly to fab-

You can keep the fizz in champagne for hours if you slip the handle of a metal teaspoon down the neck of the bottle. I don't know why it works, but it does!

rics. Treat perfume stains with Zout® Stain Remover and launder as soon as possible. If the fabric is dry-clean only, be sure to point out the stain to your dry cleaner.

- Never iron an area that has been sprayed with perfume. You might set the stain, or worse, remove the color from the fabric!
- Perfume stains can be removed from sturdy fabrics with a lather of Fels-Naptha Soap® and warm water. Work well into the stain, let sit 15 minutes and launder as usual.
- Stains from massage oil can be removed with a good waterless hand cleaner, such as GOJO®. Rub it well into the fabric—*massage* it in if you'd like!—then flush with warm water. A paste of liquid dish soap and 20 Mule Team® Borax will also work. Launder as usual using your normal detergent and the hottest possible water for the fabric. One-half cup of 20 Mule Team® Borax will ensure that all residue is removed.
- Oil stains on carpets should be covered quickly with baking soda. Allow the baking soda to absorb the oil—this may take several hours—then vacuum it up using the attachment hose to concentrate the suction. Vacuum very well with the hose before vacuuming with a beater bar to remove all of the baking soda. Finish off with your favorite carpet cleaner.

March

It's spring! The flowers are blooming, the birds are singing, everything's fresh and new, and you can't wait to get started with your spring-cleaning. Yikes! Did I say spring-cleaning? That has no part in my spring fantasy. How about yours? Spring-cleaning was a necessity a long time ago when log cabins were boarded up to keep out the winter cold. The arrival of spring presented the first opportunity to clean out all the soot and grime that had accumulated during the long winter months—hence the term spring-cleaning. Those of you living in log cabins may want to continue this practice, but for the rest of us, well, there are better things to do.

That's not to say that there aren't certain times of the year when you'll want to clean a little more thoroughly. It may be just after Christmas, it may be right before Aunt Martha's next visit . . . it might even be spring. *When* you do it is entirely up to you. As for *what* to do, read on.

Spring Forward

Don't Clean Your Clutter

The hardest part of cleaning is working around the accumulation of all those things you've somehow acquired. If you really want to streamline your cleaning process, take a few minutes, go room to room and take stock of what's in sight, as well as what's hiding in your cupboards. I'll bet my crown (the cheap cardboard one . . .) that you have things that haven't been used in three, five, ten years or more. Think carefully. Do you really want to keep that purple giraffe? Do you really want to clean it?

If you can't bear to part with your collectibles (I love cats and pigs—don't ask), consider storing some and displaying others, rotating your selection from time to time. You'll have less to clean.

If you have a lot of treasures, think about investing in a glass-fronted display cabinet. The glass will protect your ornaments from dust, and you shouldn't have to clean them more than once a year.

Are you really going to read all those back issues of *National Geographic*? Don't be timid. Throw them out.

If that cat figurine that Aunt Lucille gave you 10 years ago is missing a paw and part of its tail, look at it, smile at the memories and then say good-bye. Don't keep things that are broken and can't be repaired.

Think before you purchase the latest gadget. If you don't buy it, you won't have to clean it.

Can't find any twist ties and the trash bag is full? Just use dental floss or a rubber band. Both are tough and water resistant, so you don't have to worry about the rain.

A Word About Cleaning Products

Gather all your cleaning products together in one container before you start your rounds—something with a handle is ideal. If you have more than one bathroom, think about purchasing a set of cleaning products for each. It may cost more at the time, but you'll save yourself the aggravation of toting products from one floor to the next.

Make sure you have plenty of clean cloths and vacuum bags. If you anticipate throwing out a lot of garbage, make sure you have lots of good, strong bags. Check supplies of soaps and any all-purpose cleaners that you may use. There's nothing worse than starting a task only to have to stop halfway because you don't have what you need at hand.

The most expensive products are not always the best. Try store brands and homemade solutions—they can work just as well as their more expensive counterparts.

Try not to depend on harsh chemicals. Things like baking soda, white vinegar, 20 Mule Team® Borax, Fels-Naptha Soap®, lemon juice, salt and club soda work just as well and aren't harmful to your family or the environment. Baking soda is a great deodorizer and a wonderfully mild abrasive. White vinegar is a terrific cleaner, especially for soap scum and mildew. Borax is a never-be-without laundry additive, and Fels-Naptha Soap® is great for stubborn stains. And let's not forget the club soda, lemon juice and salt. Club soda works on all sorts of spills; lemon juice is a great natural bleach; and salt can be used on just about everything, from artificial flowers to clogged drains.

Look for odor eliminators instead of cover-ups. Make sure to purchase products without scent. Try using baking soda or a good, natural odor eliminator such as ODORZOUT™.

Don't forget to change that little box of baking soda in your fridge. Pour the old box down the drain, and chase it with a ½ cup of white vinegar, and you'll create a little volcano to naturally clean and freshen drains.

Smells in old trunks and drawers can be

Be wary of using too many antibacterial products. Unless you're prepping for surgery, good old soap and water work just fine.

eliminated with a slice of white bread placed in a bowl and covered with white vinegar. Close the trunk or drawer for 24 hours, and when you remove the bread and vinegar the odor will be gone!

Fresh, dry coffee grounds will remove smells from refrigerators.

A pan of cat litter will remove musty smells in closets and basements.

Place crumpled newspaper in drawers to remove musty odors.

Put dryer fabric softener sheets in luggage, storage containers, closets and drawers to leave a clean, fresh scent.

"Housework can't kill you, but why take a chance?"
—Phyllis Diller

First Things First

Decide on your approach and be consistent. If you decide to clean for an hour, stick to it. If you decide to clean one room now and another tomorrow, stick to that. Indecision and distraction can really affect how well you clean. If you start out doing one thing and end up doing another, you'll have a houseful of half-finished projects, and you won't feel as if you've accomplished anything. That can be very frustrating, to say the least.

Remember: If it isn't dirty, don't clean it!

I like to start with the room that requires the least amount of effort, and that's generally the one that's used the least. It may be the guest room, the living room . . . it may even be the kitchen. Hey—no judgments. Think of it as a sort of warm-up. Start with the lightest task and you'll see results fast. That will motivate you to keep going!

Generally speaking, work from top to bottom. Dust from the light fixtures, tops of furniture, etc., will fall onto the carpet and floors. So do floors last and you'll know that your house really is clean.

Don't backtrack. Finish one task before moving to another. Put on some high-spirited music to set the pace and keep you going.

Let's Get Started

Dusting comes first. But don't just pick up any old cloth, and don't, for heaven's sake, use a feather duster. They may be some man's fantasy, but they just scatter the dust all around. Really, they're worse than useless. Try lambswool dusters. I strongly recommend them. You can buy lambswool dusters in many varieties, including dust mitts and telescoping dusters, which are great for those hard-to-reach corners.

Use a telescoping lambswool duster to clean ceiling fans.

Don't just move ornaments while you're dusting. Make sure to dust them, too!

After you've dusted your electronic equipment, it's a good idea to give it a wipe with some rubbing alcohol. Apply with a clean, soft cloth, then buff dry. Make sure to turn the power off first, though.

Once you've dusted, give the upholstery a good going-over. Use the appropriate attachment on your vacuum cleaner—the small brush for cushions and arms, the long nozzle for crevices and hard-to-reach areas. If you own a sofa bed, make sure to open it up and vacuum the mattress. (Most sofa bed mattresses are one-side only, so don't try to flip it.) Don't forget to vacuum scatter cushions.

Climb the walls, I mean clean the walls, by tying a towel over the head of a broom and pulling it down the wall. Shake out the towel as necessary, and change it when it becomes soiled. Work up and down the wall—not side to side—and use strokes that are comfortable for you. Complete one room at a time.

Walls don't need to be washed every year unless you're a smoker. So don't wash walls that don't need it. If, however, a room looks grimy, a good wall wash could save you the effort of painting.

Floors

Grit can scratch wood floors, so they should be swept before washing. Use long, directed strokes, moving from the corners to the center of the room. Sweep all the grit—that means crumbs, cat litter, and all that unidentifiable stuff—into a dustpan.

Now you're ready to wash with your favorite, gentle floor cleaner. Make sure the cloth is damp, not wet. Overwetting the floor could warp it or damage the finish. Just in case I haven't been clear on this: *Yes, I am suggesting that you get down on your hands and knees.* Sorry, but anything else is just a shortcut, and if you want to clean your floors thoroughly, this is the only way to go.

- Start at the edges and move your hand across the floor, using a small circular motion.
- Keep the cloth well rinsed and continue until the entire floor is done.
- For vinyl or tile floors use the same cleaning method, substituting 1 gallon of warm water combined with 2 tablespoons of 20 Mule Team® Borax for the tea.
- For marble floors try the ACT Natural® Microfiber Mop. It uses nothing but water and thousands of little scrubbing fingers that pick up the dirt without scratching. It won't leave a film, either.

And Don't Forget . . .

- Give the inside of kitchen cupboards a wash with a simple solution of warm, soapy water. Anything sticky can be removed with a little baking soda.
- Grind some lemon rinds and ice cubes in the disposal to keep it clean and sharpen the blades, too.

* Vacuum your mattress with the upholstery attachment, then flip it for even wear. A plastic bag, such as a dry cleaner's bag, placed between the box spring and mattress will help ease the strain of this task. (Best not to take any chances, so if you have young children leave out the bag and let your muscles do the work.)
* Since you're flipping your mattress, don't forget to wash your mattress pad, blankets and pillows before putting the bed back together.
* Yes, even that self-cleaning oven needs to be cleaned.
* Draperies should be cleaned once a year. Please read the care label carefully and don't try to wash curtains that should be dry-cleaned.

> You can extend the life of your window coverings by vacuuming them frequently.

* Not every room requires the same effort or attention, so decide before you begin what clean means to you.
* If you use the space under your bed for storage, remove the storage containers, vacuum the carpet and clean the containers before you put them back.
* If the woodwork on your walls is dirty, you should carefully wash it even though you do not wash the walls.
* Take down the globes from the overhead light fixtures, wash them and put them back up. While you're at it, when the lightbulbs are cool, dust them, too.
* If hinges are squeaking every time you open a door, lubricate them with a quick spray of silicone.
* Don't overlook door handles—wash and polish them. They get used constantly and seldom get washed.

Wearing of the Green Doesn't Have to Mean Grass Stains

Now that winter white is starting to disappear, just make sure that the greens of spring don't appear on your clothes!

Grass stains can be removed from clothing with the help of a little white, nongel toothpaste. Brush the toothpaste into the stain using an old, soft toothbrush—rinse and then launder. Zout® Stain Remover will also do the trick. Work a liberal amount into the fabric with your thumb and forefinger, then wash as usual.

Grass stains on jeans should be treated with rubbing alcohol. Saturate the stain, let sit for 10 to 15 minutes, then pop the jeans into the wash. Check to see that the stain has come out before you put the jeans into the dryer. Heat will set the stain and make it impossible to remove, so if you need to repeat the procedure, it's best to find out *before* you use the dryer.

For grass on white leather athletic shoes, try molasses. You heard me—*molasses!* Massage the stain with a dollop of molasses and let it sit overnight. Wash the shoes with soap and water the next morning, and the grass stains should come off along with the molasses.

Fabric shoes such as Keds® can be cleaned with baking soda. Dip a wet toothbrush into some baking soda and brush vigorously. Rinse well and dry out of the sun. No baking soda? Use white, nongel toothpaste instead.

If those blue suede shoes have had a meeting with the green, rub the stain with a nylon sponge that has been dipped in glycerin. Rub until the stain has been removed, then blot with a cloth dipped in undiluted white vinegar. Brush the nap to reset in the right direction, and allow the shoes to dry out of the sun.

Grass stains on carpets should be removed with a good-quality carpet cleaner such as Spot Shot Instant Carpet Stain Remover®. Just follow the directions on the can. For stubborn stains, apply rubbing alcohol; wait 10 minutes, blot, then treat with your favorite carpet cleaner.

21 April

Allergy season *and* tax time? If it weren't for Easter, April really would be the cruelest month. Don't fret. You can shorten the sneezin' season by allergy proofing your home. As far as taxes are concerned, well, I can't tell you how to pay less, but I can help with things like pencil marks and sweat stains. So turn your attention to Easter and the beauty of the month—those blue skies that remind us that the best things in life are free.

Spring Fever

The experts say that allergies are reactions to harmless substances that don't bother most people. Huh! If that's the case, why do so many people suffer from them? Seasonal allergies are caused by factors such as trees, grass and pollen. Year-round allergies are reactions to things like dust particles, animal dander, mold and dust mites. Whatever their cause, allergies can make us sneeze, sniff, cough and generally feel miserable—but you don't have to take it lying down.

Can You Do Without It?

Many detergents contain petroleum distillates—a major irritant for allergy sufferers. If freshly laundered clothes make you sneeze or itch, consider changing detergents. Be selective. Look for products marked "dye and perfume free," and check the label for colors or perfumes—you'll want to steer clear of them. I like PUREX®, a gentle detergent that does a great job on laundry. People with severe allergies or asthma may benefit from environmentally friendly products, such as those manufactured by Soapworks®. If you or anyone in your family suffers from allergies, you owe it to yourself to shop around.

Dryer fabric softener sheets can exacerbate allergies—best to do without them.

Allergy sufferers should use pump dispensers rather than aerosol sprays, which can fill the air with minute particles of irritants.

* If you must use hair spray, apply it outside the house so that the fumes won't linger.
* Look through your cleaning supplies and eliminate those with a strong scent, those loaded with chemicals, and those you've had for a long time. Products can undergo changes after time, and irritants can increase.
* Don't mix chemicals.
* Look for natural cleaning products such as baking soda, lemon juice, club soda, white vinegar, etc.
* Furniture polish can attract dust and dust mites. Best not to use it.

* Stuffed animals are huge dust collectors, so if your children have allergies, it's best to limit their exposure. Any cloth or fuzzy toy can be a potential allergy problem. If your child is having difficulties with allergies, remove toys one by one to determine those that can be tolerated—and those that can't.

DID YOU KNOW?

Stuffed fabric toys that can't be washed can still be cleaned. Just place in a plastic bag with some baking soda and salt and shake vigorously a few times a day for several days. This should remove dust, dirt and odor.

Filters: Not Just for Coffeemakers

* If there's a filter, clean it! This means vacuums, fans, air purifiers, etc.
* Change the furnace filter at least once a month or invest in one that can be washed. Make sure to wash it frequently.
* If your allergies are severe, consider wearing a filtration mask while vacuuming and dusting.

Don't Get Hauled on the Carpet

* Dust and dander cling to carpets, so if you have severe allergies you may want to consider hard floors such as wood, laminate and ceramics. These floors can be washed frequently and will do a lot to keep allergy symptoms at bay.

- If you have severe allergies but are unable to remove carpets, apply benzyl benzoate dry foam or 3 percent tannic acid, then vacuum using a cleaner with an effective filter system. Tannic acid breaks down mite allergens, and benzyl benzoate dry foam actually kills mites and helps remove them—and their waste products—from carpet.
- Vacuuming can stir up dust mites and their droppings, so don't vacuum too frequently. Once a week is fine.
- Vacuum hard floors prior to mopping so that you don't stir up dust.
- Wash all hard floors with a quality cleaner created with allergy sufferers in mind. Try At Home All-Purpose Cleaner from Soapworks®.
- Damp-mop hard floors with a good-quality mop that can be washed in the washing machine. Try the ACT Natural® Microfiber Mop.
- Change the bag in your vacuum frequently. If you have a vacuum with a collection canister rather than a bag, empty it each time you vacuum.

Avoid placing houseplants directly on carpets and rugs. Moisture in the plant can cause condensation, and that in turn can cause mildew—a powerful irritant to allergy suffers.

Sofa, So Good

- Stay away from fuzzy or flocked fabrics that are difficult to clean. Buy only upholstered pieces that can be cleaned with water.

* Vacuum upholstered pieces weekly.
* Stay clear of furniture with ruffles or fringes. They're notorious dust catchers and notoriously difficult to clean.
* When shopping for upholstered furniture, look for pieces without loose pillows. Buy tailored pieces in tightly woven fabrics.

And So to Bed

* Sealing your bedroom door with weather-stripping will give you more control over your sleeping environment.
* Keep pets out of your bedroom.
* Something as innocent as wallpaper can cause mildew, so keep walls—especially bedroom walls—clear of papers and fabrics.
* Use an air purifier in your bedroom.
* Vacuum your mattress frequently. Invest in a good mattress cover—one that forms a protective cover but still allows the mattress to breathe.
* Wash all bedding in 130-degree water at least every 10 days. That includes blankets, pillows, comforters and mattress pads.
* If you can't wash pillows and comforters as frequently as you'd like, try placing them in the dryer on air fluff. That will help.
* Keep bedspreads, dust ruffles, decorator pillows, etc., dust free. Better yet, get rid of that dust ruffle.
* Stay away from down and feather pillows. They can aggravate allergies, even if you're *not* allergic to them. Use foam pillows encased in hypoallergenic covers that can be zipped shut.

And Don't Forget . . .

- Wash windows and screens frequently.
- Keep the house closed up as much as possible, especially on windy days.
- Plant flowers and trees that produce as little pollen as possible, such as ivy, African violets, and leafy plants such as philodendrons, piggyback plants, creeping pileas, and prayer plants.
- Install an air cleaner on the furnace or invest in a stand-alone air purifier.
- Don't keep fresh flowers indoors, no matter how beautiful.
- Keep your fireplace clean and make sure the damper is closed.
- Use natural lambswool dusters. The lanolin traps the dust and keeps it from spreading.
- If you don't like to use lambswool dusters, use a clean, damp cloth.
- Insects love stagnant water, so don't allow water to stand in fountains and plant bases.
- Remove dried flower arrangements. These dust catchers are very hard to keep clean.
- Invest in a dehumidifier and maintain it well. Empty it weekly and clean it, too. Wash it with a solution of 1 quart warm water and 2 teaspoons of chlorine bleach. Make sure you wipe down the coils, and pay special attention to the container that catches the water.
- Make sure your curtains are made of synthetic fiber. Natural fibers contain more lint and may aggravate allergies.

✳ Dust mites survive in dampness, so do everything in your power to keep the air dry—except moving to my house in Arizona!

✳ Keep cooking pots covered to eliminate steam.

✳ Use an exhaust fan over the stove when you cook.

✳ Don't hang clothes in the house to dry.

- Brush your pet outside and often. Try to wash him weekly—if he'll let you!
- Allergy sufferers should avoid cleaning litter boxes. If that's not possible, use a filtration mask and dispose of waste outside, never in a trash can.
- If your pet hates a bath, wipe his coat with a damp ACT Natural® Microfiber Cloth. This will remove loose hair, dander and dry saliva—all of which contribute to allergy problems.
- Don't take your dog for a run in the woods, through fields, or in tall grass where he can pick up allergy-causing mold spores, dried grass, leaves and pollen. Hmph. . . . Dogs!

Taxing Times

Now that we've dealt with allergies, it's time to deal with those other seasonal irritants—taxes! Read on to find out how to deal with those stains and other little annoyances that come up at this time. Just think of me as your own personal support group!

First, stock up on aspirin. You can use it to treat underarm stains, as well as that tax-season headache! (What do you mean you're not sweating?)

No, I'm not going to tell you how to launder your money.

For underarm stains on T-shirts and other cottons, dissolve 8 to 10 aspirin tablets to 1 cup of warm water, then saturate the underarm area of the garment. Allow to sit for 30 minutes and then launder as usual. If you're wearing the same tee night after night (hey, no judgments), rub the underarms with a bar of Fels-Naptha® Laundry Soap—then go change your shirt!

Pencil marks? Just take a nice, clean, soft eraser and gently rub the mark away.

If you're one of those confident types who prepares her taxes in pen, treat ink stains by soaking the garment in milk for several hours before laundering. You can also blot with rubbing alcohol or Ink Away®, available at office supply stores.

Paper cut? After disinfecting, secure it with a piece of Scotch® tape. The tape will protect the cut from the air and will also help to ensure that it doesn't get pulled farther apart. And if it doesn't get pulled farther apart, it won't hurt!

If you don't have any tape on hand, even a dab of super glue will help. Really—it's a great little healer. A little dab on the paper cut and no more pain! Is it dangerous? No, just don't use it on deep cuts, and please, don't glue your fingers together. Uncle Sam will not accept that as an excuse for late filing! You did glue your fingers together? A little acetone polish remover will unstick you—fast!

Okay, you're almost done. You've prepared your return, made out your check, sealed the envelope and are just about to leave the house for the post office when you realize you've forgotten to enclose the check. Dang! Don't despair. Reach for Un-Du™. It will open the envelope right up. No tears, no muss, and you'll be able to reseal it safely. Un-Du™ is available in home centers, drugstores, hardware stores and discount stores. It has such a wide range of uses. Use it to remove

kids' stickers from walls, price stickers from anything but fabric and bumper stickers when you change party affiliations. No home should be without it.

If you don't have any Un-Du™, try putting the envelope in the freezer for an hour or so, then roll a pencil under the envelope flap. With a little bit of care that envelope will open right up faster than you can say "Mata Hari!"

You don't owe? You're my hero! You say you're getting a refund? Give me a call. . . .

It's Easter

Now it's time to turn our attention to something more cuddly than the taxman! I have such fond memories of gathering around the table to dye Easter eggs with Dad and the Queen Mother. It's something the King and I love to do, too, and we love to include as many friends and family members as possible. The Queen Mum always insisted on covering the kitchen table with an old plastic tablecloth to prevent those stains from spills (where did you think I got it from?) so that our creations wouldn't harm the table. Here's what else you can do:

Place a clean washcloth or pot holder in the bottom of the pan and add cool water. Gently place the eggs in the pan, being careful not to overcrowd them. The cushion on the bottom of the pan will help prevent cracks, but if you add a tablespoon of white vinegar you'll be sure to avoid them altogether. (Vinegar will seal any cracks and help the egg to congeal.) Turn the heat on to medium and bring the eggs to a gentle boil. Continue to boil gently until they are done—about 20 minutes.

- Keep raw eggs fresh in the refrigerator by applying a light coat of solid vegetable shortening. The shortening seals the egg, which keeps the air out and helps the egg last longer.

* If you drop a fresh egg during any of this process, just sprinkle it with a heavy layer of salt, wait several minutes then wipe up with a dry paper towel. The salt will "cook" the egg so that it is easy to remove. A turkey baster also works well.

* Prepare for coloring by putting out several glasses of hot water (plastic will stain). Add 1 tablespoon of vinegar to each cup. The acid in the vinegar will help the dye adhere to the eggs.

Check your eggs for freshness by placing them in a bowl filled with cold water. Eggs that float to the top are old and should be discarded.

* You can use natural things to make great Easter egg dyes. Mustard and turmeric create a wonderful yellow shade, coffee and tea turn eggs tan to brown, red onion skins soaked in water create a purple dye, hot cranberry and cherry juice make vivid reds, and heated orange pop gives you orange! Use your imagination and create additional colors or mixtures.

* Remember: If you plunge hard-boiled eggs into cold water as soon as they are cooked, you won't be bothered with that gray ring on the inside of the egg white.

* Need to know which eggs are boiled and which are raw? Just give them a spin on the counter. A hard-boiled egg will spin easily, whereas a raw egg will wobble.

* One last important piece of information. If you are going to allow your colored Easter eggs to sit out in baskets, don't eat them. Eggs spoil rapidly at room temperature and can cause anyone who eats them to become very sick.

22 May

May is one of my favorite months. The uncertain weather of early spring is a thing of the past, and the whole summer seems to stretch out before us. What better time to get reacquainted with the garden? I came by my love of gardening naturally: I inherited it from my mom! The Queen Mother taught me to garden the natural way, with minimum fuss and no chemicals. I'm going to pass that along to you! I'm also going to share some recipes for homemade personal care products because there's nothing nicer than pampering yourself after a warm afternoon in the garden. And because May is the month of Mother's Day, why not treat her, too?

A Garden of Ideas

Before You Get Started

Get a head start on summer! Plant seeds in an egg carton to which you have added a small amount of soil—don't pack it too hard, and don't let it spill out over the sides. Keep the soil moist, taking care not to overwater. When you've seen the last frost, it's time to pop the seedlings out of the egg container and plant them in the ground. Still impatient? Speed up germination by laying a piece of plastic wrap over the seedlings to keep them moist and warm. Leave the plastic in place until the plants start to poke their heads through the soil.

* Try latex gloves in the garden instead of cloth. They're easier to clean—you can just rinse them under the hose and let them air-dry—and they don't stiffen up like canvas gloves do.

Tie a used fabric softener sheet around your belt to keep mosquitoes away while you garden.

* For a moisturizing treat while gardening, rub your hands with hand cream or petroleum jelly before donning your gloves.
* Don't like to wear gloves? Scraping your fingernails over a bar of soap before you get started will prevent dirt from penetrating under your nails and will protect them from breaking.
* Use a little wagon to haul your supplies around the garden. Check garage sales for good deals.
* Carry a quart spray bottle filled with water and a squirt of liquid dish soap. If you see bugs attacking your flowers, just give them a squirt and they'll vamoose!
* Need a kneeling pad? Take a 2- or 3-inch piece of foam, wrap it in plastic or put it in a large resealable bag and you're all ready to go.

Fertilizers

* Crushed eggshells worked well into the soil make a wonderful fertilizer. Terrific for gardens and houseplants, they aerate the soil, too.

- Bury some used coffee grounds in your garden to provide much-needed acid to soil that has a high alkaline content. You'll notice much greener greens!
- Fish tank water is loaded with nutrients. Use it for gardens and houseplants.
- Plants love starch, so save the water each time you boil noodles or other pasta. Just make sure to let the water cool down first.
- Dampened newspapers placed on the ground around plants will help keep the soil moist and hold weeds at bay. Wet the newspapers well—you need the weight of the water to hold them down—then sprinkle lightly with soil. The papers are biodegradable, so they will eventually dissolve.

Pest Control

- Keep pests such as aphids, mites, and whiteflies off roses, geraniums, hibiscus, and other plants by spraying them with a combination of 1 quart of water and ½ teaspoon of liquid dish soap. Reapply the solution every 2 weeks.
- Dissolve 1 to 1½ teaspoons of baking soda in 1 quart of water to kill bugs on flowering plants. Spray every 7 to 10 days.
- Powdered milk can kill aphids on roses. Mix ⅓ cup of powdered milk in 1 quart of warm water, and spray. The

Planting garlic, parsley or basil among your flowers will deter bugs. Marigolds also work well. Just plant them as an edging around the garden.

aphids will get stuck in the milk and die. Hose the roses down occasionally and reapply as needed.

* Here's a great natural way to control black spots on roses. Add 1 tablespoon each of baking soda and vegetable oil to 1 gallon of water. Then add 1 drop of liquid detergent and shake well. Spray directly on the foliage, and spray every 5 to 7 days during humid weather. Make sure to wet both sides of the leaves.
* Chase away pests that feed on your tender plants by mixing 1 tablespoon of hot mustard or red pepper with 1 quart of water. Spray directly on the foliage. One hot taste and the pests will be gone!

Who Knew?

Cutting roses and trimming bushes can be a prickly job, but if you grip thorny stems with barbecue tongs or clothespins . . . no more pierced fingers!

* Old panty hose make great ties for plants and tomatoes. They're strong and flexible, but soft enough so that they won't cut into the plant.
* Tuck a bar of soap inside a mesh bag and tie it around the outside faucet. After gardening cleanups will be a breeze.
* Hands that are very dirty can be cleaned with a thick paste of oatmeal and water. Rub well into hands before rinsing and washing as usual.
* Kill weeds with a natural toddy of 1 ounce of white vinegar, 1 ounce of inexpensive gin, and 8 ounces of water. Pour on the weeds and say good-bye.

Keep on the Grass

Morning is the best time to water your lawn. Grass that's damp with dew will absorb water better than grass that's fully dry. Parched grass can be resistant to moisture, so don't wait till your lawn is dehydrated before you bring out the sprinkler. And try not to water your lawn at night if you can avoid it. Night watering can encourage fungus.

You can cut grass that's still damp with morning dew by spraying the blades with vegetable oil. The wet grass won't stick, and you can get on with the rest of the day. Car wax works well too, but it's probably best to skip the drive through the car wash!

How do you know when it's time to water the lawn? I like the barefoot test. If you feel comfortable walking across the grass barefoot—if the lawn isn't crackly and springs back up when you walk across it—there's no need to water. But if the grass feels unpleasantly spiky and lays down flat after you've left the area, it's time to water.

A good soaking of water will promote a healthy lawn. That means strong roots and good color. I put a small empty can of Zack's cat food on the grass when I water the lawn. When the can is full I know I've given the grass about an inch of water, and that's plenty.

Try not to cut grass too often. A closely manicured lawn may be fine for the golf course, but longer grass is actually healthier because it holds moisture longer. Use the high setting on your mower for best results.

Just Tooling Around

Take good care of your garden tools and they'll last you a lifetime.

Keep a container of sand in the garage or shed, and push your shovels and trowels into it when you've finished your chores. Sand is a wonderfully natural abrasive. It will clean your tools and stop them from rusting. Not only will this tool-time sandbox prevent dirt from spreading around the garage area, but you'll always know where to find your garden tools!

Bothered by moles and gophers? Some people swear by castor bean plants, but the leaves and seedpods are poisonous to children and pets—yikes, that's me! Try human hair instead. Hair is an irritant to these small rodents, but it won't harm them or anything else. Ask your hairdresser for a bag of clippings and stuff the hair into the hole. It won't be long before these little critters move on. (If you have any hair left, you could try knitting a toupee for your uncle Jack.)

If dogs, raccoons or other animals are tipping over your garbage cans, tie a couple of rags soaked in ammonia to the handles. All it takes is one sniff and your garbage can will no longer be attractive to critters. *Dogs . . . sheesh!*

Discourage fleas and flies from gathering around your pet's outside eating and sleeping area by planting rue *(Ruta graveolens)* nearby. You can also rub rue on furniture to keep cats . . . like me, from scratching. Just use care that you don't discolor upholstery.

Keep the neighborhood dogs and cats out of your flowers by mixing equal parts of mothballs and crushed dried red pepper (cayenne) in and around the flower beds. No more four-legged visitors! Not that I would ever do such a thing . . .

Paint the handles of your yard tools a bright color and they will be easier to spot among the green of your yard. Not only that, you'll be able to identify your tools if you loan them out.

If rust has disfigured a metal tool, try rubbing with a stiff wire brush. Scrape a metal file across dull edges and they should come back to life if they're not too dull. Naval jelly sold at hardware stores is also a good alternative for rust on metal. Follow the directions on the container.

You can help protect your tools by applying Clean Shield® Surface Treatment or a thin coat of paste wax to the metal. The wax will form a barrier between the metal and the elements and should retard the growth of rust.

Rough handles mean rough hands, so make sure to take care of your tools. Wood handles that have become jagged and coarse can be made smooth again with a good rubbing of some light-grade sandpaper. Apply a generous coat of linseed oil when you've finished sanding and you'll protect the wood from cracking and splitting.

Spray your garden tools with nonstick cooking spray each time you use them. The dirt will be easy to remove when you are done. In fact, it should fall right off.

If you still find the handles too difficult to hold, try wrapping them in tubes of foam insulation, the kind used to insulate water pipes. Slit the foam lengthways, slip it onto the handle, and wrap lightly with heavy-duty tape. Not only will the foam protect your hands from the wood, it will also protect the wood from the elements.

Don't forget to store your tools out of the elements.

A Mom for All Seasons

When you hear the words "Mother's Day" I'm sure you think of your Queen Mother just as I do mine. Naturally, we all want to do something nice for our mothers . . . and naturally is what it's all about. So read on to find out how you can make your own collection of personal care products that are easy to make, and natural too. Give these to your own Queen Mum and every day can be Mother's Day!

Let's Face It

An oatmeal scrub will treat dry skin and draw impurities from your complexion. Mix ¼ cup of oatmeal, 1 teaspoon of honey and enough milk, buttermilk or plain yogurt to make a paste. Apply liberally to your face—making sure to avoid the delicate eye areas—then gently massage in small circular motions. Allow the mask to dry before you rinse with warm water. Once the mask has been removed, give your face an invigorating finish by splashing with cool, clear water. Apply your favorite moisturizer, or for a more thorough facial, follow with the tightening oatmeal mask.

Grandma loved this tightening oatmeal mask, and you will too. Mix 1 tablespoon of oatmeal with the white of 1 egg. Apply to your face and allow to dry. Rinse off using cool water.

> Prone to breakouts? Apply a thin mask of milk of magnesia once a week. Allow to dry and rinse with cool water.

Very dry skin? A little mayonnaise added to the tightening oatmeal mask will give you a smooth finish.

Need a four o'clock revival? Try witch hazel. Keep a small bottle in your desk at the office, along with some cotton balls. Dampen the cotton balls with the witch hazel, then blot your face and neck . . . prepare to be revived! It's that easy. Keep the witch hazel in the refrigerator if you can. And for an extra treat, pour some in a spray bottle for an after-workout spritz!

The Eyes Have It

These remedies aren't new, but they're worth repeating.

- A slice of chilled cucumber on each eyelid will relieve tired eyes. And that 15-minute rest won't do you any harm, either!
- Cold tea bags are great for puffy eyes, so keep some on hand in the refrigerator.

* A little bit of Preparation H® helps keep puffy eyes at bay. Just make sure to avoid tear ducts and the eye itself.
* Dab some castor oil on the skin around your eyes before going to bed at night. Stay well away from the eye area, and make sure not to use too much oil.

Your Crowning Glory

Restore luster to dry hair with a light, natural oil such as corn oil or sunflower oil. Those of you with very dry hair may like to use olive oil, but make sure to use a light touch. Olive oil can be extremely difficult to wash out. Another warning: Oil heats up very quickly and can cause severe burns, so avoid the microwave. The best and safest way to warm oil for a scalp treatment is to place the oil in an egg cup, then put the egg cup inside a mug or small bowl that you have filled with hot or boiling water. Heat the oil to lukewarm—about 1 teaspoon should do—and apply to dry hair with the palm of your hands. Make sure that the shaft and ends are well coated (not saturated, though), but avoid getting oil on your roots, which will weigh hair down. Cover your hair with a plastic bag and try to leave it on as long as you can—overnight is best. Finish with a thorough shampoo, lathering twice. Skip the conditioner and get ready for the compliments!

Mayonnaise also works well—it's a combination of egg *and* oil.

I HATE IT WHEN THAT HAPPENS . . .

Static electricity causing your hair to stand on end? Rub your brush and comb with a fabric softener sheet before brushing your hair. No more annoying static!

Don't heat the mayonnaise or it will separate. Just remove a quantity from the jar—a couple of tablespoons should be fine, unless you have very long hair—and let stand at room temperature for a few hours. Rub on just enough mayonnaise to soak the hair thoroughly (remembering to avoid the roots), and comb through. Leave on for 30 minutes, shampoo well and rinse with water and lemon before that final rinse of cool, clear water.

Let's See a Show of Hands

Make your own hand cream by mixing 2 parts glycerin to 1 part lemon juice. Massage a little into your hands after washing and at bedtime. This absorbent cream works well and smells lovely!

Soften hardworking hands and feet by rubbing with equal proportions of cooking oil and granulated sugar.

Cuticles may be softened by soaking in a bowl of warm olive oil. Push them gently back with a cotton swab. If cuticles are really dry, coat them with olive oil at bedtime.

Lemon juice is great for removing stains and whitening hands. Bottled or fresh-squeezed, just massage it into hands before washing with good old soap and water.

Your nail polish will last longer if you apply a little white vinegar to each nail. Just coat each nail with a cotton swab prior to applying your nail polish. The acid in the vinegar encourages the polish to stick to the nail so you get better coverage and longer-lasting wear.

Speed up the time it takes to dry nail polish by plunging freshly polished nails into cold water. Shake hands to dry. And to prevent nicks and chipping, brush baby oil on just-polished nails!

Let's Dish!

Of course, nothing says "Mother's Day" like breakfast in bed!

ORANGE BLOSSOM FRENCH TOAST

12 slices bread
6 egg yolks
½ cup half-and-half or whole milk
⅓ cup orange juice
1 tablespoon grated orange peel
¼ teaspoon salt
¼ cup butter

Leave bread out to dry overnight.

Next morning, in a medium bowl, slightly beat egg yolks, then mix in half-and-half, orange juice, orange peel, and salt. Dip bread in batter, turning to coat both sides.

Heat butter in skillet and cook bread on both sides until golden.

Serve with syrup and love. Makes 6 servings.

23

June

Summer—it's finally here. The kids are out of school and it's time to hit the road on the family vacation. Frightened of an endless chorus of *Are we there yet?* It doesn't have to be that way. The kids don't have to be bored and neither do you. There are many things you can do to make that trip a good one—enjoyable *and* safe. So let's put our imaginations to work and have some fun.

Hit the Road, Jack

You're going on a family trip . . . in the car. You may be in there for hours. If that strikes fear in your heart, you're not alone. Hit these pages before hitting the road.

Before You Leave

It's fun to take a little time away from home. And if you take some time to prep the house before you leave, your homecoming will be that much sweeter.

- Lock the doors and windows, but leave the shades up and curtains open. Put the lights on automatic timer.
- Clean out the refrigerator and remove any perishables.
- Want to know if your freezer has shut off while you've been away? Take a child's ice pop—the ones that come in the clear plastic push-up wrapper—lay it flat to freeze, then prop it against the freezer door. If the freezer goes off while you're away the pop will be hanging over the inside of the door instead of standing straight up. You'll know then that freezer food *isn't* safe to eat.
- Store your valuables in a safe place. The freezer, jewelry box and lingerie drawer are not secure choices.
- Turn off small electrical appliances. Unplug decorative lights and fountains.

If you've read about it in a book or newspaper column, chances are it's not a safe place to store your valuables. Burglars read, too. Use your imagination and your discretion.

- Smokers will want to make sure that ashtrays are empty. Odor from cigarette butts can linger long after the cigarette has been extinguished, and there's nothing worse than coming home to a house that smells like a stale ashtray!
- Suspend delivery of the newspaper and the mail.
- To keep plants watered when you're not at home, gather them

up and sit them in the bathtub in about an inch of water. The plants will absorb the water gradually, enough to last a week or two. For those plant pots that don't have a hole in the bottom, fill a glass with water, insert one end of a coarse piece of string in the glass, and bury the other in the plant. Believe it or not, this homemade water wick will keep most plants moist while you're away!

* Leave a key and contact number with a trusted neighbor who will keep an eye on things during your absence.

What to Pack

No two vacations are alike, so consider what you want from your trip *before* you start to pack. If your weekday routine dictates that you wake at 6:30 to head off for work each morning, then chances are the last thing you want to hear is the ringing of your alarm. If, however, you want to be first in line at Disneyland, you're going to need that clock.

Here's a sample list to get you started:

* Small sewing kit
* Travel hair dryer
* Umbrella or raincoat
* Hunting or fishing license
* Alarm clock
* Swiss army knife
* Small fold-up tote for all those extras you'll buy
* Small amount of laundry detergent for those "oops!"
* Exercise gear

Take along an almost empty liquid soap container filled with water. It makes a handy cleaner for all those little emergencies.

* Camera and film
* Batteries
* A few plastic garbage bags for holding dirty laundry
* Bathing suits
* Plenty of tee shirts
* Tweezers—they come in very handy
* Gallon-size Ziploc™ bags for damp swimsuits, etc.
* A few clothespins and some safety pins

Spray the front of the car with nonstick cooking spray before you hit the road. Bugs and grime will wash right off.

And Don't Forget These Necessities

* Personal medicines and spare eyeglasses
* Children's aspirin and remedies for upset tummies
* Sunglasses, suntan lotion, insect repellent
* A first-aid kit, some paper towels and tissues
* Proof of insurance—auto and health
* A duplicate set of car keys
* A spare tire, car jack, flashlight, windshield scraper and emergency repair kit
* A few gallons of fresh water—for you and your radiator
* Maps
* A 1-800 number for credit card companies
* A small notebook and pen
* Picture ID

Backseat Drivers

Traveling with children requires special care and preparation, not to mention a good dose of imagination and patience. So plan ahead. Keep children occupied and try to avoid mishaps before they happen. You'll be glad you did.

Do's and Don'ts for a Safe Trip

✓ Do lock all doors and teach your children not to play with the door handles.

✗ Don't permit children to ride with their heads, arms or hands outside of the car through open windows.

✓ Do set a good example for your children by buckling up each time you enter the car.

✗ Don't leave children or pets in the car alone—even for a short time.

✓ Do make sure that children sit in the backseat.

✓ Do make sure to make frequent stops so that children can stretch their legs.

✗ Don't allow children to suck on suckers while riding. A sudden stop could be disastrous.

✓ Do make sure to take plenty of cold water.

We're Not Finished Yet

Children are resilient, but their little bodies can be especially sensitive to the environment. Keep a close eye on small passengers, and be on the lookout for any signs of car sickness and upset tummies. Sometimes a quick stop for some fresh air is all it takes to avoid a problem.

* Keep a new toothbrush in the glove box, along with a small tube of minty toothpaste. If a little one does get carsick and vomit, brushing his teeth afterward will make him feel much better. Just make sure to stay away from sweet or flavored toothpastes, which may aggravate nausea.

Keep sugared snacks to a minimum. Children high on sugar are not going to be good travelers.

* When preparing snack foods for a car journey, make sure to avoid small foods on which a child can choke, like hard candy and peanuts.
* Baby wipes are great for wiping sticky hands and faces—for you *and* your children. They're terrific for cleaning hands after pumping gas at the self-serve, too.
* Little ones will need a change of clothes. Everybody will benefit from having a spare, fresh T-shirt. And don't forget the diapers!

Now for the Fun Stuff

* Children love to play with office supplies such as Scotch® tape, paper and Post-it® notes—and they can't hurt them-

selves, either. Don't give children pens or pencils, though, and don't give them scissors.

* Play money is great fun. Your child can set up her own mall in the backseat! Just make sure to avoid giving coins to small children.
* Squares of aluminum foil are great for making sculptures and jewelry, and they can be used again and again. (Don't give foil to young children who may be tempted to put it in their mouths.)
* High-tech kids can still enjoy singing songs and reciting rhymes. Encourage children to make up their own verses. Don't be afraid to get creative!
* Paint books—the kind that already have the paint on the page—are very popular with young children. All you need is a little brush and an inch or so of water in a cup. No fuss and no paint to spill.
* Don't forget the classics. Hangman, tic-tac-toe and "I Spy" are great, as are crossword puzzles.
* Don't forget the bubbles!
* Have your child make some paper bag puppets before you leave. They'll be distracted with their craft, and that will give *you* some uninterrupted time to prepare for the trip. And of course, children will be pleased to take their new creations with them in the car.
* Children love to use binoculars.
* Tattoos, the kind that press on with a wet cloth, are lots of fun.
* Go Fish card games are great. Even children too young to

know the game will enjoy playing with the cards. Fifty-two pickup, anyone?

* Everyone knows that books on tape are great for long trips, but small children can get bored just listening. So why not let them record their own book? Many inexpensive cassette players have record buttons, so why not pick up a few tapes at the dollar store and let your child try his on-air talents? He can describe the scenery, make up stories and songs, record a letter to Grandma—he could even interview you!
* Kids love disposable cameras. Consider giving one to each child.

Please make sure that I'm well cared for when you're away. I need food and water, of course, but I need some company, too. I get awfully lonely when you're gone. And please make sure to put a note on the door or window that lets people know that I'm inside. Pets can get lost in all the commotion of a fire. I shudder to think of what can happen . . .

If you're taking me with you, please make sure that I have a place of my own in the car, with food and water. Bring my bed if at all possible—just keep me out of the sun.

Give dogs frequent potty breaks and some exercise. Always keep them on a leash, you know how dogs are about running away.

Don't forget my litter tray. A disposable one will be fine. Just don't expect me to go potty at 70 miles per hour with trucks speeding by. I need my privacy.

Make sure that we're wearing our tags, just in case we become lost or disoriented.

* Toddlers can use licorice laces and Cheerios® or Fruit Loops® to make necklaces and bracelets. When they get bored, they can eat their creations!
* Buy some small inexpensive toys at the dollar store—things like plastic dinosaurs and little trolls. Wrap them up with brightly colored paper and dole them out as after-snack goodies. Children love unwrapping the toy almost as much as the toy itself. Keep small toys away from little ones who may put them in their mouths.
* Cookie sheets and breakfast-in-bed trays make great portable work spaces for children. Just make sure not to give little ones sharp and potentially dangerous objects such as pens and pencils. The slightest bump can mean disaster when these items are at hand. Crayons and jumbo markers are best.
* Yahtzee® is still a great traveling game.

At the Car Wash

A long trip can take its toll on your car. Here's what to do to get it looking good again—fast!

* Use a paste of baking soda and water to clean the outside windshield so that it shines.
* Put some baking soda in your car's ashtray. It may not discourage smokers, but it will help neutralize the odor.

> Rust spots can be removed from car bumpers quite easily—just rub with a ball of tinfoil! If the rust is stubborn, try dipping the foil in a glass of cola! (Don't ask ...)

* Keep some used fabric softener sheets in your glove box. Use them to wipe the dashboard, clean the air vents, and polish the rearview mirror. Store them in a Ziploc™ bag and you'll still have room for all those maps and fast-food coupons!

* If birds leave you an unwanted gift on the car, simply take some waterless hand cream, working it in well with an old rag. Let sit for several minutes and it should rub right off.

"Never lend your car to anyone to whom you've given birth."

—Erma Bombeck

* Remove road tar by saturating it with linseed oil. Apply the oil liberally to the tarred area, let soak for a while and then wipe with an old rag that has been dampened with more linseed oil. Be sure you dispose of the rag outside in the trash.

* Make your own windshield washer fluid by mixing 2 quarts of rubbing alcohol, 1 cup of water, and 1 teaspoon of liquid dish soap. This will not freeze at 30 degrees below. In summer, add 1 pint of rubbing alcohol and 1 teaspoon of liquid dish soap to the car washer container and fill with water. This will keep the windows clean in rain and warm weather.

* Baking soda on a soft, wet cloth is great for cleaning chrome, headlights and enamel.

* Wipe down windshield wiper blades from time to time to remove road film.

* Wash the car in the shade to prevent streaking.

* Use a couple of squirts of liquid dish soap in a bucket of warm

water to wash the car. Start at the roof and wash and rinse in sections so that the soap doesn't dry on the car.

- Dry the car with an old bath towel, then for a super shine, rub down with a good-quality chamois.

Father's Day

You don't think we'd let the month go by without celebrating Father's Day, do you? I always think that the best gift is a gift of time. So why not give your father the day off and let him wander the links for a lovely game of golf. And when he comes home, treat his clubs to some tender, loving care . . .

Fore!

Clean golf clubs by lightly rubbing the head and shaft with dry, fine-grade (0000) steel wool. Don't wet the steel wool. Dust with a dry cloth, then use a damp cloth to give the club a final wipe before buffing dry with another clean, soft cloth.

Cleaning the grips is as easy as using soap and water—but the kind of soap you use makes a big difference. Dampen a soft cloth with warm water, then work up a lather with a moisturizing bath bar, such as Dove® or Caress®. Don't use a deodorizing soap, as that will dry out the leather. Rub well to remove the dirt, rinsing the cloth each time it becomes grimy. Repeat until the grip is clean, then reapply the soap and water one last time. Don't rinse—buff with a soft cloth instead. This will keep the grip moist and prevent it from drying out and cracking. For really stubborn dirt or older clubs, work in a little GOJO Crème Waterless Hand Cleaner® and wipe until clean. Wash with the soap formula and dry well.

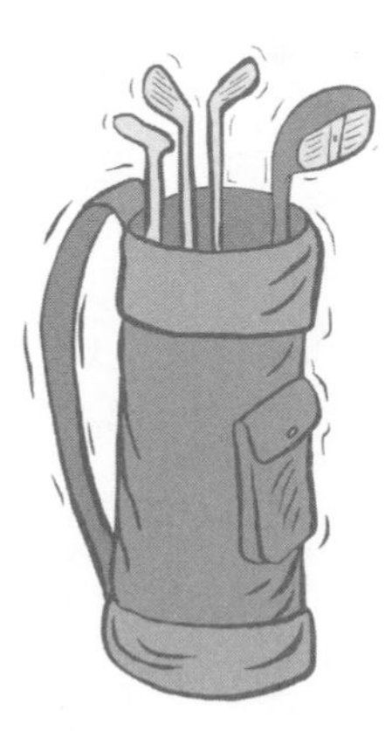

Keep the golf glove in a self-closing plastic bag to maintain softness between games. If you need to clean your glove, use the bar soap method prescribed for grips, keeping the glove on your hand to preserve its shape during the process. Work only with a damp cloth, and make sure not to saturate the glove. Finish by buffing with a soft cloth that's clean and dry, and then allow the glove to dry naturally, out of direct light. To restore a dried-out glove, try rubbing a little hand cream into it—while you're wearing it!

Golf shoes need attention, too. Brush the bottoms of the shoes with a firm brush to remove any dirt and debris. If you have been playing on a wet course, don't do this until the shoes are dry. Wash leather shoes as needed with Dove® moisturizing bath soap, removing scuff marks with a little non-gel toothpaste or rubbing with a little cuticle remover. For fabric-type shoes, brush well and spot with a damp microfiber cloth. Always keep the shoes treated with a good-quality water repellent for those rainy days and dewy mornings. Got a little odor problem? Put some ODORZOUT™ in the toe of an old nylon or sock and keep it in the shoes when you store them to eliminate odor.

Clean golf balls by soaking them in a solution of 1 cup warm water and ¼ cup ammonia. Rub lightly, rinse and lay out to dry. Store extra golf balls in an egg carton. The compartments are the perfect size!

Having trouble identifying your golf and tennis balls? A tiny drop of colored nail polish is just as good as any monogram.

24 July

Even the most devoted couch potato ventures out of the house in July. So haul out the baseball equipment, hop on that bike, put on the skates, go for a dip in the pool to cure those summertime blues. Sound too energetic for you? Then how about becoming a chaise lounge or hammock potato at a beautiful campsite for a week or so. That can be a wonderfully relaxing way to recharge your body, let the kids run off some steam, and have some quality family time, too.

Let the Games Begin!

Take me out to the ball game . . . just make sure the equipment is clean and in good working order before you do. Otherwise, it's one, two, three strikes you're out!

Wash your baseball glove with a damp cloth and Dove® Moisturizing Bath Bar. Buff with a soft cloth—no rinsing necessary. Keep the leather soft and supple by rubbing with a little petroleum jelly from time to time. Store your ball in the palm of your glove to help keep its shape.

Want to know the best way to clean your bike? Treat it like a car! Wash the frame with some hot water and a little dishwashing liquid. Rinse well, dry, then apply a coat of car wax to prevent rust. Wash the seat with a little bit of bar soap on a soft cloth and buff dry.

"My favorite machine at the gym is the vending machine."

—Caroline Rhea

Dented Ping-Pong balls? Just drop them into a bowl of hot water and let them float for a few minutes. Dings should pop right out. Sorry—balls that are cracked or have large dents can't be repaired.

Give your skateboard an occasional wash with good old soap and water. Pay special attention to the wheels by scrubbing with a brush to remove any embedded soil and stones that may slow you down.

Odor can be a problem with skates—both inline and ice. I recommend sprinkling with ODORZOUT™, a first-rate odor eliminator. Shake some into the boot, leave overnight, then gently shake out the following morning. ODORZOUT™ is an odor eliminator, not a perfumed cover-up, so your skates will stay fresher longer. Don't have any? Try baking soda instead.

Wearing petroleum jelly under your socks can prevent blisters. Apply a thin layer on tender parts before you exercise. And never wear sports socks more than one day running.

To clean skate boots, try using a microfiber cloth such as ACT Natural®. The ACT Natural® cloth can be used on its own—no harmful chemicals to damage those expensive skates.

Before you exchange that hockey equipment for baseball gear, make sure to store your pucks in the freezer. They'll stay harder and more resilient that way!

Who Says There Ain't No Cure?

Summer isn't all fun and games. There are hot nights and insect bites, sunburns to soothe and lawn furniture to clean—what we in the trade commonly refer to as the *summertime blues.* Read on for some handy cures.

- Remove dirt and mildew from a child's wading pool by flushing with warm water and baking soda.
- Sprinkle baby powder on sandy beach bodies and the sand will fall right off.
- A hot night and no a/c? Baby powder on your sheets will absorb moisture and give you a more comfortable night's sleep. What, no baby powder? Use cornstarch instead!
- Wipe exposed skin with undiluted white vinegar to discourage biting insects.
- Apply a compress of warm salt water if you're bitten by a mosquito or chigger. For long-lasting itch relief, mix a little salt and solid shortening, such as Crisco®, and dab it directly on the bite.
- Deodorant that contains aluminum (and most do) can be put on a bite to control the itch.
- Sliding doors get a lot of use in the summer, so be sure to keep tracks clean and well lubri-

That frosty film inside the carton of ice cream is not a protective coating, and it can be prevented. Just cover the top of the ice cream with wax paper and press firmly. No more "protective crystals"!

cated. The easiest way? Spritz tracks with furniture polish, then wipe with a dry cloth or paper towel. The polish will pick up grime, and will keep the tracks better lubricated than a cleanser would. If you want to add some glide between cleanings, just wipe the tracks with a square of waxed paper. Works every time!

- A plastic shower liner makes a great tablecloth. It's washable and inexpensive.
- Sheets make better beach blankets than blankets. They don't hold sand and they're easier to launder when you get home. Pick up some spares at a thrift store.
- Black pepper will deter ants. Just sprinkle under rugs or cupboard liners. Silverfish can be kept at bay with Epsom salts: Just shake some in cupboards and under lining paper in drawers.
- Put sunburned kids in a cool (not cold) baking soda bath for half an hour. This also works well for chickenpox and mosquito bites.
- No need to use chemicals or expensive products to clean lawn furniture. Just rinse with warm water and baking soda. Sprinkle dry baking soda directly on stubborn marks—this natural abrasive will take them right off!

I HATE IT WHEN THAT HAPPENS . . .

Tar on bare feet? Remove it by rubbing vigorously with toothpaste.

Camping

If slow room service is your idea of camping, you may want to skip this section.

The Necessities

- Campsites can be very dark in the evening, so make sure to bring along a torch, a candle or a flashlight. Even better, bring along all three. And don't forget the batteries!
- Remember that Swiss army knife you got for Christmas three years ago? Now's the time to use it. You'll need some good kitchen knives, too, so don't forget to bring those as well.
- Toilet paper in a lidded coffee can to keep it dry. Need I say more?
- Bring a few candles, a votive or a tea light.
- Make sure to bring along a little dishwashing liquid, a scouring pad and some absorbent towels.

> Rubbing two sticks together to make a fire is highly overrated. Don't try to be macho. Bring along matches or a lighter.

- A cooked breakfast is one of the joys of camping, but bacon and eggs are *not* finger foods. Don't forget the cutlery, cooking utensils, a pot to boil water in, and a frying pan.
- Bring along a length of nylon rope. You can use it for dozens of things, such as drying clothes, elevating food so that animals don't get at it, and knocking up an emergency shelter. You can even use it to replace those lost guy ropes. Use your imagination . . . just don't tie up the kids!

- Bandannas are wonderfully versatile. They make good napkins, facecloths, bandages and slings. Tuck one under the back of your baseball cap to keep the sun off your neck, foreign-legion style!

- A first-aid kit is a must. Make sure yours is stocked with bandages, antiseptic, tweezers, a thin needle for splinters, Imodium® for those tummy troubles, aspirin or aspirin-substitute, sunscreen and sunburn relief, insect repellent and a whistle to call for help in an emergency.

Cell phones are great, but the batteries on whistles never run down.

- Bring soap. You can find the water when you get there.

- Dental floss and a darning needle will come in handy for quick repairs to holes in clothes and tents.

- Duct tape is indispensable.

Fire Starters

There's an easy way to dry out wet kindling. Construct a small tepee out of your kindling, making sure to leave an opening into which you can insert a tea light or votive candle. Insert the lighted candle, then watch as the kindling crackles and dries. You should have a fire under way by the time the candle has burned down.

Pinecones make great kindling. They heat up fast and burn for a long time.

Bring along a few cardboard tubes from paper towels or toilet paper. Twist a few sheets of newspaper to fit inside the tube (I find the business section works best), making sure to leave some paper hanging out the ends. Toss a few of these in with twigs and wood and you'll have a roaring fire in no time!

My dad and I learned—quite accidentally—that grease from cooking pans makes a great fire starter! Use paper towels to wipe up the grease from pots and pans, then store them in self-closing plastic bags. The next time you need to start a campfire, wrap some twigs in the paper and set them alight!

Keeping matches dry can be a challenge, but if you dip the match head and part of the matchstick into some candle wax, it will resist water. Light as usual—the act of striking the match will remove the wax. (This only works on wooden matches, not cardboard.)

Rub the outside of pots and pans with a bar of soap before you use them. Do this to both the bottom and sides of the pan, and soot will wipe right off, along with the soap.

Loitering Within Tent

- Rocks, twigs and other sharp objects may damage your tent, so make sure the ground is clear before you set up camp.
- Avoid wearing heavy shoes inside the tent.
- Use extreme caution around open flames. Nylon tents melt easily.
- Pack tent poles carefully to avoid punctures.
- Prolonged exposure to direct sunlight can weaken tent fibers, so wherever possible, set up the tent in a shaded area.
- A strip of glow-in-the-dark tape wrapped around tent stakes will ensure that you never trip over them again!
- Drive tent stakes twelve inches into the ground to provide adequate stability, even in the wind. The stakes should be at a

45-degree angle, slanting *away* from the tent. Paint each stake at the 12-inch mark and you'll never have to guess again!

Cleaning Your Tent

Make sure to store your tent correctly—that means cleaning it first. With proper care your tent can last for years.

Shake off all loose debris before packing and storing the tent. Clean any spots with a wet brush rubbed over a bar of Fels-Naptha Soap®, then rinse. Air-dry thoroughly. A damp tent is a breeding ground for mildew.

Stakes should be stored alongside the tent, but make sure to put them in a canvas bag or even a few old pillowcases—something to ensure that the stakes will not tear or puncture the tent itself.

Take action at the first sign of mildew—an organic rotting odor, black spots or a powdery white smudge. Sponge the tent with a solution of ½ cup of Lysol™ and 1 gallon of warm water. Allow to dry on the tent (think *leave-in conditioner*) and air-dry thoroughly prior to storing. For advanced mildew use a combination of 1 cup of lemon juice (real or bottled) and 1 gallon of warm water. Rub onto visible mildew and allow to dry facing the sun.

Spray zippers with a silicone lubricant to ensure smooth action and prevent freezing. Rubbing with paraffin or candle wax works well, too.

Repairing Your Tent

Stakes and tent poles cause the majority of tears in canvas tents. Either the pole slips and tears the fabric next to the eyelet, or the canvas itself is tied too tightly to the ground stakes. Bear this in mind when setting up your tent.

Canvas is too heavy for most home sewing machines, so if your tent is generally in good condition, you may want to consider getting it repaired by a tent or sail maker.

For a cheaper alternative, glue an appropriate-sized square of canvas to the tent. Make sure you overlap the tear by about one to two inches. Putting a patch on both sides of the tent will reinforce the repair. Use fabric glue or even a hot glue gun and remember to waterproof the repair once the glue is dry.

Duct tape is great for making emergency repairs. Just make sure to tape both sides of the tear. And remember: This is just an interim measure. Have your tent properly repaired once you get back home.

> Never underestimate the power of a large darning needle and dental floss.

Nylon or cotton hiking-type tents can be repaired on a home sewing machine. Look for patch kits, available where tents are sold.

It's in the Bag

Keep your sleeping bag clean and mildew free by washing it in a large-capacity machine. Add ½ cup of 20 Mule Team® Borax to the water along with your detergent, and ½ cup of white vinegar in the rinse instead of fabric softener.

Make sure that the sleeping bag is totally dry before storing to prevent mildew. When ready to store, place about a quarter cup of ODORZOUT™ in a nylon stocking and tuck inside the sleeping bag to prevent odors. A good sprinkling of baking soda will help to keep it fresh, too. Store your sleeping bag inside a king-size pillowcase to keep it clean.

25
August

Where did the summer go? Seems like only yesterday we were preparing the garden for spring, and now we're thinking about how to make the most of this final summer month. I hate to be a drag, but it's time to give your house the once-over before autumn starts. That means paying attention to those tasks that everybody seems to ignore—cleaning the driveway *and* the gutters. It's not all chores, though. We still have some time for that last summer picnic!

Driveway Dilemmas

Driveways take quite a beating, but we never seem to pay much attention to them—until they're covered with oil spills and weeds. Put off caring for your driveway, and like most jobs, it will become more difficult and time-consuming when you finally do get around to it. So sweep your driveway regularly—say, once a month in the summer—and wash it thoroughly once a year. You'll be glad you did.

Give your driveway a good sweep. Use a stiff push broom or long-handle brush, and make short, brisk strokes to direct debris away from the center of the driveway.

- Wash concrete driveways with a simple solution of water and washing soda. Dissolve 1 cup of Arm and Hammer® Washing Soda in a bucket of warm water and apply to the driveway with a long-handle brush or stiff push broom. Scrub well, then rinse with clear water.
- Oven cleaner works well for those really tough stains. Spray it on, let sit for a few hours, and then rinse well. Just make sure to keep the kids and pets a good distance away.
- For old marks and blotches, apply a heavy layer of a good laundry stain remover, such as Zout®, and allow it to sit for five minutes before sprinkling with powdered laundry detergent. Apply a small amount of water to get a good lather going, then scrub with a stiff broom and rinse well.
- Kitty Litter™ is good at absorbing oil. Just make sure to grind it into the stain with your feet.
- Patio blocks can be cleaned with washing soda or laundry stain remover. Don't use the oven cleaner method, though. It can remove color and damage the blocks.
- Kill weeds that grow through the cracks in driveways and patios by saturating them with 1 gallon of warm water to which you have added ¼ cup of salt.
- Prevent weeds from growing in these cracks by sprinkling salt

directly into the crevices. That's all there is to it—just let nature do the rest.

Get Your Mind *into* the Gutter!

Gutters are designed to carry rainwater and melting snow off your roof and away from your house. They are not storage places for leaves, Frisbees™, and tennis balls. Keep them clean.

Check your gutters to see if they're in good working order by spraying a hose directly into the trough. If the water runs through the trough and out the spout, you're in good shape. If, however, the water flows over the sides, it's time to give those gutters a good cleaning.

Use a ladder to clean gutters. Never approach them from the roof. That's asking for trouble. If the ground beneath your ladder is soft, sit the legs of the ladder into a couple of small cans, such as those from tuna fish. The cans will help distribute the weight, and the ladder won't slope or sink into the ground at uneven levels.

Once you're confident that the ladder is secure, climb to the height of the gutters and, wearing rubber gloves, scoop out the debris that's collected there. Hang a couple of shopping bags onto your ladder and use them to hold the debris. When one is full, just toss it to the ground and start filling the next. (Just don't forget to shout, "Look out below!")

Once you've removed the debris, flush the spout with water to make sure it flows freely. Usually, a forceful stream of water directed down the spout will be strong enough to push out anything that's blocking it. If that doesn't work, try inserting the hose *up* the spout. That should loosen the debris. One final blast of water from the top down should then be enough to dislodge whatever is blocking it.

You can avoid a lot of this hassle next year by placing a screen or netting over the gutters, which will prevent leaves and other debris from settling.

Time for a Picnic

A sunny day, a brightly colored checkered tablecloth, something good to eat . . . sounds like heaven to me! There's nothing quite like a picnic to round off an afternoon of outdoor fun, but insects and food poisoning can ruin the day. Read on to find out how to ward off those uninvited guests, as well as for advice on how to relieve that burn from the last of the summer sun. Oh, and let's not forget how to care for and clean that barbecue grill!

Don't Bug Me

- Insects are attracted to intense colors—bright *and* dark. Bear this in mind when selecting tablecloths and paper plates, as well as your clothes for the day. This is not the time to be bold!
- Citronella candles are great standbys. No picnic should be without them.
- Insects love grapes, melon, and sweet fruit drinks, as well as strongly scented foods, such as tuna, strong cheeses, and meats. Think about this as you prepare your picnic.

> Flies ruining your picnic? Keep them away by wiping the table with some undiluted white vinegar or laying some citrus peels on the tablecloth.

- Choose a picnic site that's away from rivers, lakes, and streams. Insects tend to gather around water.
- Odors can broadcast mealtimes to insects, so keep foods sealed in plastic containers until you're ready to eat.

* Make sure to cover serving plates so insects can't touch down on your meal—even for a moment. Domed food covers are great, as are pieces of inexpensive nylon netting. Don't have either? Try turning a large bowl upside down over platters.

* Don't let a bug surprise you in your soda or juice. Cover the glass with a piece of aluminum foil and then push a straw through it.

* Ants can't make it through water, so the best way to deter them is by sitting the legs of your picnic table in tin cans filled with water. Disposable pie tins or old Frisbees™ work well for tables with thicker legs.

* Entice insects away from your picnic by giving them a picnic of their own. Put a pie plate filled with water and sugar several yards away from your eating area. The bugs will rush to their meal, leaving you alone to enjoy yours! (Don't forget to pick up the pie plate before you leave.)

Cuts and scrapes may come with outdoor fun, but the *ouch* that comes with bandage removal doesn't have to. Just rub some baby oil around the bandage before pulling it off.

Food for Thought

Picnics may be the ultimate in casual eating, but that doesn't mean you should be casual about the way you prepare and store the food. Bacteria thrive in hot weather; that's why it's easy to become sick from food poisoning. So take a few precautions and have a lovely, stress-free day.

* Keep hot foods hot and cold foods cold. That means making sure you have one cooler set aside for cold foods, and one for hot.

A tear or hole in a picnic cooler can be repaired with candle wax. Gently warm the bottom of a candle over a flame, then rub it on the tear until the seam can no longer be noticed. A wax scar will form, and that should prevent further splitting.

* Insulate foods by wrapping them in layers of newspaper or brown paper grocery bags.
* Large blocks of ice keep food colder and last longer than their smaller counterparts, so use your imagination when choosing containers for ice. Milk cartons, for example, do a great job! Rinse out the carton (no need to use soap), fill it with water about two inches from the top, then pop it into the freezer until you're ready to go. Don't cut the top off, and don't tear it open, either. Resealing the spout once you're ready to go will ensure that this ice block stays cold a long time.
* Think of that foam cooler as your "hot chest." Put all of your hot foods together, wrap them well in layers of paper, and the combined heat will create a thermos to keep everything hot for a few hours.
* Add mayonnaise to foods when you're ready to eat them, not before. It's not the mayonnaise that's the problem; it's usually

I HATE IT WHEN THAT HAPPENS . . .

Ketchup too slow for your liking? Tap firmly on the *side* of the bottle, and the ketchup will come right out.

the foods you mix with it that carry bacteria. Mayonnaise deteriorates quickly in warm conditions, and can act as a host for bacteria-growing food.

- Ketchup and mustard deteriorate in hot weather, so leave the big bottles at home. Now's the time to use up all those extra packets of ketchup and mustard you picked up at fast-food restaurants.
- Don't eat picnic leftovers or food left out for more than two hours.
- If it smells or looks bad, throw it out. Don't take chances.

Grill of My Dreams

Never use gasoline or kerosene to start a fire. These substances are extremely flammable and very difficult to control—and they're not safe to use around food, either.

Don't try to revive a smoldering fire with a squirt of charcoal lighter fluid. The fire could flare up and you could be engulfed in flames. Revive a fire by dampening a few fresh pieces of charcoal with lighter fluid and carefully placing them—one at a time—in with the old coals.

Dispose of ashes with care. Douse them with water, stirring them with a metal fork, then douse with yet more water. You can also dispose of ashes by dumping them into a metal can. Wait at least 24 hours before putting in with other garbage.

> Grilling at the beach? Clean the grill rack by rubbing it with sand!

Clean the exterior of gas and charcoal grills with GOJO Crème Waterless Hand Cleaner®. Dip a paper towel into the GOJO®, work it into the outside of the grill, and watch the dirt, grease and barbecue sauce come right off! Buff with a clean paper towel and the grill will sparkle like new—with the added benefit of a nice protective coating.

The easiest way to clean a grill rack? Lay the cool rack upside down on the grass and leave it overnight. The dew will work to soften any burned-on food and the next morning you can simply wipe it off!

Place a layer of sand in the bottom of a charcoal grill to prevent the charcoal from burning through the bottom.

Remove burned-on foods with black coffee. Just pour the coffee over a hot grill rack and wipe with aluminum foil.

The Hot News on Sunburn

Ouch! You forgot the sunscreen and now the damage has been done. It happens to the best of us. Sunburns hurt. Bad. But there are some steps you can take to cool the heat and soothe the pain. Read on.

- A cool bath helps. Shake in some baking soda, or about ½ cup of salt. Soak for about 30 minutes or so, then apply aloe gel to still-damp skin to keep the temperature down. (Works on mosquito bites and chickenpox, too!)
- A thin layer of Preparation H® is soothing to hot, itchy skin and is especially good on delicate facial areas. Yes, I am serious.
- Make up compresses of 1 part milk to 3 parts water, then lay on burned areas for soothing relief. The protein in the milk will draw out the heat.
- Moist tea bags can offer much-needed relief to eyelids that are burned and swollen. Lay the cold bags over closed eyes, then relax for 30 minutes or so.

* Heavy lotions can trap heat rather than soothe it, so try gels instead, particularly those containing aloe.
* Your grandmother may remember this old-fashioned remedy: Whip 1 egg white with 1 teaspoon of castor oil, then apply to affected areas. Let dry. Rinse off with cool water.
* Spraying on a 50/50 solution of cider vinegar and tepid water will cool the burn on contact.
* Vitamin E is a wonderful moisturizer for burned skin.

Don't you hate it when pet food gets dry and sticks to the bowl? I know I do—and I'm not the one who has to clean it out! There is a solution, though: Give the bowl a quick spritz of nonstick cooking spray before dishing out the food. No more stuck-on food. No more difficult cleaning jobs.

A little bit of oil in my food will also help with that bowl cleanup. And it's also good for my coat!

A lot of people like to use Dustbusters® to clean up scatterings of cat litter (apparently not all kitties are as fastidious as I am), but not many of them know that a used dryer fabric softener sheet makes a great addition to the filter. Easy to clean and fresh smelling too!

26
September

Children are grumbling. Parents are rejoicing. It must be September—back to school! Doesn't matter if you're dealing with a first grader or a high school senior (or whether you yourself are heading back to college), going back to school can be exhilarating—and stressful. So get organized. Plan ahead. Establish rules. Consider your schedule and your family's needs, and with a little bit of imagination, you can get the school year off to a good start.

School Daze

First Things First

Try not to buy any new clothes for your kids without taking stock of what you have on hand. Go through their closets first, *then* hit the back-to-school sales.

Take an afternoon—a rainy one if you can—and sift through your children's closets. If they're at an age when they're interested in what they wear, enlist their help and consider it a joint project. This is a terrific opportunity to show them the benefits of being organized. Come armed with a few large plastic bags and some silly jokes. Let them pick the music to play and let them decide (with your help) what stays and what goes. The more you involve your children in the process, the more likely they are to cooperate. And if there are any squabbles down the road, well, remind them that the choices were made by both of you!

The first step to an organized closet? Get rid of anything that's too small or that you know won't be worn anymore. If repairs are needed, now's the time to do them. Hem hems, fix zips, sew on buttons and tend to any mending that you can. Then make use of those large plastic bags and get rid of whatever can't be used. Can't find a mate to that sock? Get rid of it. Elastic gone on those underpants? Use them as cleaning rags. Be ruthless. If an item of clothing is not up to the task, throw it out. Those torn jeans may be old favorites, but if they're ripped beyond repair, let your son say farewell to them and put them in the trash. That pink blouse may have been your daughter's favorite, but if it didn't fit her last year, it's not going to fit her now. Donate the blouse to a thrift shop and move on to the next item. This is no time to be sentimental. You've got a closet to organize.

Now look into that pared-down closet and see what you've got left. At this point, I like to remove everything so I can organize it anew. Take all the clothes out of the closet and put them on the bed. You might find it easier to make separate piles—one for shirts or blouses, one for pants, one for skirts, sweaters, and so on. Your child's style will dictate how many different mounds of clothes you have. You don't have to be precise with your categories, just separate clothes into logical groups so they're easier to put back.

Now comes the fun part. There's only one rule when it comes to organizing: It has to work for you, and you have to be consistent. (Well, I guess that's two, but who's counting?) So, if your daughter wants to organize her closet by colors, let her. If your son wants to organize his clothes by day of the week, let him. Just make sure your child knows that he or she will be responsible for the upkeep of the system, *every single day.* Take the time to talk to your child. Offer her some choices. Blouses here, T-shirts there, skirts over here and pants down there. If your daughter rarely wears those two blue dresses and is keeping them for special occasions, you may want to suggest that she keep them near the back of her closet and bring more frequently worn items to the front. If your son wears mostly tees and sweatshirts, ask him if he'd rather keep these items in baskets. (Do you know a child who *likes* to hang up his clothes?) Talk about the best ways of organizing and you may come up with some nifty ideas that will suit your child well. Be imaginative and flexible. The more realistic you are in planning the closet, the more likely your child is to keep it tidy. And isn't that what it's all about?

A few suggestions:

* Make it easy for your child to put his clothes away by installing hooks at easy-to-reach levels.
* Install low bars so that little ones can hang up their own clothes.
* Baskets and buckets are great for holding children's socks and underwear.
* Let your child select some bright hangers in her favorite colors. Clothes are less likely to end up on the floor that way.
* A baseball-cap holder is great for that Little-League enthusiast.
* Everyone knows that an over-the-door shoe rack is great for shoes. It's also great for T-shirts, gym clothes, swimsuits and dance gear.
* Use plastic storage bins to hold clothes that aren't used daily. And make sure to label them well. If your child is too young to read, let him draw pictures so he knows what's inside.

* Encourage children to make use of all of the racks and shelves in their closets—the ones they can reach, anyway.

* Give each child a colorful laundry hamper, and let older children know that they're responsible for bringing their laundry down to the laundry room.

New school shoes causing your child to slip? Score the soles with the tines of a fork.

One last thing: Now that your children know the work that goes into organizing a closet, you might want to remind them of that old adage *Work saved is work done.* Encourage your children to keep their closets organized and their clothes clean. Remind them to put away their school clothes when they remove them, not several hours later when the wrinkles have had time to set. Who knows . . . they might even listen!

Clothes Calls

* When hitting those back-to-school sales, remember to save some money for those new fads that show up the first few weeks of school—those things the kids *just can't* do without.

* Read the care labels on new clothes. Make sure you know whether an item has to be handwashed or dry-cleaned *before* you buy it.

* If your child is having problems with a zipper, try rubbing a pencil over it a few times. The graphite will help the zipper to glide as smooth as ice!

* If new school clothes are too stiff—a problem with jeans especially—break them in by throwing ½ a cup of table salt in with the wash. They'll come out nice and soft!

Just Five More Minutes

I wish I could give you more time in the morning, but I'm a Queen, not a magician. There are, however, some things you can do to make your mornings less hectic.

The school bus leaves in ten minutes and all across the country kids are screaming, "I can't find it!" Don't let this happen to you. Help each child select a designated spot for books, homework and sports equipment—plus anything else they need to take to school in the morning. Baskets are great, as are bright plastic buckets. Canvas bags hanging on coatracks are good, too.

Designate another safe place for report cards (did I just shiver?), notes from teachers, and permission slips that need to be signed. And let your children know, firmly, that the morning of is *not* the time for signatures.

An over-the-door shoe rack in see-through plastic can be great for holding those small items that kids never seem to be without—and never seem willing to leave the house without. Label a few pockets for each child and tell them it's their own little holding bay. These pouches can be used to hold skipping ropes, GameBoys™, caps and small toys, not to mention hats, scarves and mittens. Give top pockets to older kids and save the easy-to-reach pouches at the bottom for the little ones.

> Television is a great distraction. Keep the TV off in the morning and you'll all save time.

If kids want to agonize over what goes with what (not to mention who's *wearing* what), that's fine. Just remind them that 8:00 in the morning is not the time to be doing it. Save yourself a headache and let the kids select what they want to wear to school, but get them into the habit of setting out their clothes *the night before.*

Who's on First?

A large family calendar is a must. Keep it displayed in a location that's prominent *and* convenient. Older children can be taught to log in their own events; just make sure they tell you first. Use the calendar for school functions, sports events, doctor's appointments and birthday parties. Keep a bulletin board nearby. You can use that to hold any relevant papers, like invitations, cards and notes.

A daily visit to your family calendar is not a bad idea. It just takes a minute or so to prevent overlaps that may lead to conflicts.

Get your children in the habit of looking at the calendar, too. Show them how their week is shaping up *before* they enter into it. Let your children know that four busy days in a row might not be such a good idea, and encourage them to use their calendar to make choices. Everybody needs to be reminded that they don't have to say *yes* to everything.

If nothing's scheduled on a particular day, why not use the calendar for other things? Jot down a knock-knock joke or an encouraging word about a child's performance. An organized life doesn't have to be boring!

Accept the fact that things don't always run smoothly. Some days *are* better than others. Take a deep breath and don't sweat it. Tomorrow offers another chance to get it right.

Get It off Your Chest

Now that you're in the mood to get organized, why not extend the project for just a few more minutes and tidy up your medicine chest? This small but important project could mean a lot to your family's safety.

Remove everything from the cabinet and place the contents onto a large, flat surface, such as a table. Again, organize the contents into logical groups. Medicines here, bandages there, and so on. Now:

* Toss out anything that doesn't have a label.
* Get rid of any medicines that have passed their expiration dates.

* Take note of any duplicates you may have but don't, for heaven's sake, combine them. You may have two half-empty bottles of aspirin, but putting them together in the same bottle to save space is a bad idea, especially if they have different expiration dates.
* Blister-pack pills are often separated from their boxes. If you aren't certain of the medication or if you don't know the date of expiration, get rid of them. This is no time to be frugal.
* Chances are, you have at least one tensor bandage that's lost its elasticity. Get rid of it.

Cleaning out a medicine chest is similar to cleaning out a closet, except you don't have to sew on any buttons!

Unwanted medications can still be dangerous, so make sure to dispose of them safely. Flushing them down the toilet may be satisfying in a dramatic sort of way, but that can be bad for the environment. Don't just toss pills in the garbage, either. They can be deadly to children and animals. The best way to get rid of medication is to put it in a child-proof container, then in another jar (which you seal), and then safely in the garbage. Don't take chances.

Take this time to clean out the shelves of your medicine chest. Metal shelves can be cleaned with a little bit of baking soda and water. Glass shelves can be cleaned with vinegar. Make sure that surfaces are dry before restocking, and take this opportunity to be a rebel and store anything *but* your medicines in your medicine chest. That's right!

Store your medication in a place that is clean, dry and safe from curious youngsters. Save the medicine chest for the cotton balls.

Despite its name, the medicine chest is probably the worst place to store medicines. Not only does it suffer fluctuations in temperatures, but it's damp and steamy, too!

The most important thing to do to protect yourself and your family is to purchase a carbon monoxide detector. It's not expensive, but it may turn out to be priceless.

The Last Word, and a Very Important One at That!

Carbon monoxide is a tasteless, odorless killer. It can be released by wood-burning stoves, fireplaces, furnaces, kerosene lamps and gas-fired heaters, and it occurs when these items burn without enough oxygen. When fresh air is restricted, carbon monoxide can build up in your home and cause an irregular heartbeat, headaches and fatigue. In very high amounts, it can cause death.

Please, take the following precautions against this silent killer:

- Ensure that adequate air is available in any room that contains a gas-burning appliance.
- Have your furnace, chimneys and flues checked regularly for cracks and leaks.
- Make certain that door and stovepipe connections fit tightly on all old wood-burning stoves.
- Use a range hood and fan with a gas stove.
- Keep a window slightly open when using a space heater that operates on oil, gas or kerosene.
- Never barbecue in a house or closed garage.
- Always make sure the garage door is open when running the car.

27 October

The days are getting shorter. The nights are getting longer. And that nip in the air tells us without a doubt that the seasons are changing. I hate to be the one to mention this, but it's time to get ready for the colder months. So, let's store our summer clothes and soon-to-be out-of-season sports and gardening equipment. Then let's move inside and turn our thoughts to brighter things, like lighting fixtures. Once we've done that, we can get dressed up in costumes and scare the living daylights out of the neighbors. What else is Halloween for?

Storing Summer Clothes

Summer is finally over and now it's time to store your warm weather clothes. Try to avoid the temptation to just push them to one side of your closet. You'll feel better organized all year long if you make the effort to adjust your closet to the seasons. You won't have so many items to sift through when looking for something to wear, and your clothes are less likely to become wrinkled in the crush.

Clothes should be washed before storage; otherwise, stains will have a nice long time to set, and you'll never get them out. It's best to have everything laundered (or dry-cleaned, as the case may be), even if they seem to be clean. Some stains are hard to detect and only materialize over time, like a rash. Best to tackle them right away.

> Try to avoid using fabric softener on clothes you're about to store. Fabric softener can leave grease spots, which can attract undesirables and weaken fibers. Best to forgo the softener, or use a vinegar rinse.

Another good reason to launder clothes before storing them? Moths are attracted to your scent.

For surprise spots on washable clothes, try using ½ cup of hydrogen peroxide and 1 teaspoon of ammonia. Saturate the stain and allow to sit for 30 minutes. Then launder. Zout® Stain Remover is also great on old stains; use as directed.

Make sure that swimsuits are washed before storing them. Chlorine residue can damage fibers and may give you a nasty shock when you head to the beach next year. It's best to wash swimsuits using your machine's gentle cycle and cold water along with your favorite laundry detergent. (If you have been swimming in salt water, soak the suit in cold water for 15 minutes *before* washing.) If you handwash your suit, make sure to rinse well to get rid of all detergent. Air-dry your suit out of the sun. Don't put it in the dryer. Heat can break down the elastic and spandex that keeps the shape of your swimsuit.

Don't forget to protect your natural fibers from those natural predators: moths. Mothballs work well, although some people find the odor offensive. Cedar chips are also reliable. Just insert a handful into the container with your clothes. Perhaps the best deterrent, though, is this lovely homemade citrus remedy: Take some oranges, grapefruit, lemons or limes, remove the peels and cut them into thin strips. Place the strips on a cookie sheet (making sure it's clean) and leave in a warm place to dry. You can also speed the drying process by placing the tray in a 300-degree oven. Preheat the oven, then turn it off before putting in your citrus tray. Prolonged heat will burn the peels. Once the peels are dry and cool, put them into clothes pockets, storage drawers or boxes. No nasty smells, and no damage from moths, either.

Suitcases come in handy for storing seasonal clothes, but I like under-the-bed storage boxes best. Choose between cardboard or plastic, whichever suits your space and budget. I like the transparent plastic boxes because they allow me to see at a glance what's inside. Nevertheless, I also tape a list of the contents to the top of the box so I can get to things in a hurry, if need be. (I *am* an organized Queen!)

Don't store clothes in plastic dry cleaner bags. They can cause yellowing.

Be creative as to *where* you store your boxes. Under-the-bed storage boxes don't have to go under the bed. Look at the unused space in children's closets, for example. And who says that the linen closet it strictly for linens? Just be careful of storing clothes in the basement, attic, or other places where mold and mildew can damage clothes.

Give some thought as to how you want to pack the boxes *before* you start the process. Use separate storage receptacles for each person, try not to overstuff boxes, and be sure to group types of clothes together. You'll be glad you did when, next summer, you find how easy it is to unpack boxes that have already been organized with care.

Bring the Outdoors In

Now that summer is drawing to a close, it's time to take a few steps to make sure that your tools and summer gear are safe and dry for the winter ahead. A word of caution: If you store your seasonal equipment in the garage (and most of us do), don't forget to leave room for your car!

* Lawn chairs and summer gear can be suspended from the ceiling of your garage with sturdy hooks.
* Open rafters make great storage space, too. Secure items there with bungee cords.
* Don't overlook the simple solutions. A shopping bag hung on a nail can be great for storing small and medium-sized balls.
* An inexpensive string hammock, the type you might use to display a child's collection of stuffed animals, makes a great home for soccer balls and other large items.
* Pegboards are endlessly versatile. Use them to hold hand tools and other small equipment. There's a reason they've stood the test of time!
* Sand doesn't freeze, so store your small gardening tools in the same container of sand that you've been using all summer.
* Garden hoses can crack and split in severely cold weather, so store them inside. Just make sure they're empty first. Pockets of water can collect and freeze in cold weather, and that can result in a tear.
* Take steps to ensure that your lawn mower will start in the spring. Old, unleaded fuel can solidify over winter and that will clog up the workings on your mower. Empty the gas tank and then run the mower till it stops. Only then should you store it for the winter.

Let There Be Light

Now that it's too cold for outdoor lanterns and citronella candles, let's turn our attention to indoor lighting, namely, the main light in your dining area. It may not be the chandelier from *The Phantom of the Opera,* but the light over your dining room table is still important. Keep it clean and sparkling—it will reflect well on you.

Chandeliers have a reputation of being difficult to clean, but it doesn't have to be that way. First, turn off the light and give the bulbs a chance to cool down—don't start until they're cool to the touch. Place a small, plastic snack bag over each bulb and secure with a twist tie to prevent moisture from seeping into the socket. Next, position a table directly under the chandelier, covering it with a sturdy plastic table cover and a good layer of old rags (towels work well). This will give you a work base and will also catch the cleaning solution as it drips off the chandelier.

> Use a premoistened alcohol wipe to quickly shine chandelier crystals—no drips and lots of sparkle!

Now for the cleaning solution: Make a mixture of 2 cups of warm water, ½ cup of rubbing alcohol and 2 tablespoons of an automatic dishwasher spot stopper, such as Jet Dry™. Pour the solution into a spray bottle—you can pick them up quite cheaply at the dollar store—then spray the chandelier liberally. Allow it to drip-dry. Pour the leftover solution in a cup and you can use it to hand-dip the crystal teardrops or other decorative hanging pieces. No need to remove them from the chandelier; just dip them and let them drip-dry. The chandelier will be sparkling.

But wait: You're not finished—not until you clean the bulbs themselves. Lightbulbs collect dust and that prevents the beauty of the light from shining through. Make sure that the bulbs have had a chance to cool down, then wipe them with a soft, dry cloth. Don't apply much pressure to the bulb—it may break.

Of course not all overhead lights are chandeliers. You may have traditional fixtures with a flat base attached to the ceiling. You may have track lighting or lights connected to a fan. The glass may be clear, frosted or colored. No matter, it still needs to be cleaned. Remove fixtures carefully. If

I HATE IT WHEN THAT HAPPENS . . .

If a lightbulb breaks off in the socket, just grab a bar of soap and push it into the jagged edges. Turn the soap counterclockwise and presto! You've safely removed the broken bulb!

the light is hard to reach, make sure you use a step stool or ladder to remove it—easier on you, and easier on the light. Keep one hand firmly on or under the fixture while you undo the screws or brackets that hold the fixture to the ceiling, and remove with great care. You don't want to chip the edges.

Now, place an old towel in the bottom of your sink. That should prevent the fixture from hitting the hard bottom and breaking or cracking. Fill the sink with warm water and a little bit of dishwashing liquid. Wash the fixture gently, then remove it from the water and sit it safely to one side on another towel. Empty the sink, then fill it up again with warm water, this time adding ¼ cup of white vinegar. You'll need to put another towel in the water, too. Place the fixture in the sink one last time and leave it there for a minute or so before removing. Gently remove excess moisture with a soft, lint-free cloth, then allow to air-dry thoroughly. Use this dry-time to gently wipe down any metal components with a damp cloth. Buff well with a dry one, and wipe down the lightbulb(s) with a soft cloth. Be sure the fixture is shut off and the bulb and metal are cool. Now you can put the fixture back in place and let the light shine through!

Trick or Treat

Okay, the chores are done and now it's time for fun. And because it's October, that can mean only one thing—Halloween!

The Treat

* Makeup is much safer for children than masks, which can obscure their vision.
* Remove glitter makeup and heavy dark makeup from kids' faces with petroleum jelly. Gently work in the jelly (use care with glitter makeup not to get it into the eye area), then tissue away the makeup. Wash face well when done.
* Make sure to leave plenty of room for your child's clothes under the costume. And make sure the costume isn't trailing on the ground. You don't want your child to trip!
* Make sure to check your children's candy before you let them eat it. If little ones are impatient, give them a piece of the candy you bought until you've had time to check the bounty.
* Put some reflective tape on costumes and shoes so that your child will be visible. Consider making a cute flashlight part of the costume.
* Did you color your hair green for Halloween only to discover that the color won't come out? Don't give up hope. Reach for the baking soda, liquid dish soap and shampoo. Make a paste the consistency of thick shampoo, work it well into your hair—concentrate on your hair, not your scalp—then rinse thoroughly. No more green!

The Trick

Sometimes those little pirates and princesses come home with a lot more than candy. Here's how to treat those muddy problems.

* Wet mud on your clothes can be treated by flushing the

wrong side of the fabric with lots of cool water. Hold the garment under a faucet and direct a forceful stream of water at the clean side of the garment. (Flushing the dirty side with water will only grind the mud into the fabric.) Once the water runs clear, work some Fels-Naptha Heavy Duty Laundry Bar Soap® into the area and launder as usual.

* Muddy shoes should be allowed to dry, then vigorously brushed with a shoe brush. Use fast, downward strokes rather than circular motions, which could grind the mud into the shoes. If mud remains on leather shoes, clean with a bar of soap (Dove® Moisturizing Bath Bar works well) and a soft cloth. Canvas or athletic shoes should be cleaned using Fels-Naptha Soap® and a nailbrush.
* Mud on car upholstery, whether fabric or leather, should be allowed to dry before treating. Use the attachment hose on your vacuum to remove all the mud you can. For fabric upholstery, use your favorite carpet and upholstery cleaner (I like Spot Shot Instant Carpet Stain Remover®), following the directions on the container. On leather, wash the area using a moisturizing bar soap, such as Dove® and wipe with a clean soft cloth.

The Pumpkin Patch

Pumpkins decay and mold quickly, so make sure to put something under your pumpkin, such as a couple of paper plates or a plastic tablecloth. You don't want to have a black stain as a reminder of the holiday.

If you already have a black stain you may be able to remove it with one of the following remedies.

For pumpkin mold on a porch or concrete, try cleaning the area with oven cleaner. Spray the area with the cleaner and allow to sit 10 minutes, then agitate with a brush and rinse well. Do this on a cool day, and make sure to keep kids and pets away.

For wooden tabletops, use a little nongel toothpaste on a damp cloth and rub in a circular motion. You can also try some fine-grade (0000) steel wool dipped into turpentine. Do this in a very small, inconspicuous spot first. Apply some lemon oil to the area when you are done, let it soak in and buff with a soft cloth. You can avoid that stain altogether by making pumpkin pie out of that pumpkin.

Let's Dish!

DAD'S FAVORITE PUMPKIN PIE

2 cups canned pumpkin

1 can evaporated milk and ⅓ cup regular milk to equal 2 cups

1 cup granulated sugar

2 eggs, well beaten

½ teaspoon ginger

1 teaspoon cinnamon

½ to ¾ teaspoon nutmeg

½ teaspoon salt

1 deep 8- or 9-inch pie shell

Using a mixer, combine all ingredients thoroughly.

Pour into pie shell. Bake for 15 minutes at 425 degrees, then turn down temperature to 350 degrees and bake until a knife pushed into the center of the pie filling comes out clean, approximately 30 minutes. Serve with whipped cream or nondairy topping.

28 November

It's November, and the year is almost over! Where did it go? Thank heavens for Thanksgiving and the time to pause, to give thanks for what we have. Thanksgiving is a time of tradition—a big turkey dinner with all the trimmings, Grandmother's silverware, Aunt Jean's china, and Uncle Jim's bad jokes. Nobody wants to keep Jim's bad jokes, but the silverware and china, well that's something we hope to have for a good long time. That's why proper cleaning and maintenance is a must. Take the time to care for these precious heirlooms, and not only will you enjoy them for years to come, but you'll be able to pass them along to your children, your grandchildren, and perhaps even your great-grandchildren! Oh, and when you're finished with the china and silverware, take a moment to get ready for the snow. November is the gateway to winter after all.

Traditions at the Table

The China Syndrome

First things first. You'll need to evaluate what you have, so remove everything from the cabinet and place it on the dining table. Don't put the china on a bare table (you could scratch the finish), and don't put it on the floor where you might break something—those *I Love Lucy* situations are best avoided!

Now's the time to get tough. If you're *really* going to repair that teacup—you know, the one that's been broken since the Carter administration—now's the time to do it. If it can't be repaired, and if it doesn't really have any sentimental value, throw it out. Bear in mind that cracked dishes can be unsafe to eat off of because food and debris can settle in the cracks and not come out during washing. If in doubt, throw it out.

If you have a piece of china that has great sentimental value but is broken beyond repair, consider putting it in a sturdy paper bag and giving it a good whack. Collect the pieces (there won't be a million—trust me) and glue them around a picture frame or on a trinket box. Add some jewels, pearls, or artificial flowers, letting your imagination run wild. You'll end up with a lovely keepsake.

Dishes that don't get regular use should be cleaned before use. Soap and water will generally do the trick. Just make sure to rinse well. For special challenges, like black cutlery marks on china plates, use nongel toothpaste on a soft cloth to rub the marks away. If you have fine, hairline cracks in old china, soak it in warm milk for 30 to 60 minutes. The cracks should disappear when you remove the plate from the milk. Wash as usual and dry well. If food has left any stains on the china, make a paste of lemon juice and cream of tartar, and rub gently. Rinse the piece well when you're done.

> Never use the dishwasher for antique china, china with metal trim or hand-painted china.

The next step is to dust the cabinet shelves with a soft cloth. Then wash them with a cloth that has been immersed in a mild, soapy solution (1 teaspoon of liquid dish soap to 1 gallon of warm water) and then wrung out until just damp. Wash well and dry thoroughly with a soft, lint-free cloth. You may prefer to wash the shelves with a solution of brewed tea (1 quart of warm water and 1 tea bag). Allow the solution to cool to room temperature and wash the shelves using a soft cloth. Then dry thoroughly. A damp microfiber cloth can also be used.

Glass doors should be cleaned with a solution of 2 parts warm water to 1 part rubbing alcohol. Apply the solution directly to the cloth, then wipe gently in small circular motions. Make sure to clean the corners of the glass, too. Buff with a dry, lint-free cloth.

> Never spray glass cleaner directly onto glass doors, picture frames or mirrors. The solution can seep into the wood and cause damage to the surrounding areas.

Sliding doors have tracks that need to be cleaned from time to time. The crevice attachment on your vacuum cleaner is perfect for this. After you've vacuumed, wash the track with a damp, soapy toothbrush and dry with a soft cloth. Keep the track and doors running smoothly by rubbing them with a little lemon oil or spraying with some furniture polish.

Okay. You've cleaned your cabinet and evaluated its contents. Now's the time to put everything back. Take stock of what you have before returning items to the shelves. What are your favorite pieces? What do you want to display, and what would you rather conceal? Bear this in mind as you arrange your cabinet. Put larger pieces at the back of the cabinet, smaller items in front. Create groupings. Keep one set of china together, silver together, and crystal together, and so on. Put the things you seldom use in the back or on the shelf that's most difficult to reach, and keep them clean by covering with plastic wrap. Always empty sugar from the china sugar bowl.

Stack dinner plates, dessert plates, saucers and other flat items together, and insert a napkin or paper towel between each one to avoid scratches. Sit groups of these flat items on each other to make the most of your space. Cups are more delicate and easily broken, though, so don't stack them more than two deep. Be creative with your groupings. Try putting some of your old and new pieces together. You may just see things in a whole new light!

If you plan to wash your china in the automatic dishwasher, take one piece (say, a cup) and wash it over the course of a month to determine if it's dishwasher safe. Just leave the cup in the dishwasher and let it run through the wash with your everyday dishes. Take a look at the piece every few days or so. If it appears that the trim is changing color, the pattern is fading or small cracks are occurring, you'll want to stop the experiment. If the piece remains unharmed, you can follow with the rest of your set. For best results, use the "china" or "short" cycle, as well as the "energy saver" or "no heat" drying cycle. (You'll save energy and money, too!) I wish I could tell you another easy test you could try, but there isn't one. If you are buying a large set of china, you might want to consider buying one extra, inexpensive piece to try this dishwasher experiment.

Crystal that stands up securely in the rack can be washed in the dishwasher. It should not lean, lay sideways or hook over the prongs on the dishwasher rack. Don't allow crystal pieces to bump against each other during washing—they'll chip. Avoid water spots on crystal by adding 1 teaspoon of 20 Mule Team® Borax to your automatic dishwashing detergent.

When handwashing crystal, wash only a few pieces at a time and make sure not to overload the sink. Crystal should be cleaned in hot water, but not too hot. As a general rule, if the water is too hot for your

Place a towel in the bottom of the sink when handwashing crystal. The towel will cushion the crystal and prevent breakage.

hands, it's too hot for the crystal. Sudden changes of temperature can cause crystal to crack, so place it sideways into the water instead of bottom first. For a squeaky clean finish, add 1 tablespoon of white vinegar to the water, along with your liquid dish soap.

Cranberry stains on that tablecloth? Remove them with a little Wine Away Red Stain Remover™. Works like a charm.

Crystal should be stored upright, as you would drink from it. A lot of people like to store glasses upside down to prevent dust from accumulating in the goblet or flute, but it's not a good idea. Moisture can be trapped inside the glass, causing damage to the crystal and the shelf on which it's stored.

Hi Ho Silver

Acidic foods and their residue can tarnish silver and may even cause it to pit. Salt, egg yolk, fish, broccoli, mayonnaise and mustard are the biggest offenders. Get into the habit of rinsing your silver right after you clear the table. You may not be able to wash the dishes right away—I know it's not *my* idea of an after-dinner treat—but a thorough rinsing will go a long way to prevent permanent damage.

Wash silverware in hot water and mild dishwashing liquid. Rinse well, and dry with a soft, lint-free cloth. Don't allow silver to air-dry, as this can result in water spotting. Silver *must* be dry before storing, so make sure to dry well.

- Silverware washed in a dishwasher should never be mixed with stainless steel cutlery. Pitting may occur.
- Never store silver in plastic bags or plastic wrap. That traps condensation and can encourage tarnish.
- Store silver in a tarnish-proof bag or wrap it in acid-free tissue paper. If you wear clean, soft gloves when doing this task, you

won't leave finger marks—that's where tarnish can begin.

DID YOU KNOW?

Rubber causes silver to tarnish, so don't dry pieces on a rubber mat or store it wrapped in rubber bands.

- For quick silver cleaning, put strips of aluminum foil in a large bowl, place the silver on top of the foil, pour boiling water over the silver and add 3 tablespoons of baking soda. Soak for a few minutes, then rinse and dry. Don't use this method on hollow or glued pieces.
- Make your own silver-cleaning cloths by saturating cotton squares in a solution of:

  2 parts ammonia

  1 part silver polish

  10 parts cold water

  Let clothes drip dry and use as silver polish cloths.
- Rubbing silver with a damp cloth dipped in baking soda will also remove tarnish. Or try a little nongel toothpaste on a soft, damp cloth. Rinse and dry thoroughly before using.
- Never store salt in silver saltshakers. This could lead to tarnish.
- Remove tarnish and other stains from the inside of silver coffeepots by rubbing with a piece of fine-grade (0000) steel wool dipped in white vinegar and salt.

Just boiled some potatoes? Let the water cool and then pour over silver. Allow it to soak for 30 minutes. Wash, rinse and rub with a soft cloth. The starch in the potato water will clean the silver.

* Place several sugar cubes in a silver coffeepot before storing, and you'll never have an old, musty smell. The Queen Mum taught me that one!
* Store silver teapots and coffeepots with the lid open or off so that moisture is never trapped inside.
* Clean the inside of silver teapots by filling with water to which you have added a small handful of Arm and Hammer® Washing Soda. Let soak overnight, rinse and dry well.
* Clean silver-plated items as you would real silver, but be gentle—silver plating can rub off.
* Cleaning silver is important, but be careful not to rub too hard on the hallmark. If you wear it off or distort it, the value of the set will be reduced.

If someone spills gravy on your tablecloth during dinner, sprinkle the spill with baking soda or salt to absorb it and enjoy the rest of the meal. After dinner, treat with Zout® Stain Remover and launder as usual.

Silver takes on a beautiful patina with age and with use—rather like a Queen!—so don't just keep it stored away in a drawer. A beautifully set table is an important part of a holiday meal, and your silverware is a meaningful part of that setting. So use your silverware, treat it well, and each time you set the table you'll have beautiful memories to enjoy.

There's No Business Like Snow Business

So you're thinking *What does a woman in Arizona know about snow?* Well, I lived in Michigan for more than forty years (we don't have to go into details here), so believe me, I know what I'm talking about when I talk snow!

Give Snow and Salt the Boot

- Keep boots looking their best by applying a good coat of quality paste polish and following up with a spray of water protectant.
- Damp or wet boots should be dried standing up. A roll of cardboard or a bent wire hanger will help them keep their shape. Never allow boots to dry on a heat register—the leather could crack.
- Remove salt stains by wiping with a mixture of 1 part water and 1 part white vinegar.

> Buttons on heavy winter coats have to do double duty, what with that heavy fabric and the constant on-and-off as you go from indoors to out. Try sewing them on with dental floss. It's stronger and longer-lasting than most thread, so you'll never be bothered with missing buttons again. If your coat is dark, just finish off with a few loops of dark thread to avoid an ugly contrast.

Car Detail

- Don't wait until it's too late. Schedule a tune-up and winterizing appointment for your car.
- Give your car a thorough cleaning before the winter sets in. Don't forget to vacuum the carpet and upholstery, and treat it with a good-quality fabric protector.
- Make sure the dashboard and defroster are clear from obstructions.

Prevent frozen locks in your car by covering the lock with a couple layers of masking tape. The tape will keep the lock free from moisture, and that's what causes the ice to form.

* Rubber mats with deep, diagonal grooves really help to capture melting snow. They're a good investment.
* Locks frozen in your car? If your car is in the garage near an electrical outlet, use a blow-dryer on the low setting to direct the warm air into the lock, from a distance of about six inches. That should do the trick. If your car is outside, heat your key with a match or lighter and insert it into the lock. Leave it there for a few minutes, and then gently turn the key. You may have to do this a few times, but it should work. *Don't try this method if your lock has an electronic device.* You could damage the chip.
* Rub Vaseline™ on the gaskets so doors don't freeze.
* Getting stuck in the snow can be a real pain in the radials, so keep a bag of Kitty Litter™ in your trunk for some much-needed traction. A few layers of newspaper work well, too.
* Don't run out of windshield washer fluid. One part rubbing alcohol to 1 part water, and a few drops of liquid dish soap, work well on winter windshields. And if you treat them first with Clean Shield® (formerly Invisible Shield) protectant, they'll be that much easier to clean. Snow and grime will wipe right off.
* You can shave a few minutes off your morning snow detail if you place an old beach towel on the windshield the night before a forecasted snowfall. Tuck the towel beneath the windshield wipers before the snowfall, pull it off afterward, and you

won't have to scrape your windows. Just give the towel a good shake and dream of sunnier days. A mitten placed on your sideview mirror will save you time, too!

* It's always a good idea to keep an emergency kit in your car during winter. Nobody leaves the house saying, "I think I'll get stuck in the snow today," so be prepared. Take along the following:

  Blanket

  Flashlight and some extra batteries

  Two bottles of water

  Chocolate bar (for emergencies only!)

  Piece of red cloth to tie to the car

Give your snow shovel a coat of nonstick cooking spray before you start to tackle the driveway. You won't be bothered with those annoying clumps that stick to the shovel!

Shovel It

Every year hundreds of people suffer heart attacks from shoveling snow. Follow these simple rules to minimize the hazards.

* Never shovel snow after a heavy meal.
* Dress in layers and always wear a hat.
* Don't shovel snow after you've been drinking.
* Don't overload your shovel—snow can be very heavy.
* Always bend from the knees.
* Make sure someone knows where you are.
* Pace yourself. Take frequent breaks.

29 December

Christmas comes but once a year, which is a good thing if you're the one who has to do all the work. Try to make Christmas as stress-free as possible by planning ahead and enlisting what help you can. Don't be a holiday hero. Involve even the youngest members of your family, and don't decline those offers of help. Make lists. Plan ahead and try not to abandon your family's routine. The closer you follow yours—regular meal-times and bedtimes, for example—the more you'll be able to enjoy the excitement of Christmas without the chaos. So go ahead and deck those halls . . . just don't forget to dust them first.

Holiday Hints

Ten Time Savers

1. Tell your children that Santa only comes to a clean house. Don't laugh—it worked on me for years!

2. Take the time to clean your house *before* you bring in the tree and all the decorations. Sure, you'll probably need a quick vacuum once you have the tree in place, but it's easier to clean a house when you don't have to maneuver all those holiday adornments around. Trust me on this one.
3. Make lists and stick to them. It's amazing how much time and effort you'll save.
4. Never say no to those offers of "Can I bring something?" or "Can I help?"
5. Shop early in the morning or late at night when stores aren't as crowded. Make use of the Internet and catalogs whenever possible.
6. Consider these quick gifts: a phone card, a wine club membership, a framed photo of a special time, this book, a gift certificate for a favorite coffeehouse, and pretty stationery with stamps.
7. Use gift bags instead of wrapping paper.
8. Make your own frozen dinners by preparing extra portions when you're cooking a big meal. Great for dinner when you're rushed, and great for the kids when you're on your way out to a party.
9. Get your holiday clothes cleaned and ready in advance. Hang the clothes and accessories together and you will have time for a leisurely bath, too!
10. Remove the word "perfection" from your vocabulary.

It's a Family Affair

- Enlist the whole family in a quick cleanup. Small children can dust, older ones can vacuum, your spouse can do the dishes, and you can tidy up and put things away. It's amazing what you can accomplish in 30 short minutes.
- Involve children in sending out Christmas cards. Older ones can address the envelopes, and little ones can attach the stamps!
- Let your children bake some Christmas cookies. They're easy to prepare and require little supervision—just make sure to keep small hands away from the oven. You can make things easier by giving cookie cutters a quick spritz of nonstick cooking spray to prevent dough from clinging. And for those stubborn cookies that won't come away from the baking sheet? Slide a length of dental floss under each cookie and they'll glide right off.
- Children love to make pictures with artificial snow, but it can be difficult to wash off. Prevent snow from sticking by preparing the surface with a light misting of nonstick cooking spray. If you forget this step you can still remove it easily: Just rub with a little bit of white, nongel toothpaste.
- Let the kids wrap some gifts. The outcome may not be just as you'd like, but the kids will have fun and they'll be proud of their accomplishment.

O' Christmas Tree

- Know the height of your living room before you select your tree. Make sure to allow for the stand (about a foot) and the treetop. Size does matter!

* Older trees are dry and will drop needles when shaken, so make sure to shake the tree before you buy it. Choose one that has sturdy, flexible needles and a strong, fresh scent.
* The first thing to do when you bring your tree home is to cut off a small diagonal section at the base of the trunk. Trees need a lot of water, and this small act will help them to absorb it.
* Pine tree needles will last longer if spritzed first with fabric sizing or spray starch. Just make sure to do this *before* you put the lights on.
* Put a plastic tablecloth under the base of your tree to help protect your carpet from spills.
* If you do have a spill from your Christmas tree, clean it up as soon as possible or you'll have mold on the carpet. Slide the tree carefully to one side, and blot up all of the water by standing on some heavy towels placed on the carpet. Absorb all you can. Clean the area with your favorite carpet cleaner, and let a fan blow across the area until it is thoroughly dry, at least 24 hours.

Nourish your Christmas tree with a mixture of 1 quart of water, 2 tablespoons of lemon juice, 1 tablespoon of sugar and ½ teaspoon of liquid bleach. If you want a simpler solution, try 2 ounces of Listerine® or 1 tablespoon of maple syrup.

* Add water to the reservoir of a Christmas tree with a turkey baster, and you'll keep spills to a minimum.
* Make sure to water your tree daily.
* Rub a little petroleum jelly on the trunk of your artificial tree

before inserting the branches. They'll be easier to remove in the new year.

* Put lights on your tree before adding any other decorations. And when choosing your lights, remember that white bulbs give off more light than colored ones.

Protect your door by securing a piece of weather stripping under your wreath.

* Ran out of hooks and hangers? Use paper clips, bobby pins, twist ties, pipe cleaners or dental floss. These makeshift hooks work well, but they're not very attractive, so try putting these ornaments deeper in the tree, where you're less likely to see the fastener.

At the Table

* Finding your good napkins wrinkled from storage can be frustrating. Don't despair. Just throw them in the dryer, along with a damp towel. After 10 minutes or so the creases will relax and you won't have to iron them.

* Don't throw away those empty rolls of wrapping paper. If you make a slit down the side of the roll and slide it over a coat hanger, you can use it to hang tablecloths without worrying about creases.

* Clean your dining table the natural way, with tea! Make a pot of tea. Sit down, have a

Put a few layers of foil in the basket before you add the napkin and rolls. Your bread and buns will stay warmer longer. Just about everybody likes warm buns!

cup yourself, and wait until the tea is cool to the touch. Pour the liquid into a small container, saturate a clean, lint-free cloth, and wring it out till barely damp. Then wipe the table and leaves in the direction of the wood grain. Buff dry with a soft, dry cloth.

* Remove white marks from your table with a little bit of mayonnaise. Just make sure it's regular mayonnaise—low-fat

Christmas may be an exciting time for people, but it can be a little nerve-racking for those of us with four legs. Here are a few things to watch out for:

- Holiday plants such as holly, poinsettia and mistletoe can be toxic. Please keep them away from us—and from small children, too.
- Cats love to play with tinsel, but we also like to eat it. This can wreak havoc on our intestinal tract. Please keep the tinsel and other stringy decorations out of our reach. If you want to put tinsel on the tree, avoid the lower branches.
- We may like to eat rich foods, but they're not good for us and can make us sick, especially chocolate. If you can't resist our soulful faces staring up at you while you're eating dinner, give us some carrots and a small piece of turkey without gravy. Of course, it's best not to feed us from the table at all, but don't ever say I told you that!
- Bear in mind that I may not be the party animal you think I am. If you're having lots of company, please put me in a room by myself, with my food, water and litter box. Better include a chew toy for the dog—you know how they get . . .

won't do the trick. Mix the mayonnaise with table salt or cigarette ash. Massage the mixture into the mark for about 45 minutes. Yes, 45 minutes! It's a long time, but it's the massaging that gently buffs the mark away. Allow the mixture to sit for several hours, preferably overnight. Linseed oil and rottenstone (both available in hardware stores) work well, too.

* Use wax sticks or crayons to cover scratches. Make sure you get these from the hardware or furniture store (your child's crayons won't work here), and take care to match the shade of the stick to the table. Once you've applied the crayon according to the manufacturer's instructions, heat the area with a blow-dryer and buff firmly with an old rag for an almost invisible repair.

It's a Wrap

* Keep rolls of wrapping paper handy by standing them up in a wastebasket or in a small, clean garbage can.

* Empty wrapping paper rolls can also be used as kindling. Slide small twigs, dried leaves and broken bits of pinecones in the tubes to make the foundation of a wonderful, crackling fire.

* Run out of wrapping paper? Recycle some old gift wrap by spraying the back with spray starch. Press with a warm iron and you're ready to go!

Be creative when wrapping packages. Fabric, wallpaper, maps, T-shirts and sheet music all make great gift coverings.

- Keep the end of the tape from disappearing by folding it over a paper clip. You'll never have to pick at bits of tape again.
- Don't burn foil wrapping or magazines in a fireplace—they emit noxious, dangerous gases.
- Recycled Christmas cards make great gift tags.

That Oh-So Common Cold

Christmas may be a time of giving, but nobody wants a cold. Here are some things to minimize your chances of getting this seasonal nuisance. If you do get a cold, look here for some comforting remedies . . . and some solutions for the stains those remedies can cause on your soft flannel sheets!

An Ounce of Prevention

- Contrary to the old wives' tale, you can't catch cold from being out in the cold weather. Colds are caused by viruses. Avoid the virus, avoid the cold.
- Wash your hands frequently and wash them well. Use water that is comfortably hot. *Always* use soap.
- Avoid touching your eyes, nose and mouth.
- Use tissues instead of handkerchiefs, if at all possible. Tissues are more easily disposed of, along with their germs!
- Don't leave tissues in an open

> Help prevent colds by washing your hands for as long as it takes to sing "Happy Birthday" . . . twice! That's the amount of time you'll need to wash your hands properly.

Be particularly vigilant about sharing phones. Use a soft cloth dipped in Listerine© Mouthwash or rubbing alcohol to swab down phone mouthpieces, door handles and computer keyboard. Alcohol wipes work well, too.

trash can. Dispose of them in a plastic bag kept just for that purpose. You don't want anyone else picking up your germs!

- Try not to share things with someone who is ill. That includes towels, glasses and cooking utensils.
- Continue to share kisses—there's nothing like a little love when you're sick. Just confine it to the cheeks.

Cold Care

- Keep your feet warm. Believe it or not, cold feet can cause your nostrils to become cold and dry, and that can aggravate your cold.
- Wash bedding and pajamas in the hottest possible water.
- The fragrance of fabric softener can irritate delicate noses, so soften flannel sheets and cotton towels with ¼ cup of white vinegar when you have a cold.

Make sure you check the date on those cold medicines *before* you take them.

- ✳ Rubbing some Vicks Vapor Rub® on the outside of your throat and chest will soothe that congestion, no matter how old you are.
- ✳ Put a dash of wintergreen oil in a basin of hot water, lower your face to the water (no closer than twelve inches, though), and put a towel over your head to create a tent. Breathe deeply for some much-needed relief.

Prone to cold sores? Dab on some Pepto Bismol® when you feel that first tingle, and, chances are, the sore won't make an appearance!

Humidifier Heaven

Moist air is heaven to dry throats and nasal passages, but if you don't keep your humidifier clean and free from mold, you may find your cold aggravated by airborne pollutants.

Remove mineral deposits from detachable parts, such as the plastic rotor tube and locking ring, by submerging them in a pot of hot white vinegar. Bring a pot of vinegar to boil, remove it from the stove, and then immerse the tube and ring in the vinegar for about five minutes. Rinse well in clear water and make sure that all parts are dry before returning them to the unit.

Clean a humidifier by swishing around a solution of 1 cup of bleach in 1 gallon of water in the container that holds the water, allowing it to soak for a few minutes, if necessary. Scrub any mineral deposits with a brush and then rinse. Make sure the humidifier is cool and empty before you start.

Baby wipes are great for removing stains caused by medicated ointments. Rub the stained fabric firmly with the baby wipe, then pretreat and launder as usual.

What to Do for Those Cold Medication Stains

Rubs, liniments, eardrops and ointments are oil-based stains, so you should treat these as soon as you can. Rubbing the stain with a good waterless hand cleaner such as GOJO Crème Waterless Hand Cleaner® is your best bet. Apply directly to the stain, and rub it in well with your thumb and forefinger. Wait 10 minutes, then apply a good stain remover, such as Zout®, before laundering in the hottest possible water.

Cough syrups and other red-based stains can be removed quite effectively with Wine Away Red Wine Stain Remover™ or Red Erase®. Apply liberally, as directed on the container, then launder as usual. Alternatively, soak the stained area in 1 cup of warm water and 1 tablespoon of salt.

Fabric stained from hot toddies and medicated drinks should be flushed under cool, running water as soon as possible. Be sure to direct the water to the *wrong* side of the fabric. Next, make a paste with 20 Mule Team® Borax and cool water. Use about 2 parts borax to 1 part water, adding more water as needed to create a pastelike consistency. Apply to the fabric, then have a cup of tea and watch your favorite sitcom. Once 30 minutes have passed, it's time to loosen the mixture by applying more cool water. Work the loosened mixture between your thumb and forefinger, then launder as usual in the hottest possible water for the fabric type.

Americans suffer from more than one billion colds a year. That's nothing to sneeze at!

Let's Dish!

Mom made these cookies every year for as long as I can remember. When I got old enough I got to "help"—I loved the decorating part best and I admit to sneaking a bite of the dough, not a healthy thing to do.

THE QUEEN MOTHER'S CHRISTMAS COOKIES

2 cups flour
1 teaspoon baking powder
½ teaspoon baking soda
½ teaspoon salt
½ cup shortening
1 cup sugar
¼ teaspoon nutmeg
¼ teaspoon lemon extract or grated rind
2 eggs

Mix together the dry ingredients in a bowl.

Using a mixer, cream together the shortening, sugar, nutmeg and lemon extract until well blended and light in color. Beat in the eggs and add the dry ingredients a little at a time, beating between additions.

Chill the mixture in the refrigerator for an hour or so, and then bake in one of the following ways:

Roll out the dough and cut with cookie cutters and place on a greased cookie sheet.

Drop by rounded tablespoons onto a greased cookie sheet and flatten with the bottom of a drinking glass dipped in flour.

Decorate the cookies by placing a raisin or nut in the center. Sprinkle with granulated sugar—colored granulated sugar is nice for Christmas.

Bake in a 375-degree oven for 10 to 12 minutes. Do not overbake. Makes about 3 dozen cookies.

Think I'll go call my mom . . .

Laundry Day

30

Care and Control of the Washing Machine

How difficult can it be? You add water and detergent, drop in the clothes, select the cycle and walk away. When you come back the clothes are clean. Okay . . . but have you ever considered how clean your washing machine is after all that hard water and *all* those dirty clothes?

Your washer needs some TLC from time to time, especially if you have hard water in your area. So if the clothes seem dull and gray, maybe you don't need that new and improved detergent. Maybe all you need to do is clean the washing machine. Here's the easiest way I know.

Fill the washer with hot water. Add 1 quart of chlorine bleach (no detergent, please). Run the washer through the longest wash cycle. When the washer is still wet—this should be immediately after the bleach cycle—add 1 quart of white vinegar and run the washer through the same cycle again. This will clean out soap scum and mineral deposits from the spin basket and also from the hoses. If you live in an area with hard water you really need to do this every three months—otherwise, every six months will do. You'll be amazed at the difference it will make.

If you start to notice little brown, rusty-looking spots on clothes when they come out of the washing machine, well, it probably *is* rust! Look your spin basket over carefully when this occurs, and check for any chips in the finish. Chipped areas rust and transfer to clothes, and the only way to remedy this problem is to replace the spin basket. Check with your appliance dealer and be sure to get the right basket for your machine. And a word of caution: Take care when using detergent balls or fabric softener balls. They can chip the spin basket with their weight.

When you don't have time to give your machine a really thorough cleaning, just fill the washer with hot water and pour in 1 gallon of white vinegar. Run through the entire wash cycle.

For information on removing rust stains from clothes, turn to the spotting section. It's easier than you think.

Cleaning the Fabric Softener Dispenser

Clean the automatic fabric softener dispenser every month to 6 weeks to keep it working well and to prevent it from leaving softener stains on clothes. (Liquid softener can leave blue spots on clothes; marks from dryer sheets can look like small grease patches.) To clean the dispenser you first must warm 1 cup of white vinegar (I use the microwave), and pour it into the dispenser as you would softener. Make sure you use warm vinegar, and make sure you do this when the washer is empty. Large pieces of sticky fabric softener will occasionally be flushed out during cleaning, and they could adhere to clothes. Not a pretty sight. I suggest cleaning the fabric softener dispenser when you are cleaning the machine with one of the methods recommended in this chapter.

Cleaning the Bleach Dispenser

It is equally important to keep the bleach dispenser clean. Clean any removable parts by washing with hot water and dishwashing liquid. When you clean the washer with white vinegar, be sure to add some to the bleach dispenser too.

Use less detergent and you will have less soap buildup on clothes *and* in the washing machine. Use ½ cup of Arm and Hammer® Washing Soda and about half the amount of detergent you would usually use. Adjust this formula by increasing or decreasing detergent per your individual needs.

Tips on Buying and Placing a New Washing Machine

If you don't have space for a washer and dryer to sit next to each other, remember that you can buy some very efficient stackable units. Just make sure to measure the area *before* you buy.

A front-loading washer is definitely a space saver—the top makes a great work space for spotting clothes. You'll need to protect the top of the washer if you are going to work off it, though. A plastic breadboard is ideal.

Another good feature of front-loading washers is the way they tumble clothes. They generally tumble clothes the way a dryer does, and that's gentler on fabric than agitating. It is also less wobbly when spinning. The downside is that front-loaders generally have a smaller capacity than top-loaders, and they're usually not as good at cleaning heavy, ground-in dirt.

There are many top loaders to choose from. Consider your needs carefully. You may want an extra-large capacity washer if you wash large loads of towels and sheets, but do make sure you don't overbuy. It's a waste of money to buy bells and whistles you don't need—and there's more to go wrong, too!

Give your washing machine plenty of room to vibrate. Allow an inch of space all the way around the machine.

To keep the exterior of your washer and dryer clean and shiny, make sure you apply a coat of Clean Shield® (formerly Invisible Shield®) as soon as you buy your machine. This will put an invisible nonstick finish on the surface that will keep it looking like new. Water will bead up and wipe off, as will detergent and spotters. Reapply as needed.

Important: If your washer's power cord does not reach the outlet, have the outlet moved or the power cord replaced with a longer one. Absolutely never use an extension cord between the washer's power cord and the outlet. If water touches the connection between the extension cord and the power cord, you could be electrocuted.

Do not install your washer in an unheated garage or utility room. Water that is trapped inside can freeze and severely damage the machine.

One last installation tip: If you are installing a washing machine in a vacation home that is not heated during cold weather, have it drained completely by an appliance service technician before shutting up the home for the winter. Again, trapped water can freeze and damage the machine.

If I can leave you with a final piece of advice concerning washing machines it would be this: NEVER leave home when the washing machine is running. It only takes seconds for a hose to break or a malfunction to occur and that can cause damage and flooding in your home. I cannot tell you how many water damage cleanups we did when I owned my cleaning and disaster restoration company in Michigan. The amount of water that can pour from a small hose is unbelievable. So is the damage that can be done—not only to things that can be cleaned or replaced but also to precious treasures that can never be saved. It's heartbreaking.

31

Care Labels: What Are They Good For?

Care labels are very important. You should read each and every one of them before you purchase a garment, and each time you have it cleaned.

The Federal Trade Commission (FTC) requires manufacturers to attach a permanent label to textile garments indicating directions for care. This label must be easily located. It should not separate from the garment, and it should remain legible during the lifespan of the garment. The label must warn about any part of the recommended care method that would harm the garment or other garments being laundered or dry-cleaned with it. It must also specify if a garment cannot be cleaned without damage.

When you examine a label, do you look at the size and nothing else? Well, you're missing out on a lot of valuable information.

Symbols may also appear on a care label to supplement written instructions. When a garment carries an international symbol tag, all care methods will usually be listed.

May I remove the care label? Garments are required by law to have a care label attached at the time of sale. Removing the care tag does entail some risk, though; you may forget the proper cleaning instructions and your dry cleaner will not have access to some valuable information.

If you do remove care labels, mark them with a description of the item and put them in a safe place where they can be easily located. You might remember today that your favorite summer dress should be washed in cold water and laid flat to dry, but by next summer you may have forgotten this entirely. A corkboard in the laundry room is wonderful. Care directions will be at your fingertips and at those of other family members who may surprise you by doing the laundry sometime. Remove labels from the board when you no longer have the item.

No law can take into account a woman wearing a little black dress with a big white care label hanging out the back.

Cleaning Instructions

Dry-clean: A garment marked "dry-clean only" can be cleaned using normal dry-cleaning fluid found in any commercial or coin-operated dry-cleaning establishment. Be aware that dry cleaning, despite its name, is not necessarily dry. Water may be involved in the process, whether by moisture added to the fluid, or by steam press or steam air-form finishing.

Professionally dry-clean: If your garment is marked "professionally dry-clean," then it is restricted to the dry-cleaning methods possible only in commercial dry-cleaning plants. A label marked "professionally dry-clean" must be accompanied by further information, such as "use reduced moisture," "low heat," or "no steam finishing." Your dry cleaner should be alert to these labels, but there's no harm in pointing them out.

Machine wash: Indicates use of either a commercial or home washing machine. Other information may be included, such as specific washing temperatures, size of load, or drying instructions.

Does "washable" mean it can also be dry-cleaned? If a garment care label says "washable" it may be safely dry-cleaned—and it may not! Unfortunately, there is no way of telling from the label. A manufacturer is required to list only one safe method of cleaning, no matter how many other methods can be safely employed. And be warned: Manufacturers are not required to alert you to care procedures that *may not* be safe.

"There never seems to be enough time to do it right. But there always seems to be enough time to do it over."

—Anonymous

32

Taking the Dread Out of Dry Cleaning

Not everything we wear can be laundered, and that means a trip to the dry cleaner and the dreaded game of "will that spot come out?" Most people end up at the dry cleaner because they have clothing stains they can't get out themselves. Luckily for us, professional dry cleaners, with their special solvents, equipment and training, can remove some of the most disastrous-looking stains fairly simply. Successful stain removal depends on three things: the nature of the stain; the type of fabric; and the colorfastness of the dye. Remember to check your care labels. Not all fabrics and dyes are made to withstand the use of cleaning or stain removal agents.

Invisible stains: Many stains that are caused by food, oily substances, or beverages may become invisible when they dry. Later on, with exposure to heat or the passage of time, a yellowish or brownish stain will appear.

You have probably seen this on clothes you have hung away and pulled out months later. This is caused by the oxidation of the sugar in the staining substance. It is the same thing that makes an apple turn brown once it is peeled and exposed to the air.

You can be a better dry-cleaning customer and help your dry cleaner do a better job for you by pointing out such stains when you take a garment in to be cleaned. The cleaner often treats these stains prior to cleaning, much as you prespot your laundry at home. This pretreatment is vital since the heat of drying or finishing may set the stain, making it impossible to remove.

Oxidized stains can be recognized by their irregular shape on the fabric. Oily stains can be removed easily during the dry-cleaning process provided they have not been there for an extended period of time. Once they are yellow or brown, they are almost impossible to remove.

DID YOU KNOW?

When an oily substance is exposed to heat or ages in a piece of clothing for a long period of time, it oxidizes.

Perspiration stains: Perspiration can also cause problem stains, especially on silk and wool clothes. Perspiration left in a silk garment can eventually cause deterioration of the fibers.

Repeated exposure to perspiration and body oils can leave clothing with a permanent yellow discoloration and even an offensive odor. Perspiration can react with the dye in the fabric, making it even more difficult to remove the stain.

If you perspire heavily, have your clothes cleaned more frequently, especially in the warmer months. You'll save money on costly replacements.

Important Reminders

Make sure that you point out any unusual care instructions to your cleaner, and make sure that you point out spots and spills, identifying them wherever possible.

- Whether you are doing the cleaning yourself or a professional is doing it, treatment of spots and spills with the right spotter is essential.
- If you remove the care tag, it's a good idea to label it clearly—that is, identify the garment to which it belongs—and pin it to a corkboard in your laundry room for future reference.

Now the part we never want to hear—the dry cleaner's responsibility. Dry cleaners are responsible for attempting to remove stains in accordance with professional practice. Sadly, not all stains can be removed, despite the dry cleaner's best efforts.

The more information you give to your dry cleaner and the sooner a garment is brought in, the greater the chance of success in stain removal.

33

The Dirt on Home Dry-Cleaning Kits

You've seen them—those home dry-cleaning kits available in all the stores. What are they good for? Well, if you expect to open the dry-cleaning bag and find clean, sharply pressed clothes straight from the dryer, you'll be disappointed. If, however, you want to extend the time between professional dry cleanings, these kits may be for you.

I have found home dry-cleaning kits to be effective on items such as sweaters, cut velvet, velvet, dry-clean-only blouses—and those garments that are delicate and hard to hand wash and lay flat to dry. They are also great for freshening small blankets, bedspreads, comforters and draperies. Do not force a large bedspread or blanket into the bag. It will be filled with wrinkles when you remove it.

Home dry-cleaning kits do work on suits, although you'll give up the sharply pressed finish. (You may even find occasional spotting on the suit's lining.)

All of these kits come with treated cloths and reusable dryer-safe bags. Some come with separate spotting solution and spotting blotters. They all work relatively the same way:

First, you spot the garment, either with the same sheet that you toss in the bag during the cleaning process, or with a separate spotting liquid. Spotting the garment well is important because, as we all know by now, heat can set stains. Take your time with the spotting procedure and look over the garment well.

Carefully follow the directions on the kit you have selected. Do not overcrowd the dryer bag or your clothes will be very wrinkled and require a lot of work with the iron—and that defeats the purpose.

Are these kits worth the money? Ultimately, that's up to you to decide. If you have a lot of things you want to freshen between cleanings, and if that crisp, pressed look is not vital to you, then yes, give them a try. If, however, your wardrobe consists mostly of business suits and crisply creased trousers, you will probably be disappointed. Will these kits replace your regular trips to the dry cleaner? I don't think so. And I don't think they were intended to.

"If at first you don't succeed, try, try again. Then quit. No use being a damn fool about it."

—W. C. Fields

Special Hints from the Palace

- Remove the clothes from the dryer bag immediately, and hang or fold them—whichever is appropriate. Some pressing may be required, depending on the type of fabric.
- Do not use any bag other than that which is provided in the kit, and do not use any additional cleaning chemicals.
- If you don't like the odor of perfume fresheners, check out each kit individually and try several. Some have more perfume than others.
- Again, follow the directions closely.

34

Doing the Laundry Sorting Boogie

Some people like the "grab and stuff" laundry method: grab the clothes—no matter what fabric or color—and stuff them into the machine, as many as you can at one time. These people are easy to recognize. They're the ones with pink underwear, color-streaked clothes, shrunken sweaters, short pants, and clothes that are otherwise "challenged."

Separate

* Dark fabrics from white and light-colored fabrics.
* Lightly soiled clothes from heavily soiled garments such as work clothes.
* Fabrics by water temperature (hot—warm—cold).

* Fabrics that will shed lint on other fabrics (terry cloth, corduroy, etc.).
* Lingerie, hose, and delicate fabrics that should be washed in a mesh bag.
* Clothes that may have fugitive color and bleed onto others.

Sort your laundry for best results. You'll thank me for this advice, I assure you.

Now It's Time to Pretreat

* Check for spots, spills, stains, etc., before putting a load of clothes into the washer.

Do This Before You Wash

- Button buttons.
- Hook bras.
- Zip zippers.
- Tie sashes, cords, straps, etc., to prevent tangling.
- Check pockets for coins, tissues, pens, etc.
- Remove anything on the garment that cannot be washed.
- Repair tears so they don't become larger while agitating.

* Pretreat these with one of the spotters you'll find in Chapters 36 and 37, or go to the stain removal guide for help.
* Soak heavily soiled garments before laundering. *Do not* soak wool, spandex, silk, or fabrics that are not colorfast.

Mark the Spot

Use a brightly colored clothespin to mark the stain, or use a rubber band and wrap it around the area that needs to be spotted prior to laundering. Have family members do this *before* they put their clothes into the hamper. This will make spots and stains easier to locate and easier to treat. Spots will be obvious, so you don't need to examine each article as you sort.

Now You're Ready to Wash!

Add detergent to the washer as it fills up with water. If you are using cold water with powdered detergent and you have a problem with the detergent dissolving, mix it with a little hot water before adding it to the machine—or consider switching to a liquid detergent.

* Add additional laundry aids such as bleach, water softener, laundry booster, etc.
* Load the machine, but do not overload. If you stuff too many garments into the machine the clothes will not clean well, and they'll have more wrinkles too.
* Make sure your load is balanced—not all bunched on one side of the agitator—especially if you are washing one large or heavy item, such as a blanket or bath mat.

If you have room in your laundry or closet areas, provide several different colored laundry baskets for family members to sort dirty clothes as they are removed—a basket for whites, colors, jeans (if your family wears a lot of them), and delicates. You'll be off to a good start and the whole laundry sorting boogie will go faster. Use these baskets after washing to hold clothes that need to be folded and to carry clothes that can be put away. Normally I don't like to use the f-word . . . but not everything can be hung on a hanger. There are some things that simply must be *folded.* Don't worry, though. You don't have to be the empress of elbow grease to quickly fold clothes and put them away.

Remember: **Don't leave the house while you're doing laundry.**

Snap, Zip, and Hook! (No, It's Not a New Breakfast Cereal!)

The best advice I can give you is zip your zippers, snap your snaps, hook your hooks, and button your buttons.

If you don't, you run the risk of catching, pulling, or tearing fabric, damaging the interlocking mechanism (zipper) and pulling the buttons off during the washing process.

Just Zip It!

If you have a zipper that sticks and doesn't want to pull up, rub it with a little soap, paraffin, or candle wax. This will lubricate the teeth and get it moving.

If your zipper on slacks, skirts, etc., doesn't want to stay up, add a button, snap, or some Velcro just above it.

To give your zipper a little extra "stick," spritz it with hair spray. That will help it stay zipped.

Button Bonus

To keep buttons from falling off, dab a little clear nail polish on the thread in the center of the button. This will keep the thread from wearing through so easily.

For buttons that get hard wear, stitch them on with dental floss. It may not be as pleasing to the eye as thread, but the buttons won't fall off!

35

It Doesn't Have to Be a Soap Opera

I don't think there is a greater laundry challenge than walking down the soap and detergent aisle and deciding what products to buy. We are constantly bombarded with ads about how well this one cleans, how well that one smells . . . this one contains bleach, that one contains optic brighteners, and that one over there . . . well, it contains every cleaning agent known to man—and woman. Argh! But what really matters in a laundry detergent? When is more just too much?

I have a rule that I follow with laundry detergent: less is more.

When I want a laundry detergent or soap I want that and only that. Period. I want to be the one who determines when I need bleach, softener, or other additives, so I opt for the simplest product that basically does one thing: removes and suspends soil from my clothes and leaves them clean and fresh. Now by fresh, I don't mean have a smelly odor after the wash. I like to leave the house without advertising what detergent I use by the way I smell. I like the labels that read "FREE." I don't want odor or artificial color, just the cleaning product. It is healthier for the body and the clothes. If I want to have a fragrance, I will choose the perfume. I don't want to smell like combinations of soap and softener and other laundry products all mixed together.

Basic laundry detergent: This is where it all starts. Choose your laundry product (bear in mind my lecture above), and measure it into the machine. Remember to adjust the amount of detergent used to the size of your load. (You may need to adjust the amount if you have hard water.) More is not better where laundry soap is concerned. It's just harder to rinse out. Detergent residue makes fabric sticky, and that makes it attract soil faster.

What laundry detergent do I use? I've tested them all, and believe me, that was a challenge. Sometimes the detergent that gets out the most spills and spots is not the one that is best for your clothes, or your family. Some laundry detergents are particularly hard on colored fabrics, fading them and giving dark colors a whitish cast.

After more testing than you can imagine, I have picked one detergent that I believe can be all things to all people: PUREX®. It is gentle on clothes and gentle on you, and available in enough varieties so that you can decide whether you want additives and fragrance, etc. It is gentle on colors, tough on whites, and with the addition of 20 Mule Team® Borax, can remove the very worst messes. For general laundry, just follow the directions on the box or bottle. I am a liquid soap kind of Queen, because I like to measure out my detergent in the cap, and then do a little prespotting with it before I toss the clothes and the balance of the detergent in the machine.

Laundry additives: If you have a particularly soiled load of clothes and feel that your detergent needs a kick, try a safe additive like 20 Mule Team®

Borax Laundry Booster. This will help detergent work better without bleach. It removes soils and stains, brightens clothes, and freshens laundry without an artificial smell. It's been around since 1891, so it's definitely passed that test of time! Use about ½ cup per wash load when you need that extra cleaning power for things such as work clothes, towels, rugs, etc.

Allergy-free products: Many people, particularly children, have allergies and asthma problems that seem to be directly related to the cleaning and laundry products we use in our homes. If your family appears to be allergic to its underwear (no, I'm not kidding), it may be your detergent. I've been researching allergy-free, nontoxic cleaning products for a long time, and I'm happy to tell you that I have found environmentally friendly products that work to avoid these reactions. I've tested these products. They work safely on laundry for the whole family, babies to adults.

DID YOU KNOW?

20 Mule Team® Borax is great for diapers. It's completely safe for baby clothes and hand washables.

The following products are made by a company called Soapworks. They were created by a woman in direct response to her son's severe, life-threatening asthma.

Try the Fresh Breeze Laundry Powder™ or the Fresh Breeze Liquid™. It is made from natural ingredients such as coconut and palm kernel soap.

A WORD TO THE WISE . . .

There is something for everyone in the laundry aisle, but a word of caution: not all clothes require those heavy-duty products. They can be hard on fabrics and on the environment. Grandma didn't need those additives, and her clothes lasted a long time.

This can be used to safely spot clothes and presoak too, and has a light, fresh scent of natural ginger. Cost for the powder soap works out to about 5 cents per load compared with about 18 cents a load for a reasonably priced detergent.

They also make Sun Shine Liquid Soap™ for dishes and washing delicates, and Soapworks Brilliant Bleach™, a hydrogen peroxide-based bleach.

36

Be a Spot Hot Shot!

I love natural products, and I love things that I can make for pennies and still have them work better than the products I could buy at the store. Here are some of my favorite laundry spot removers. Use them just as you would over-the-counter products, but take note: many of them are designed to take care of specific spots and stains.

Start with a clean spray and/or squeeze bottle, and always be sure to label any product you make. It's important to know what the bottle contains and what it was intended for. I like to include the recipe on the label too—that way I can mix up additional product with ease. Cover the label with clear packaging tape or a piece of clear adhesive sheet to protect the label from moisture.

These spotters are all intended for washable fabrics. If in doubt, test in an inconspicuous spot, such as a seam.

General All-Purpose Laundry Spotter

Combine the following to make a generic spotter that works on a wide variety of stains:

1 part rubbing alcohol

2 parts water

If you use a large spray bottle you can add 1 bottle of alcohol and 2 of the alcohol bottles filled with water. Spray this on spots and spills, wait a few minutes, and then launder as usual.

Beverage, Fruit and Grass Remover

Combine equal portions of:

white vinegar

liquid dishwashing soap

water

Shake well and work the solution into the spot. Let stand a few minutes and then launder as usual.

Non-oily Stain Remover

Combine equal portions of the following ingredients:

ammonia

liquid dishwashing soap

water

Shake well, and work the solution into the spot. Let stand a few minutes and flush with water. This solution works well on stains such as milk, blood, perspiration and urine. *Do not use on washable wool, silk, spandex, acrylic and acetate.*

Oily Stain Remover

Combine the following:

1 tablespoon glycerin
1 tablespoon liquid dishwashing soap
8 tablespoons of water

Work the solution into grease and oil stains. Let sit a few minutes, flush with water and launder as usual.

Remember: All of these spotters are for washable fabrics only and none of them are for silk, wool, spandex, acrylic and acetate. When in doubt, test first!

37

Bringing Out the Big Guns

It's time to talk about the big guns of laundry spotters. We all need them from time to time. But what's best? What really works? Read on. I've tried them all, so you won't have to!

A quick disclaimer: Remember, I am counting on you to test a small, inconspicuous area on the fabric for colorfastness *before* you use any of these spotters. Don't let laundry spotters dry. Launder soon after spotting to prevent the spot from becoming a stain. Don't let me down!

Energine Cleaning Fluid®: This is a terrific "can't be without" spotter for dry-clean-only clothes. Blot it on until the stain is gone and then blow-dry to avoid a ring.

Fels-Naptha Heavy Duty Laundry Bar Soap®: This is that old-fashioned brown bar soap that your grandmother used. It has been around 100 years—literally!—and it's a great spotter for numerous spots and stains. Wet the bar and simply rub the stain, working it in well. Let it sit a few minutes. This spotter still works even if allowed to dry on the fabric. Great for ring-around-the-collar and perspiration stains.

Ink Away™: Ink and marker can be a challenge to remove, but this product, made by the makers of Goo Gone™, really proves its worth. Follow package directions carefully and be sure to read the list of things *not* to use it on *before* you start.

Spot Shot® Instant Carpet Stain Remover: This one wins the prize for the most unusual laundry spotter, but it's *still* one of the Queen's favorite products. Yes, that's right, it's not just for carpet. It's also a great laundry prewash spotter—and boy does it work. It is safe for all colorfast washables and works in all wash temperatures. Spray the stained area thoroughly, saturating the stain. If the stain is difficult or stubborn, work it between your thumbs. Allow Spot Shot® to sit at least 60 seconds, then launder as usual. *Do not* allow it to dry on the fabric and do not use it on silks, fabrics labeled "dry clean only" or noncolorfast fabrics. This product works on oily stains, ink, pet stains, cola, shoe polish, lipstick, blood and others. A must-have in the laundry room.

Wine Away Red Wine Stain Remover™: Don't let the name fool you, this product is much more than a red wine stain remover. It works great on Kool-Aid™, grape juice, red pop, cranberry juice, orange pop, coffee and tea, as well as red wine. I even took red food coloring out of a shirt with it. Wine Away™ is made from fruit and vegetable extracts and is totally nontoxic—I love that!

Zout® Stain Remover: This is a superconcentrated stain remover that works great on ink, blood, grease, fruit juice, grass and hundreds of other stains. A little goes a long way with this. Simply saturate the stain, work it in, wait 5 to 10 minutes, and then launder as usual.

38

Bleach 101: Whiter Whites, Brighter Brights

Are you one of those people who thinks that directions are what you read to find out what you did wrong? Then pay attention. I'm going to give you my dos and don'ts of bleach basics.

Do's

- ✓ Read the directions on the container of bleach.
- ✓ Check the labels on the fabric you wish to bleach.
- ✓ Test the bleach if you are unsure. To do this with chlorine bleach, mix 1 tablespoon of chlorine bleach with ¼ cup of cold water. Find a hidden area on the piece of clothing and place a drop of the solution on it. Leave this for a minute

or two and then blot to determine if there is any color change.

- ✓ To test all-fabric bleaches, mix 1 teaspoon of the bleach with 1 cup of hot water. Again, place a drop on an inconspicuous area. Wait at least 15 minutes, blot, and check for any change in the color.
- ✓ Of course, if any color change takes place you won't want to use that type of bleach on that type of fabric.
- ✓ Always be sure to rinse bleach out of fabric thoroughly.

Don'ts

- ✗ Absolutely never allow undiluted chlorine bleach to come in contact with fabrics.
- ✗ Never use any kind of bleach directly on fabric without testing it first.
- ✗ Never use more bleach than called for. It can damage fabrics and is wasteful too.
- ✗ NEVER use chlorine bleach and ammonia in the same wash! It can generate deadly fumes.

Now let's talk about the bleaches one by one.

Chlorine Bleach

The strongest, fastest-acting bleach available, chlorine bleach is very effective on cottons, linens, and some synthetics when used properly. Used improperly it can weaken cloth fibers, causing them to disintegrate. It can even cause holes. Always follow container directions with care, and never use chlorine bleach on silk, wool, spandex, acetate, fibers treated to be flame-resistant or dry-clean-only fabrics.

Most of us have had a bad experience with chlorine bleach, so use care. Never pour it on hand washables, and never pour it onto clothes that are in the washing machine. Pour it in the bleach dispenser, if your washing machine is so equipped, or into the washer while it is filling with water *before* adding the clothes. For hand washables, dilute it prior to adding the clothes and be sure to adjust the amount accordingly for the amount of water being used.

Name brands and store brands work the same, so purchase the product of your choice, or the one with the best price.

All-Fabric Bleach or Oxygen Bleach

This is a much milder form of bleach that works well on delicate fabrics or those requiring gentle care. It is slower-acting than chlorine bleach and is less effective in restoring whiteness to fabrics. It may be effective, though, through regular use. This bleach can be used on all fabrics, even silks, as long as the manufacturer's care tag does not say "no bleach." Add this bleach at the same time you add your detergent and do not pour directly on the clothes. More is not better, so measure, don't just pour.

A New Generation of Bleach

Soapworks has come up with a new generation of bleach that is effective, user friendly, and safe for use by people with allergies and asthma. It is hypoallergenic, nontoxic, biodegradable, 100 percent natural, safe for septic tanks, contains no chemicals, no dyes and no fragrances.

This product is called Brilliant®, and it is just that! Created with hydrogen peroxide—which is the safest, natural whitener and brightener for fabrics—this bleach can be used effectively on whites and colored fabrics both.

Clothes can be soaked safely for 24 hours or more without harm to either fabric or color.

Brilliant® is also a softener, so no additional softening agent is required. Add ¼ cup to the washer as it fills with water. As with any bleach product, test in an inconspicuous area when in doubt.

Making Your Own Bleaching Agents

Yes, you *can* create your own forms of bleach with things you already have at home.

Lemon juice: Nature's bleach and disinfectant, lemon juice can be used to whiten clothes.

Take 1 gallon of the hottest water possible for the fabric you're bleaching and add ½ cup of bottled lemon juice or the slices of one or two lemons. Soak the clothes for 30 minutes or even overnight. This works especially well on white socks and underwear, and is safe for polyester fabrics. Don't use on silks, though.

Automatic dishwasher detergent: This is another wonderful bleaching agent for white clothes. Fill a bucket with the hottest possible water for the fabric you are working with, and add 2 tablespoons of any brand of automatic dishwasher detergent. Soak white clothes for 30 minutes or even overnight. Dump into the washer and launder with your detergent as usual.

To use this bleaching technique in the washer, fill the machine with water and add ¼ cup to ½ cup of automatic dishwasher detergent. Agitate for several minutes and then add clothes. Soak as directed above and then add detergent and launder as usual.

Hydrogen peroxide: This can be used to bleach delicate items such as wool or wool blends. Soak them overnight in a solution of one part 3 percent hydrogen peroxide to eight parts cold water. Launder according to care directions.

Bluing

Bluing is a whitening and brightening agent that has been around for a long, long time. Available in liquid form, bluing contains blue pigment, which actually counteracts the yellowing that occurs in some fabrics. Always dilute this with water as directed on the bottle, and never pour directly on clothes or spill on other fibers or surfaces. Look for it in the laundry aisle at the grocery store. This product will even remove the yellow from gray hair!

39

Cry Me a River—The Color Ran!

Ever turned your underwear pink? Then you know what I'm talking about when I say that some dark colors bleed during initial washing. Not all colors are what we call "colorfast," so you must be careful to prevent the dye of one garment from running on to another.

Is It Colorfast?

How do you know if an item is colorfast? Test it! Try this simple colorfast test before you launder new fabrics. You'll save yourself a lot of time and heartache if you do.

* Place a drop of water on an inside seam or another inconspicuous spot. Blot with a white cotton ball or towel.
* If the cotton ball remains clean, it is safe to wash with other clothes. If it picks up some color from the fabric, then you must wash the garment separately.

Be careful not to drip-dry fabrics that are not colorfast. The color can streak. Instead, roll these clothes in a towel to absorb excess moisture, then hang to dry, away from other fabrics.

Uh-Oh . . .

What happens if a pair of new black socks were somehow washed with your favorite white blouse? Fugitive color happens, that's what! Don't despair. Some products can help you do away with color runs.

Synthrapol®: This is a wonderful product used by quilters to eliminate color runs in quilts. Used in a basin or in the washing machine, it will remove fugitive color without damage to the original color or fabric. In simple terms, if you washed a white T-shirt with a red T-shirt and the hite T-shirt turned pink, Synthrapol® will remove the pink and return the shirt to its original white.

Synthrapol® works best on cottons, but I've had success with polyester and blends too. Try it in an inconspicuous spot first, unless the item is a total loss and you feel you've got nothing to lose. This is a fairly strong chemical, so be sure to follow the directions carefully.

Carbona® Color Run Remover: One box of Carbona® will restore a whole wash load of clothes dyed from mixed-wash bleeding. You must test the fabric to be sure that it's colorfast, otherwise the garment's original color will be removed along with the fugitive color. Follow the directions carefully and use great care. This, too, is a strong chemical. It may be harmful to synthetic materials, denim, or bright, fluorescent and khaki colors. Zippers, buttons, etc., may become discolored, so you might want to remove what you can prior to treatment.

Retayne®: A color fixative for cottons, Retayne® is an interesting product that you should use before washing a garment that is likely to bleed. Just think of this as an ounce of prevention.

For best results, treat the garment with Retayne® prior to laundering for the first time. Not only will this prevent bleeding, it will also help to keep colors brighter, longer. Again, as with everything, try in an inconspicuous area first and read the directions carefully.

Important: All three of these products contain chemicals that can be harmful to children and pets, so please make sure to take adequate storage precautions.

40

The Hard Truth About Water Softeners

If you live in an area that has hard water you will be well acquainted with the graying or yellowing effect that hard water minerals can have on your clothes. You may also have noticed that, rather than suds in your washing machine, you have gray-looking water and, sometimes, scum on the water surface.

Not sure if you have hard water? You can check your local water supply office—they will tell you the degree of hardness in your water. If you have well water you might want to call a water treatment company. They'll be able to test your supply. Of course, you can also look out for these telltale signs:

* Fabrics look dull and gray.
* Fabrics feel stiff instead of soft.

* Soaps and detergents don't lather well.
* White residue appears around drains, faucets, and on glassware.

If your water is not too hard (less than 10.6 grains of hardness per gallon), you can help alleviate the problems associated with hard water by adjusting the amount of detergent you use. Again, start by using half the amount of detergent called for. You can also give your detergent a "kick" by using Arm and Hammer® Washing Soda, or 20 Mule Team® Borax along with your detergent, following package directions. These products are found in the laundry additive aisle at the grocery store or at discount stores. If you find that your clothes still do not have the degree of cleanness and softness that you desire, you may need to try a liquid softener that you can add to your laundry along with your detergent, or go to a mechanical means of softening.

Making Your Own Water Softener

Combine the following in a labeled one-gallon container. Plastic gallon milk jugs, washed well, work great.

½ lb. of Arm and Hammer® Washing Soda

¼ lb. of 20 Mule Team® Borax

1 gallon of warm water

To use: Add 1 cup of the solution to each load of wash water along with your normal laundry detergent.

If you still find that your wash is dingy and you are not getting any lather from your bar soap in the shower, then you may need to turn to a mechanical softener that is attached to the house water system.

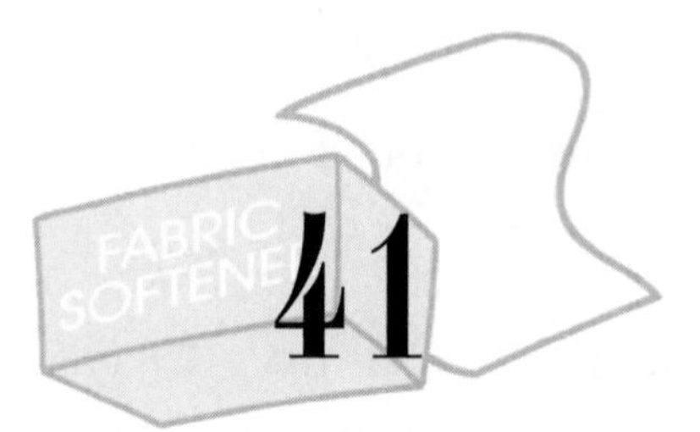

The Soft Sell—
Fabric Softeners

Fabric softeners are used to make fabrics soft and fluffy, and to minimize static cling. They can also reduce wrinkling and make ironing easier.

Liquid softeners: These should be added to the final rinse cycle by the automatic dispenser (if your washing machine has one), or by hand if not. Carefully follow the directions on the label, and make sure to measure: too much is not better, nor is too little.

If using an automatic dispenser, add the softener then follow with an equal amount of water to help disperse the liquid softener. This will also help to eliminate softener spots on clothes.

Dryer-added softeners: These paper-thin sheets soften clothes, and they also work with the heat of the dryer to reduce static electricity in the load—which means that your dress won't cling to your panty hose and your trousers won't cling to your socks! I find store brands work just as well as higher-priced varieties, so go ahead and make your choice by fragrance or price. Whatever suits you.

A word of advice. Dryer softener sheets can cause buildup on towels, and that can make them feel slippery and reduce their absorbency. Use the softener only once every two to three washings to avoid this.

Dear Queen of Clean:
I use dryer sheets, but sometimes static cling is still a problem. Anything I can do?

Clingy in Cleveland

Dear Clingy:
Try smoothing your skirt with damp hands. A little bit of hand cream on top of your panty hose works well too.

Retired Softener Sheets

Once you have used the pesky little sheet, remember my earlier advice: use it to clean off the lint filter in the dryer before you toss it. Here are some other uses for those retired sheets.

- If you have a casserole or pan with burned-on food, fill with hot water, toss in a softener sheet for several hours (overnight is fine), and the burned-on food will slide right out.
- Run a needle and thread through the sheet to prevent static from tangling the thread.
- Wipe the television screen, venetian blinds, or any other surface that attracts dust with a used sheet to reduce the static electricity that attracts dust.

- Place a sheet in a coat pocket to avoid the shock you get when getting in and out of the car in winter.
- Place a used sheet in luggage, drawers, closets, trashcans, under car seats, and in your laundry bag or hamper to provide a fresh scent.
- Tuck a used sheet into shoes before placing them in your luggage. Shoes will smell fresh and you can use the dryer softener sheet to buff shoes and remove dust after wearing.
- Polish chrome to a brilliant shine after cleaning.
- Use it to wrap Christmas ornaments or other fragile things before boxing for storage. The dryer sheet will protect them and you can wipe Christmas ornaments prior to hanging on the tree to reduce static electricity and repel dust.
- Wipe car dashboards with a used sheet to shine and repel dust.

Retired dryer fabric softener sheets have plenty of uses left, so don't waste them. And don't use new softener sheets for any of these purposes. Pick up a *used* or, as I like to call them, *retired* sheet instead! I put my used dryer sheets in an empty tissue box I keep in the laundry room. This way they are always handy.

Making Your Own Dryer Fabric Softener Sheets

Believe it or not, you can make your own dryer fabric softener sheets. Simply take an old washcloth, mist it with 1 part of your favorite liquid fabric softener and 2 parts water, then toss it in the dryer with the clothes. Remist for each new load of clothes and occasionally launder it when doing towels to remove any softener buildup and soften the towels at the same time.

I keep a mixture in a small spray bottle on the shelf in the laundry room along with a few old washcloths. I find that ⅓ cup liquid fabric softener and ⅔ cup of warm water makes a good quantity. Shake prior to spraying on the cloth, and *always* label the bottle of any mixture you make yourself to keep it from accidentally being misused.

If your detergent already contains softener (read the label) you may not need additional softener unless you are getting a lot of static cling in your clothes.

Fabric Softener Spots on Clothes

No matter how hard you try, at some point you will probably pull out a load of clothes and find either blue spots from liquid fabric softener or "grease"-type spots from dryer softener sheets on your clothes. Here's what to do:

Liquid softener spots: If spotting occurs, wet the item and rub with undiluted dishwashing liquid, then rewash. Wetting and rubbing with shampoo seems to work too. Do *not* rub with laundry detergent. It won't remove the spot—in fact, it may set it in.

If liquid softener has been allowed to freeze, dissolve the required amount of softener with warm water before adding to the wash.

Dryer fabric softener sheet spots: If spotting occurs, rub the area with a wet bar of soap, such as Dove®, and then relaunder.

To avoid spots, place the sheet on top of the clothes in the dryer rather than mixing it in, and start the dryer immediately. Do not use the sheet when you are using the air fluff cycle without heat.

Important: **Do *not* use dryer sheets on children's sleepwear or other garments labeled as flame-resistant, as they may reduce flame resistance. These sheets are *not* nontoxic, so keep out of reach of children and pets to avoid accidental ingestion.**

42

Drying: How to Succeed Without Really Trying

Keeping the dryer clean is important: A clean dryer will work more efficiently, saving you time and money. A clean dryer will also help prevent dryer fires. Dryer fires are much more common than you might think, so avoid them at all costs.

First the basics:

If you have a lint-clogged dryer venting system, your clothes will not dry properly and you will waste time and money running longer cycles to get the clothes completely dry. Turn the dryer on, and go outside and hold your hand under the dryer vent hood—you know, that metal thing on the outside of the house. If you don't feel a strong flow of air it's time to clean.

Clean the dryer vent pipe or flex exhaust hose once a year to prevent lint buildup. Try to lock a date in your mind and do it every year. I like Halloween 'cause you can extract the lint and create a dust bunny costume

Dear Queen of Clean:
What happens to that _other_ *blue sock every time I do the laundry?*

Sockless in Seattle

Dear Sockless:
Well, just to set your mind straight, there isn't a sock-devouring monster lurking in your laundry room. Missing socks can sometimes be found wedged between the drum and the machine. Check your pant legs and shirt sleeves, and check the dryer hose too. If you still can't find that missing sock, you might want to check the sock drawer of your 14-year-old son!

at the same time! Remove the duct or hose from the dryer back and the exhaust mounting, and shake it out. It may be necessary to run an old cloth through the hose to dislodge any lint that is unwilling or unable to leave the vent. Be sure to reseal the joints, using a fresh piece of duct tape if necessary.

While you have the dryer out, vacuum and wash the floor area underneath the unit. If you see any grease or oil leaks on the floor, it's time to call the appliance repairman.

On the outside of the vent, clean the hood and vent by using a straightened wire coat hanger or bottle-type brush. Push it back and forth in the vent to remove accumulated lint.

The lint filter in the dryer is no less important than the vent. Keeping it clean is vital. A clogged lint filter allows lint to accumulate and can eventually start a fire. A dirty lint filter also blocks airflow, so your clothes will take longer to dry. And that means extra money on your gas or electric bill.

Remember: Always make sure that your vent is straight. Kinks will block the airflow.

To clean the filter, remove it, wipe off the lint and replace. You can do this easily by wiping the filter with a used dryer fabric softener sheet, which will collect the accumulated lint so that you can dispose of it without additional mess. It's important to vacuum the filter periodically, and to clean the area where the lint filter is installed with vacuum attachments. (This is the opening on the dryer that the filter slides into.)

Important:
If you have a gas dryer, always use caution not to kink or damage the gas line when shifting.

Dryer Dilemmas

Now that you know how to clean the dryer, it's time to talk about some quick, easy tips to make your job a lot easier. Anyone who does laundry knows how those little OOPS! can happen and how frustrating they can be. So let's de-oops the clothes dryer!

Lint-Free Drying

If you're drying clothes that have lint—or a big oops, a tissue has gone through the washer—put a piece of nylon net in the dryer along with the clothes. The net will catch the lint effectively so you won't have to drag out the lint roller, or worse still, pick off all of the fuzz. I buy cheap nylon net from a fabric store and throw it out when it's full of lint.

Oops! I Forgot to Take the Clothes Out of the Dryer

We all know that if you take items out of the dryer as soon as it shuts off, you can fold or hang your clothes with little or no ironing. But you can't always get to the dryer immediately. Let's be honest. How many times have you gone to the dryer and found a load of clothes that were forgotten? Oops! The clothes are a mass of wrinkles! Don't go to the trouble of rewashing the clothes, and don't iron them, either. Just toss a damp towel in the dryer and rerun the load for a few minutes. The wrinkles will release and you can hang up the clothes. Remember, though, never use a white towel with dark clothes or you will give yourself another problem . . . lint!

Yikes! How Did That Get in the Dryer?

To remove crayon, lipstick or Chap Stick® from the dryer, turn it off and spray a paper towel with WD-40® Lubricant. Wipe out the dryer until all of the mess is removed. Wash out with warm water and dishwashing liquid, then dry a load of old wet rags.

Try Carbona® Stain Devils to remove chewing gum and glue. For ink, use rubbing alcohol or Ink Away™ by the makers of Goo Gone™.

Don't Even Think of Putting That in the Dryer!

Don't put stained or spotted clothes in the dryer. The heat will set the stain, making it next to impossible to remove. Re-treat the stain with one of the appropriate methods mentioned in this book, and launder again.

Important:

Do not put anything in the dryer that has come in contact with paint, gasoline, oil used on machinery, etc., or any flammable fluids. These things are fire hazards and the fumes they give off can ignite. If they come in contact with a hot dryer, you could have a serious problem. Line dry these items.

- Clean the dryer lint filter after each use.
- Always check to see that the dryer is empty before using.
- Avoid drying extremely small loads or crowding the dryer with extra large loads. Very small loads can clump, and very large loads don't tumble well. Both waste time and energy.
- Dry lightweight fabrics together and heavy fabrics together for more efficient drying.
- Dry loads one after another. That way you can utilize the heat already in the dryer.
- Don't add wet clothes to clothes that are almost dry. This wastes energy—and money!

Line Drying

We have come full circle. For years it seemed like the dryer had taken over and that clotheslines were obsolete. Now, we are returning to the days of natural fabrics, with drip-dry clothes, clothes that need to be laid flat to dry, and clothes that cannot be put in the dryer for any reason. Don't worry. You don't need a clothesline in the backyard to care for some of these hang-to-dry clothes.

The Basics

As your grandma will tell you, don't spin out too much water from clothes that you are going to hang to dry: that sets in the wrinkles. Instead, shut off the washer halfway through the spin cycle and hang the clothes on a clothesline, allowing for plenty of air circulation between clothes. Dry colored clothes out of direct sunlight (the sun fades them), but hang white clothes in the sun—this will bleach them to an incredible, eye-popping white. They'll smell great too.

Hanging clothes on plastic hangers with sloped ends will allow them to dry without those awful "shoulder dimples." You'll avoid rust that way too!

Specific Drying Tips

Trousers: Hang these by the cuffs. The weight of the trousers will usually keep the legs wrinkle-free, which means less or no pressing. We like that!

Sweaters: To prevent sweaters from having "shoulder dimples" or "clothespin points," thread the legs of an old pair of panty hose through the arms of the sweater, and pull the waist out through the neck. Attach clothespins to the feet and waist of the panty hose instead of the sweater. Just make sure to remove the panty hose before you put on the sweater. Unless you plan to rob a bank . . .

Dresses and coats: When hanging heavy dresses and coats to dry, use two hangers to absorb the weight. If hanging them outside to dry, hook the two hangers in the opposite direction to keep the breeze from blowing the garment off the line.

Lingerie and panty hose: These are better dried in the house over the shower bar, on a small bathroom clothesline, or from plastic hangers with clips.

Handy Hints

- If you do use a clothesline outside, remember to keep it clean by washing it periodically.

✳ Bedding washed and hung out to dry occasionally will be crisp and fresh-smelling. White linens will be brighter!

✳ Do not air-dry down comforters. They dry too slowly and mold or mildew may form in the process.

✳ A tension curtain rod hung in a laundry room makes a great place to hang clothes to dry. A piece of chain also works well, and you can hook hangers through the links.

DID YOU KNOW?

Strong sun will eventually weaken fibers, so keep an eye on the clothes and bring them in as soon as they are dry.

✳ If a garment label says "hang to dry," don't put it in the dryer. It may shrink, or the fibers may distort.

✳ If clothes are wrinkled after line drying, putting them in the dryer on the "no heat" or "air fluff" setting may save you from ironing them. (Do not use a fabric softener sheet, though. Without heat, fabric softener sheets can stain clothes.)

Know When to Hold 'Em, Know When to Fold 'Em

Normally I don't like to use the f-word . . . but not everything can be hung on a hanger. There are some things that simply must be *folded.* Don't worry, though. You don't have to be the empress of elbow grease to quickly fold clothes and put them away.

Consider the space your clothes have to fit into before you fold them.

It's best to hang items that wrinkle easily, such as cotton, rayon, etc. Blouses, dress shirts and dresses that are not knit are best on a hanger. Knits are best folded.

If, for example, drawer space is at a premium in your house, consider rolling things such as underwear, T-shirts, socks, towels, etc. You can fit more into a drawer or cupboard that way, and wrinkles will be minimal. Rolled clothes also save lots of room in your suitcase—an added bonus for frequent travelers.

Sweaters and sweatshirts are best folded, and you will never have shoulder dimples, either. To fold, lay the garment facedown and fold each side to meet in the middle at the back. This will avoid a line running down the center of your garment. Fold the sleeves down the back of the garment, then fold the garment in half lengthways. These items can also be rolled effectively.

Socks can be rolled toe to top. You might also want to consider investing in draw dividers made specifically for socks and hose. You will never find your socks in a tangled mess, or worse still, missing. Colors will be obvious and easy to pick out.

And by the way, just to set the record straight, washers and dryers positively *do not* eat socks. Nor is there a sock monster in your utility room who steals one sock! Missing socks can sometimes be found wedged between the drum and the machine. Check your pant legs and shirt sleeves, and check the dryer hose, too. I once found a lonely sock on the driveway—it had tried to escape by shimmying out the dryer hose and up through the vent!

Fitted sheets *can* be tamed. Fold them in half lengthwise, then fold each curved end into the middle. Now you have a square end to work with. Fold in half again and then either roll or continue to fold to the size that best fits your storage area. If you don't mind the same sheets on the bed each week, wash them, dry them, and put them back on straightaway and you will *never* have to fold them again!

DID YOU KNOW?

Folding rubber- or latex-backed rugs with the fabric side in will prevent the backing from sticking together during storage.

Consider using hooks on the back of the closet doors for robes and nightclothes. Don't use suction hooks, though. They're not strong enough to hold clothes.

If doing underwear for multiple family members together, consider buying different brands for each person to make sorting and folding go faster. Try this with socks too.

Keeping a spring-type curtain rod or shower rod set up in the laundry room makes it easy to hang clothes as you remove them from the dryer. Let each person come and claim their own hanging clothes and basket of ready-to-fold or folded clothes. This will cut your laundry time way down. A quick reminder: If the kids have to fold their own clothes, don't let them defeat your system and dress out of the laundry basket all week instead of folding and putting away their things. Otherwise, they will throw the dirty clothes on the floor all week!

Good laundry habits are easy to learn, especially when they become routine.

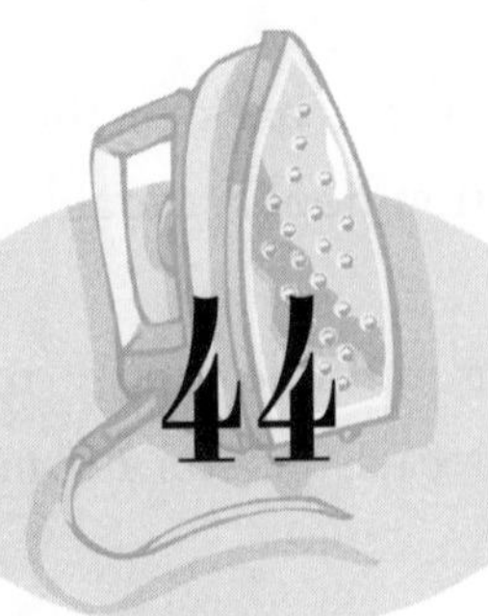

44

Taking the Heat: Ironing and Ironing Boards

Nobody likes to iron, but occasionally, no matter how carefully you launder and dry your clothes, you're going to have to iron them too. Ironing can be a nasty chore, but I have some ways to make it easier. Just think of me as Chairman of the Ironing Board!

First of all, if you have to iron, do it in a place you enjoy. Set up the ironing board in the family room or somewhere you can watch television as you work, or near the stereo where you can listen to some music or a book on tape. You might even like to set it up in a room where the family is gathered so that you can all visit as you work. You can also

> Don't assume I'm talking to Mom. Dad should be able to do the ironing just as well!

enlist family members to hang up and put away their clothes as you iron them.

Now to the basics.

Cleaning Your Iron

Irons without nonstick finishes: If the iron has a silver sole plate (the metal will be shiny), that usually means it does not have a "nonstick" finish. To clean these irons, heat the iron to hot on the nonsteam setting, and run it over table salt sprinkled on a brown paper grocery bag. You can remove residue by using white, nongel toothpaste on a damp, soft cloth. Rinse well.

For really heavy buildup, or where fabric has burned to the bottom of a cold iron: protect the body of the iron by covering it with aluminum foil, then spray the sole plate with oven cleaner. Wait 10 minutes, rinse, and clean out the holes on the bottom of the iron with pipe cleaners or cotton swabs.

Rinse the bottom well and then, using steam, iron over an old towel or rag before using the iron on clothes.

Irons with nonstick finishes: Clean the sole plate with your favorite laundry prewash on a damp, soft cloth. Do this on a cool iron. Again, iron with steam over an old cloth before ironing clothes.

Cleaning the steam part of the iron: Fill the steam iron with equal portions of white vinegar and water. Let it steam for several minutes, then disconnect the iron and let it sit for one hour. Empty and rinse with clear water and iron over an old cloth, using steam.

After cleaning your iron: When using any of these methods, remember to rinse it well and then fill with water, heat on the heavy steam setting, and iron over old fabric prior to using on clothes. This will remove any residue remaining in the vent holes.

Make the Most of Your Time at the Board

For energy-efficient ironing: Put aluminum foil between the ironing board and the cover—shiny side up. The foil will reflect the heat upward onto the garments you are ironing, so less effort is required by you!

To keep ironing boards clean longer: Spray the cover with spray starch and iron over it.

Ironing delicate fabrics: The secret to ironing these fabrics is to lay a "press cloth" over them and iron on that. Any old piece of lightweight cotton will work fine. Never lay a bare iron on delicate fabrics.

Collars: Iron both sides of the collar for a crisp, smooth finish. Start at the point and iron inward to the center to avoid pushing creases to the tip.

Seams and hems: To avoid creating a line over seams and hems, iron the garment inside out and stop just short of the seam or hemline.

Embroidery: Lay the piece of embroidery face down on a towel, and iron on the reverse side. That way you won't flatten the embroidery.

Large items: Before you start ironing, turn the ironing board around so that you are using the wide end rather than the point. You can cover more area as you iron this way. Fold items such as large tablecloths in half and iron one side, then fold in half again and iron the other two sides.

> Remember: **Don't iron dirty clothes or clothes that you have perspired in. It will set stains and damage the fibers.**

Dampening clothes: Our moms used to sprinkle clothes with water to help release the wrinkles and make ironing easier. This is still a good idea—especially with all the natural fibers we are wearing. Items that are too dry are very difficult to iron, so use a spray bottle to mist clothes that have dried. If clothes are heavily wrinkled, lay a damp towel on the ironing board and iron—with steam—over it. This works remarkably well on heavy trousers, jeans, etc.

The shoulder pad challenge: Try not to iron over shoulder pads or they will leave an ugly ring on the fabric. Just an additional note: Before you launder shoulder pads, tack the filling and the cover of the shoulder pad together so that it will not shift during the laundry and ironing process.

Steaming Strategies

* Test the iron first. If it sticks, jerks, or leaves a film on the ironing board cover, then stop—the iron needs to be cleaned before you iron clothes.
* Don't iron over zippers, buttons, or any lumps.
* Don't iron rubber, suede, leather, or stretch-type fabric.

Right Side, Wrong Side, Which Side?

- Iron cotton, net, or silky rayon right side up. These fabrics tend to wrinkle more than others, and ironing them on the wrong side will not get all the wrinkles out.
- Iron polyester on either side.
- Iron other garments on the wrong side of the fabric for best results. You'll avoid scorching, shine spots, and other fabric damage.

* Use only a cool iron on synthetic fibers.
* When in doubt, start with a cool/warm iron.
* Test iron in an inconspicuous area. If in doubt, use a press cloth to avoid "shine" on the fabric surface.
* Always empty the water from the steam iron when you are done using it to prevent mineral buildup in the water reservoir.

Yikes! The Iron Was Too Hot! It's Scorched!

Try soaking the fabric in cold water overnight. That may remove the scorch mark.

On white fabrics, try saturating a cloth with 3 percent hydrogen peroxide, lay it over the scorch, and iron over it until the mark is removed. *Do not* use this method on colored fabric.

Refer to the Spot and Stain Removal Guide (pp. 356–357) for more ways to treat scorch marks.

45

Starch and Sizing

Starches and sizing restore body to fabrics that have become limp through washing or dry cleaning. They also form a protective barrier to repel dirt. Fabrics such as cotton or linen respond particularly well to these products.

Starch: Comes in spray, liquid, and powder form. Liquid and powder starch should be combined with water—the directions on the package will tell you what proportions to use. Mix to a thick paste if you want your clothes to have a crisp starched appearance. A thinner consistency will give you a lighter look. You can also add starch to the final machine rinse if you like. Just be sure to follow the directions carefully.

The easiest form of starch is spray starch, which you apply while ironing. Just spritz it on the clothes and iron. It's that easy! Spray starches provide a light effect. Use powder or liquid if you prefer a heavier starch.

Sizing: A lighter cousin to starch, sizing is applied in the manufacturing process to provide protection and body to fabric. General wear, moisture, perspiration, and washing or dry cleaning will eventually break down the sizing, though; you may want to reapply it. Buy it in a spray can and spritz it on garments as you iron.

Do not use too much of these spray products. And don't use your iron on a high heat—the starch or sizing will flake off if you do.

46

Work Clothes

Dirty, greasy work clothes should never be washed with other clothes. Soil may transfer to the other clothes.

Prespotting stains is essential. Treat spots with a good spotter or Spot Shot Instant Carpet Stain Remover®. It's very effective on grease and oil. Launder in the hottest water you can for the fabric type, using a long wash cycle and adding ½ cup of washing soda along with your detergent.

If grease and oil are a major problem, spray the areas with WD-40® Lubricant and wait 10 minutes. Work in undiluted dishwashing liquid and launder as usual.

For heavily soiled, greasy work clothes, try pouring a can of Coke® in the washer with your detergent and launder as usual. The combination of cola syrup and sugar works like magic!

GOJO Crème Waterless Hand Cleaner® is also an effective degreasing agent. Work it into the spot and then launder as usual.

If dust and mud are a concern, prewash the clothes with the hottest possible water and ½ cup of washing soda and ½ cup of 20 Mule Team® Borax. After the cycle is complete, add laundry detergent and launder as usual.

Good water and detergent circulation is important, so don't overcrowd the clothes in the washer.

47

Perspiration Stains: They're the Pits!

Perspiration will weaken fabrics, so treat vulnerable areas with care.

The best time to treat those invisible perspiration problems is right after you wear a garment for the first time, *before* you toss it in the washer.

Moisten the underarm area—or any other spot where perspiration stains are a problem—and work in a lather of Fels-Naptha Soap®. Once you've worked up a good lather, toss the garment in the machine and launder as usual.

Working Biz Activated Non Chlorine Bleach™ into the stained fabric is also effective. Just make sure to wet the offending area first!

Always treat perspiration areas on a garment prior to laundering. If odor is present, apply warm water to the area and work in 20 Mule Team® Borax. Let sit 30 minutes or so, then launder.

ODORZOUT™ is also an extremely effective odor eliminator. Use it dry on those smelly areas. You can leave it on overnight—you can even put some in your clothes hamper.

If you already have stains, try dampening the fabric with warm water and working in laundry detergent and Biz™ . Let that soak about 30 minutes and launder as usual.

I have found that soaking garments (whites or colors) in Brilliant Bleach® from Soapworks® is very effective for removing underarm stains.

You can clean perspiration stains with heated white vinegar. Spray it on the fabric and then work in 20 Mule Team® Borax.

If the fabric has changed color, try spraying with sudsy ammonia, let sit about 15 minutes, then launder as usual.

Bear in mind that yellowed or discolored fabric may be damaged. The garment may not be salvageable.

Treat everything prior to washing for the first time and do try switching brands of antiperspirant. Never wear shirts or blouses more than one day if you have a perspiration problem. You may find that wearing natural fibers such as cottons will be less of a problem than polyester and polyester blends. If your problem is serious you may want to try underarm shields. They trap moisture before it can reach the fabric. They can be removed and thrown away each day, and can't be seen through the garment. Look for them in lingerie stores and in catalogs.

48

Socks and Panty Hose

Folklore: If the legs of stockings, panty hose, leggings or socks intertwine on a clothesline or in a dryer, the owner of the garment is assured of joy and happiness.

Socks

White socks: To get white socks really clean, soak them for an hour in 1 gallon of hot water and 2 tablespoons of automatic dishwasher detergent. Pour the socks and soaking solution into the washer and launder as usual and they'll be clean and bright like you've never imagined.

You can also whiten socks by soaking in hot water to which you have added the slices of 1 lemon or ½ cup of lemon juice. Soak several hours or overnight. Put the socks in the washer and launder as usual.

Foot odor: Turn your socks into sweet-smelling odor beaters by adding ¼ cup of baking soda to one gallon of water. Spin the socks in the washer without rinsing out the baking soda solution. Dry as usual.

To increase the life of your panty hose: Dip them in water, wring them out, put them in a plastic bag, and freeze them solid. When you remove them from the freezer, let them thaw and dry completely. They'll be ready to wear and they'll last longer! Do this before you wear them for the first time.

IT'S THAT EASY!

A run in your panty hose and no nail polish in sight? Stop the run from traveling further by rubbing it with some wet soap.

To increase the elasticity in panty hose: Add 2 tablespoons of white vinegar to the rinse water.

To wash panty hose with ease in the washer: Use an old panty hose leg to hold a pair of good panty hose. Just knot the end of the panty hose leg at the top so the panty hose won't come out during washing. Adding some fabric softener to the rinse will lubricate the fibers and make the hose last longer and cut down on electricity. Out of softener? Use some hair conditioner!

Buy two, get one free: If you are down to your last pairs of panty hose and they all have runs in one leg, take two pairs of panty hose, cut off the damaged legs, and combine the two remaining "half pairs" to make one good pair! And if they happen to be control top, you've got double the tummy control!

49

Getting in the Swim

Swimwear is expensive, but correct care, washing and storage will ensure a long life.

Always read the care label before buying swimwear. This way you will be prepared for whatever care is required.

> Remember: **Never put your suit away without rinsing it out first.**

After swimming in a chlorinated pool, soak your suit for 15 minutes or so in cold water with a little liquid fabric softener. Rinse in cold water, then wash in cool water with mild detergent. Rinse well again and dry in the shade. Chlorine is very hard on fabrics, weakening them and changing the color, so be sure to rinse the suit as soon as you can.

If the suit has been worn in saltwater, soak it for a few minutes in cold water to remove the salt, then wash in cold water with mild detergent. Rinse well and dry in the shade.

Fold the suit in shape once it's dry. Store in tissue or in a perforated plastic bag for winter. (A perforated bag will allow the fabric to breathe.)

50

Hats and Handbags

You can't toss these in the washing machine. But you can still clean them.

Leather bags: Clean these quite easily with a cloth that you have wrung out in warm water and lathered with a bar of moisturizing face soap, such as Dove®. Rub well, rinsing the cloth as needed and working the soap in until all dirt has been removed. Buff well with a soft cloth.

You may also polish the bag with leather cream or polish, following the directions on the container. Laying the bag in the sun for 15 minutes or so will allow the polish to absorb better.

Use your vacuum attachments to remove lint from the lining of your handbag, and spot with Energine Cleaning Fluid® where necessary. Again, use the blow-dryer to prevent rings.

Never store leather bags in plastic. Wrap in cloth or tissue. Never store leather and plastic or vinyl bags together. The leather will bleed color onto the other bags, ruining them.

Clean patent leather bags with a little petroleum jelly on a soft cloth. Buff to a brilliant shine, and buff once more with a clean, dry cloth.

Plastic or vinyl bags: These bags should be washed with a soft cloth or sponge and a mild soap or all-purpose cleaner. Rinse well and buff. If you want to restore the shine, apply a little spray furniture polish to a soft cloth and buff.

Suede bags: Brush suede bags frequently using a suede brush. Grease marks can be removed with a little dry-cleaning fluid, such as Energine®, or try a little undiluted white vinegar on a soft cloth. Brush the nap into position and allow to dry out of the sun, then brush again.

If the nap is severely flattened, steam the bag lightly over a pan of boiling water. Do not allow the bag to become too wet. Air-dry and then brush well.

Evening bags: Clean these gently with a soft cloth and some dry-cleaning fluid. Dry well by blotting or using the blow-dryer. Beaded bags can be lightly dusted with talcum powder to absorb dirt. Enclose the bag in a towel, wait 24 hours and then gently brush. Use care to not loosen threads holding the beads.

Dear Queen of Clean:
My lucky baseball cap is getting mighty dirty. What can I do?

Fan from Florida

Dear Fan:
That's easy. Just put your cap in the top rack of the dishwasher and it'll come out great! This works well for crowns, too!

Hats: Hats that are not washable can be cleaned by using a soot-and-dirt removal sponge, available at hardware stores and home centers. Rub the dry sponge over the soiled areas of the hat, as if you were erasing with a large eraser. Do this outside or over a trash container or sink. Continue to work until you have removed all the soiling you possibly can. This is effective for felt and cowboy-style hats, too.

Cool water and shampoo work well on nylon or knit caps. Add a few drops of hair conditioner to rinse water to soften and condition the fibers. My Canadian friends will be pleased to know that this method works well on toques!

51 Your Best Foot Forward

What article of clothing gets more wear and tear than our shoes? Many of us have a favorite pair of tennis shoes that we live in. When we come home we take them off after a hot day at work, and our family leaves the room making comments about a skunk smelling better. Now, there is a quick, easy answer to shoe odor. Taking good care of shoes will make them look better, of course, but it will also extend the life of the shoes, too.

Cleaning and Deodorizing Shoes

This method will work with any shoe. First, sprinkle some baking soda in the shoe, then place it in a plastic bag and freeze it for a night or two. Allow the shoe to come to room temperature (unless you want to cool your feet) and then shake out the baking soda and wear. It is a good idea to leave the baking soda in the shoe until the next wearing.

Stretching Shoes

Here's another freezer tip for the pair of shoes that pinches your toes. For each shoe use a heavy-duty zip closure bag, or double up two of them and put them in each shoe. Carefully pour water into the bags, until the toe area is full. Close the bags securely so the water doesn't seep out and wet the shoes. To help prevent the outside of the shoes from getting wet, put each shoe in a plastic bag. Place the shoes in the freezer for at least 24 hours. As the water freezes it expands, and as it does this the shoes will expand and stretch. You will need to allow the shoes to defrost enough to remove the bags of water when you remove them from the freezer.

DID YOU KNOW?

Damp boots can lose their shape while drying. Prevent this by rolling newspapers into the legs. As an added bonus, the newspapers will also absorb any odors.

Cleaning White Canvas Shoes

Apply a paste of automatic dishwashing detergent mixed with hot water to the shoes. Allow to soak at least 30 minutes, then scrub surface with a nail brush or toothbrush. Rinse well and allow to dry. Dry the shoes out of the direct sun. You can also put the shoes in the washing machine with several old white towels and launder as usual after soaking and brushing. To keep the shoes clean, set them on paper and apply several coats of spray starch or fabric protector. They will stay clean longer and soil will wash out more easily.

Cleaning White Leather Athletic Shoes

These can be cleaned easily with whitewall tire cleaner. Take the shoes outside if possible or spray over newspaper. Let sit 2 or 3 minutes and then wipe with paper towels or old rags. Remember, whitewall tire cleaner is a bleaching product, so rinse shoes thoroughly before wearing in the house on carpet. Pay special attention to the soles.

Polishing White Leather

Before polishing, clean well. To remove scuffs, try an art gum eraser or a paste of baking soda and water. To cover scuffs that won't come off, use liquid typewriter correction fluid prior to polishing. Prep the shoes for white polish by rubbing them with the cut side of a raw potato. The potato will help the polish go on smoothly and cover scuff marks.

When You're Out of Shoe Polish

Reach for the furniture polish. Take a rag and spray liberally with furniture polish. Rub the shoe well and buff. In a real hurry, use baby wipes! Rub on and buff.

Fixing Scuffs and Tears on Shoes

If there's a black mark on shoes, try a dab of nail polish remover, rubbing alcohol or lighter fluid on a clean cloth. For areas where the color is removed try using a marker in the same color. Wipe immediately after applying with a paper towel and then polish.

Don't throw out that hardened shoe polish. Just heat the metal container in a bowl of hot water long enough to let the polish soften.

Scuffs on Gold or Silver Shoes

Use an old, dry toothbrush with white toothpaste to remove the scuff; polish with clear polish or furniture polish.

Polishing Patent Leather

Rub petroleum jelly into patent leather and buff with a soft cloth. It not only polishes, it prevents cracking.

Scuff Marks on Vinyl or Plastic Shoes

Use lighter fluid. Be sure to dispose of the rag or paper towel you use outside.

If Plastic Tips Fall off Your Shoelaces

Easy—twist the ends of the shoelaces and dip in clear nail polish.

To Keep Children's Shoes Tied

Dampen the laces with a spray of water before you tie them. This allows you to tie the bows tighter and the laces will stay in place.

52

Ties: Don't Let Them Tie You in Knots

Ties are generally not washable, which is a shame because nothing gets more food spills and dipped into more things than ties. This does not mean that you can't successfully spot clean them, though.

If you have a tie with a food or beverage spill, first slip a pad of paper toweling in the opening between the front and the back of the tie. This will prevent the spot from forcing its way through the tie. Using Energine Cleaning Fluid®, moisten a soft, light-colored cloth (think washcloth) and blot the spotted area. As the toweling absorbs the spot and the Energine®, change it to a clean, dry section of the pad. Continue to blot until the spot is removed; then—and this is important—use your blow-dryer to dry the spot quickly to avoid a moisture ring.

When ironing a tie, lay it flat on the ironing board and cover with a press cloth (a lightweight towel will work) and press it with steam. Hang to dry completely. When storing ties, hang them or roll them (great for travel) to prevent wrinkles and creases.

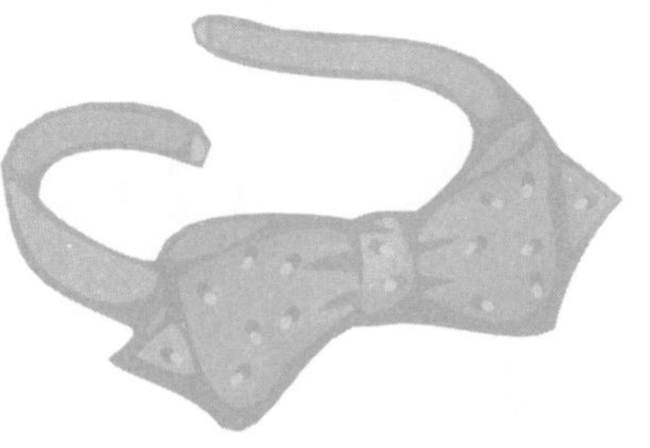

53

Let's Face the Music and Dance: Beads and Sequins

Laundering: Some sequined and beaded clothes can be washed. Here's how to keep them looking great:

* Button them completely prior to laundering.
* Turn clothes inside out prior to laundering.
* If machine washable, use only the gentle cycle set for approximately 2 or 3 minutes, with cold water and mild detergent.
* If the item is hand washable, use mild laundry soap or a little shampoo and cold water.
* Put a little hair conditioner in the final rinse if the garment is knitted.
* Always hang to dry or lay flat—never dry in the dryer.

Freshening: Spritz lightly with undiluted vodka under the arms and around the neck and cuffs. Hang to dry.

Spills: Many beaded outfits are labeled "spot clean only." Use a little club soda or Energine Cleaning Fluid®. Apply any moisture sparingly and then use a blow-dryer to dry the spot quickly to avoid a moisture ring.

54

Preserving Your Wedding Gown

Wedding gowns are expensive investments, but with so much excitement leading up to the big day, cleaning the dress afterward rarely crosses our minds. Often the dress is quickly discarded in favor of more comfortable travel attire, then it's left to lay while we trip off on our honeymoon. Yet, with just a little bit of care you can preserve the dress, for sentimental reasons perhaps, or for your own daughter to wear someday. Here's what you need to know.

First, don't leave the store without a care label. If a care label is not sewn into the gown, be sure to get written cleaning instructions from the store clerk or seamstress.

Once you have chosen your gown, it's best to leave it at the store until the last possible moment. You'll avoid wrinkling that way. If you bring your dress home prior to the big day, decide where you are going to hang it to avoid wrinkling—perhaps an over-the-door hanger in a spare room. Do not hang your precious dress in the attic or the basement. You'll only be inviting dust, dirt, bugs, dampness, and water damage.

Now what about after the wedding? Don't just throw your dress down. Hang it on a padded hanger. Assign someone to pick up the dress within a day or two after the wedding and transport it to the cleaner you have chosen. Those spots and spills and lipstick smudges from all those happy kisses will come out much more easily if you have the dress cleaned sooner, not later. Ask your mom, sister, or best friend to help out. Whatever you do, don't come home from your honeymoon to a dirty dress laying in a pile on the floor. Even if it never is worn again, you can have beautiful pillows made from the fabric and veiling to use on a bed. That's what I did!

Always have the dress professionally cleaned *before* you put it into storage. Your dress may have invisible stains from food, beverages, perfume, and body oil. If these stains are not properly cleaned, they can become permanent. Try to point out stains or spills to your cleaner *before* cleaning.

A lot of wedding gowns are beaded or lavishly trimmed. Inspect these trims with your cleaner prior to cleaning, since many of them are not made to withstand the dry-cleaning process. Beads, glitter, and pearls are made of coated plastic and may be attached to the dress with adhesives that will not weather cleaning chemicals. Some trims may yellow during the process. Some items "dyed to match" may not be colorfast and may not match after cleaning.

Look for a qualified, experienced cleaner in your area who will discuss all of these things with you and closely examine your dress for potential problems.

Follow these tips and your wedding gown will have a happy future.

Storing Your Gown

Sadly, no cleaning process or storage method can guarantee against yellowing and deterioration of the fabric in your gown. There are, however, steps that you can take to ensure the best possible results.

- Have your dress packed in a special heirloom storage box. You can have your cleaner pack the dress, or buy the box and pack it yourself. Remember to use nonacid tissue paper.
- Wrap the dress in a sheet if it is not boxed. Do not store in plastic or it will yellow.
- Stuff the bodice and sleeves with white, nonacid tissue paper to prevent permanent wrinkles.
- Store headpieces, veils, shoes and other accessories separately. A box or bag will be fine. No plastic, though.
- Store in a cool, dry place. The basement and the attic, though popular, are not good choices.
- If you decide to store your dress on a hanger, hanging it from the sewn-in straps will prevent damage to the shoulders.
- Look your gown over once a year—Valentine's Day is a memorable date—to ensure that no spots have been overlooked. If you find any spotting or discoloration, have the dress treated by a professional cleaner as soon as possible.

55

Furs: Real and Synthetic

If you have a fur coat, you know who you are, so no lectures.

Any fur garment that is worn regularly should be cleaned regularly too. This means once a year by a professional cleaner who specializes in fur. Best to have your fur cleaned just prior to storing it for the summer—this also applies to synthetic furs. A professional cleaner will remove stains, such as makeup, food, and beverages, that can ruin fur. Keeping it clean will also deter moths.

> **DID YOU KNOW?**
>
> It's a good idea to wear a soft scarf around your neck to keep stains and body oil away from a fur collar.

Treat small stains with a little Energine Cleaning Fluid®, on the fur and in the lining. Follow the directions on the can, and make sure to dry the areas that you spot clean with a blow-dryer in order to keep rings from forming. Always test in an inconspicuous spot first.

Hang furs and synthetic furs on well-padded hangers in a cloth bag. Don't use plastic. Shake the fur well when you take it from storage. You'll want to air it prior to wearing as well.

56 Sheepskin

If you have sheepskin rugs and car seats you probably know by now they are not machine washable. They can, however, be cleaned by a professional. Unfortunately, this can be costly.

If the sheepskin is not heavily soiled you can try to clean it with this method. Use a carpet cleaning powder, such as Host™ or Capture™. Both of these are excellent. They come with a machine to use on carpets, but you only need the chemical powder for sheepskin.

Sprinkle the cleaner onto the fleece and work it in well with your fingers, wearing rubber gloves. Roll up the sheepskin, slip it into a plastic bag and leave it for at least 8 hours, then shake or vacuum to remove the powder. Brush or comb the fleece and shake again before using.

If your sheepskin has a treated back and can be washed, follow the manufacturer's directions with care. Always use cool water and hang it to dry out of the sun. If you choose to dry it in the dryer, make sure to use the lowest possible heat setting. Always read the care label carefully prior to purchasing sheepskin.

57

Don't Throw in the Towel!

It's lovely to step out of the shower and wrap yourself in a clean, fluffy towel—what I call a warm fuzzy. Towels are pretty low maintenance; nevertheless there are some things you can do to keep them at their best. Read on . . . what follows is absorbing!

Washing towels in hot water with your favorite laundry detergent or soap will remove normal soiling. Add ½ cup of washing soda to a full load of towels if you want to kick your detergent up a notch and clean more effectively.

> **"What a hotel! The towels were so fluffy that I could hardly close my suitcase."**
>
> **—Henny Youngman**

Presoaking heavily soiled towels is always a good idea. Soak them in hot water and ½ cup of 20 Mule Team® Borax, and you will deodorize them as well!

Fabric softener will provide you

with soft, fluffy towels, but overuse will make the towels less absorbent. Use softener every second or third time instead of every time you launder them. You can also use ½ cup of white vinegar as a softening agent. And no, the towels will not smell like vinegar!

Dark-dyed towels will lose a considerable amount of dye during their first several washings. If you have faded towels the same color as the new ones, wash them together to restore some of the color to the old batch. Adding 1 cup of table salt to the wash water the first time you launder dark towels will keep them from fading as quickly.

Do not wash dark towels and light towels together, ever! The light towels will pick up the color and fuzz from the dark ones, and the dark towels will end up with light-colored lint all over them.

Always wash new towels prior to using to remove the sizing and make them more absorbent. If you find yourself with towels that are slick and will not absorb, here's what to do.

- Soak them in the washer in cold water and ¼ cup of Epsom salts overnight. Add detergent and wash as usual.
- Wash nonabsorbent towels several times in a row and do not add fabric softener.
- Sometimes hanging these towels to dry instead of drying in the dryer for a couple of washings works well.

If your towels have a mildew odor, sprinkle them lightly with ODORZOUT™ and let sit for a day or so, then dump into the washer (towels and ODORZOUT™) and launder as usual.

Do not wash anything else with towels. Washing things together transfers lint from item to item. Always wash towels in the hottest possible water.

58

Bedtime

We're going to wash those pillows, sheets, blankets and comforters. No sleeping on the job!

Pillows

To freshen pillows, tumble them in the clothes dryer set on air or warm for 30 minutes with several barely damp light-colored towels and a dryer fabric softener sheet. Don't use the fabric softener sheet if you have fragrance allergies.

Fiber-filled pillows: These flatten with use, so chances are you'll want to restore their bulk and softness. Clean them in your washing machine every couple of months, and choose a windy day if possible. Wash the pillows in cold or lukewarm water with a mild detergent, and use a short cycle. If you have allergies, try Fresh Breeze Laundry Soap™ by Soapworks®. Make sure the pillows are rinsed well, then spin them dry.

If you are washing pillows by hand, use cool water and mild suds, and press out all the water you can. Rinse several times to remove all the soap, then press and roll out the water.

Hang pillows to dry in a shady, breezy location if possible, turning them frequently. Finally, place pillows in the dryer on the lowest setting to fluff the filling. Adding a new tennis ball or clean tennis shoe in the dryer will help to pump up the volume!

Place pillows inside zippered pillow covers to keep them clean and fresh longer.

Feather pillows: Wash these in cool suds and dry them in the shade. Heat can release traces of oil in the feathers and cause them to give off unpleasant odors.

Make sure you allow plenty of time for the feathers to dry. Fluff and shake the pillow frequently to rearrange the feathers for better drying.

You may put feather pillows in the dryer on the air setting to reposition the feathers and add bounce to the pillows. Again, putting in a couple of tennis balls or clean tennis shoes will beat the feathers up and add fluff. Keeping feather pillows in zippered pillow protectors is also a good idea.

Other pillows: There are a lot of different pillows on the market these days, including specially formed cervical pillows. Wash them according to the care label so you don't damage the filling.

Sheets

Always wash sheets before using them for the first time.

Wash dark sheets separately from white or light colors to avoid color runs.

Use warm water for polyester and blends. Use hot water for 100 percent cotton sheets. Dry according to care label directions, usually on medium.

Flannel Sheets and Pillowcases

Launder these in the washing machine with warm water, and always make sure to wash them before using for the first time. Bear in mind that flannel sheets have an enormous amount of lint, so they may not be suitable for people with allergies (although the more they are laundered the less severe the lint will be). Rinse with warm water and a cup of white vinegar to help with the lint problem, and make sure you clean the lint filter frequently during the drying cycle the first few times you wash and dry the sheets. Wash flannel separately from all other fabrics.

Blankets

If the care label indicates that your blankets are machine washable, which most are, make sure the machine has plenty of room for movement between the folds of the blanket. Wash with mild soap in cold water and add 1 cup of white vinegar to the final rinse to remove any soap residue and keep the blankets soft. If the care tag indicates, dry in a warm dryer or out of direct sunlight over several clotheslines strung at least 12 inches apart to avoid stretching the blanket. Store blankets well by wrapping them in plastic, or inside a clean pillowcase.

For electric blankets or mattress pads, follow the care label directions carefully to avoid damaging the wiring and creating a possible fire hazard.

Bedspreads

Washable spreads should be laundered according to the care label directions. Nylon, polyester, polyester blends and cotton bedspreads all wash well. Rayons, silks and acetates should be dry-cleaned.

Chenille spreads, which are quite popular again, are easily laundered in the washing machine. Use warm water and mild detergent and rinse well. Dry in the dryer and shake well to restore the nap when you remove chenille from the dryer. Linting, which is common in these types of spreads, will stop after a few washings. Be sure to keep your dryer's lint filter well cleaned when drying these spreads.

For heavily quilted spreads you can use tennis balls or a clean tennis shoe to pump up the volume on the quilting.

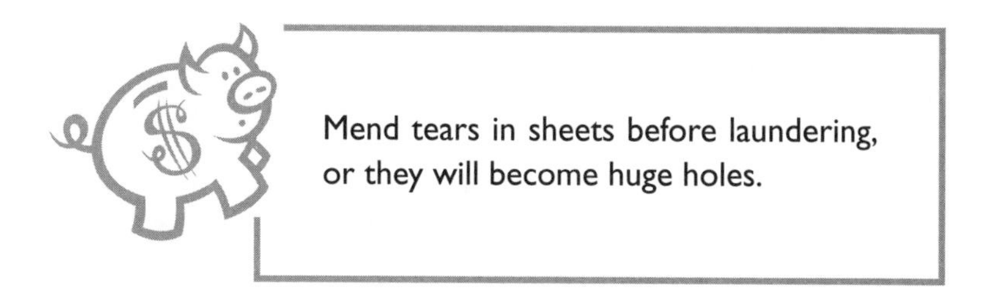

Down Comforters

I find that it's best—and also easiest—to have these cleaned professionally. If you do decide to launder yours, use a commercial-size washer, using the shortest possible cycle.

Do not wash these more frequently than you have to. Air the comforter frequently instead, and use a duvet cover or comforter cover that can be laundered as needed.

Mattresses

It's important to turn your mattress every three months to allow for even wear. Alternate between turning it end to end and side to side.

Covering a mattress with a pad or a plastic zip mattress protector is your best defense against stains, especially on a child's bed. A cloth pad is much cooler than plastic.

If you are faced with cleaning up a wet spill, such as urine, absorb all the moisture you can with paper towels or rags, applying pressure as you blot. Clean the area with Spot Shot Instant Carpet Stain Remover® and stand the mattress on its side against a wall to speed drying and keep moisture from going deeper into the mattress. Once the mattress is dry, apply a layer of ODORZOUT™ to absorb the odor. ODORZOUT™ is an odor eliminator, not a cover-up. If you can lay the mattress out in the sun to dry, it will speed up the process.

59 Window Treatments

Be sure to read the care label and closely follow instructions when you are cleaning your drapes and curtains. Never try to wash curtains that should be dry-cleaned.

You can extend the life of window coverings by vacuuming them frequently with the upholstery attachments on your vacuum cleaner. You may also take them down and shake them, or tumble them in the dryer on the air setting.

Do not allow draperies to become heavily soiled before cleaning, especially if they are labeled "dry-clean only."

Dry cleaning does not clean as well as wet cleaning, and all soil may not be removed.

If the curtains or drapes are covering a particularly sunny window, hanging a blind or shade to protect the fabric might be a wise idea.

Remove all hooks, etc., from curtains prior to washing. Follow the directions for the type of fabric on the care label directions.

Some curtains can be dried in the dryer. Check the care label. Just be sure not to overcrowd the dryer, and remember to rearrange the draperies often during the drying cycle.

If pressing is required, remove the curtains while damp and iron. This will make it easier to remove the wrinkles. For a crisp finish, use spray sizing or starch. Remember, two light sprays are better than one heavy one and will prevent white "flaking" on the fabric.

Sizing and starch will help to repel dirt as well.

If you've washed sheer or lace-type curtains, pressing them gently while damp and hanging them slightly damp will encourage them to fall into gentle folds at the window.

DID YOU KNOW?

Sunlight weakens and damages fiber and color.

Plastic shower curtains: Wash these in the washing machine with several old, light-colored towels. Add 1½ cups of white vinegar and your normal detergent, fill with warm water, and use the gentle cycle. Remove the curtain promptly from the washer and hang immediately. This method will remove soap scum and dirt. If mold and mildew are a problem, use 1½ cups of liquid chlorine bleach instead of white vinegar and follow the above directions.

60 Table Linens

Nothing makes a table look better than a beautiful tablecloth and napkins—but cleaning up after the meal can be a bit of a chore. Here are some foolproof ways to make the cleanup fast and easy.

Stain-proofing tablecloths: Spraying tablecloths with Scotchgard® Fabric Protector or a similar product prior to using will allow spills to wash out. Don't spray the cloth on top of a wood table. You'll spoil the finish.

Removing Stains from Tablecloths

Bleach white cotton and linen items. Soak colored items in heavy-duty detergent solution.

For white linens, you can also dissolve 2 denture-cleaning tablets in warm water. Spread out the stained area in a tub or sink. Pour on the solution and let soak for 30 minutes, then launder as usual.

Soaking stained table linens in Brilliant Bleach® produces beautiful results. Soak until the stain is removed—even several days—without harming the fabric.

Removing red wine stains: These methods will work on any type of red stain, including red pop, cranberry juice, and fruit punches:

Always keep some white wine handy for red wine spills. Pour the white wine on the red wine and it will remove the stain. Do this as soon as you can.

Keep club soda on hand for red stains too. Pour the soda through the stain, preferably over the sink. Pretreat and launder as usual.

One of my very favorite products is called Wine Away Red Wine Stain Remover™, but don't let the name scare you, it works great on red pop, Kool-Aid™, cranberry juice, grape juice, red food coloring, and even tea and black coffee. It is made of fruit and vegetable extracts, so it is totally non-toxic and easy to use.

Removing dried tea and black coffee stains: For tea stains, drape the stained item over a bowl or sink. Sprinkle with 20 Mule Team® Borax until the entire stain is covered. Pour a kettle full of hot water around the stain, working toward the center. Repeat if necessary and then launder as usual. For dried coffee stains, treat with a solution of 50 percent glycerin and 50 percent warm water. Rinse and blot well. Treat with laundry presoak prior to laundering.

Stains on cloth napkins: The most common stain on cloth napkins is lipstick. To remove this, spray the area with WD-40® Lubricant, wait 10 minutes, then work in undiluted dishwashing liquid and launder as usual.

As an alternative, you can work in GOJO Crème Waterless Hand Cleaner®, then launder as usual.

For food and beverage stains, treat with a commercial prespotter or one of the ones we made in Chapter 36, or use Spot Shot Instant Carpet

Stain Remover®. Be sure not to let the spotters dry on the napkins before laundering.

You can also soak both white and colored napkins in Brilliant Bleach® (Soapworks®) without damaging the fabrics or colors.

Storing Tablecloths Wrinkle-Free

Instead of folding tablecloths, fold minimally lengthwise and then roll the cloth. It takes less room to store and will not wrinkle as easily, either. Hang cloths that wrinkle easily over a hanger covered with a fabric cover. A towel works well.

Caring for Plastic and Vinyl Tablecloths

Clean plastic and vinyl tablecloths by wiping with a clean, damp cloth and rinsing well. For stubborn stains, make a paste of lemon juice and cream of tartar and work it into the stain. Allow the paste to sit on the stain for a few minutes, then rinse. Let dry before folding.

Sprinkling clean plastic tablecloths with a little talcum powder before storing them will prevent stickiness and mildew.

61

A to Z Palace Spot and Stain Removal Guide

I'm so glad that you feel safe in airing your dirty laundry with me. I am, after all, the Babe of Borax, one of the original Mold-Diggers, the High Priestess of Household Chemicals, the Vixen of Vinegar, the Deaconess of Dry Cleaning, the Goddess of Grease Stains, the Sultaness of Soap, Solvents and Solutions and of course, the Queen of Clean®! And you know what else? I'm not finished yet . . . not until I give you this, my "all you need to know" spot and stain removal guide, straight from the palace!

Now, a few words of caution before we begin. *Don't* go trying any of these spot removal methods *without* paying heed to my Royal Rules of Stain Removal. Promise?

Royal Rules of Stain Removal

- Test the spot remover on hidden or inconspicuous areas of the fabric before you proceed.
- Approach the stain from the wrong side of the fabric. Put a pad of paper toweling under the offending spot as you work. This will help to blot the stain.
- Always blot, never rub! Rubbing will spread the spot and harm the fabric.
- Do not iron or apply heat to spots or stains. Heat will set the stain and you will never be able to remove it.
- If you don't know what caused the stain, start with the weakest and simplest stain removal method.
- Make sure to consider the fabric as well as the stain.
- Remember, the faster you react to a spill or a spot, the better your chances are of removing it completely.
- Directing a blow-dryer at a freshly blotted spot will help it to dry without a ring.
- Sometimes you may still need to pretreat using your favorite laundry spotter, such as Zout®.

A to Z

ACID: Acid can permanently damage fabrics, so it must be treated immediately. Neutralize acid by flushing the area with cold running water as soon as possible. Next, spread the garment over a pad of paper towels and moisten with ammonia. Dab the spot several times, then flush again with cold water. If you do not have ammonia on hand, apply a paste of cold water and baking soda, then flush with water. Repeat this several times, then launder as usual.

Do not use undiluted ammonia on wool or silk, or on any blends containing these fibers. If you have acid on silk or wool you may dilute ammonia with equal parts of cold water and apply as directed above.

ADHESIVE TAPE: Sponge adhesive tape with eucalyptus oil, baby oil, or cooking oil. Allow to soak 10 minutes or so, then work in undiluted dishwashing liquid and rinse well. Pretreat and launder as usual.

You may also consider using De-Solv-it™, Goo Gone™, or Un-Du™ to remove adhesives from fabric and hard surfaces. Un-Du™ is so great it will remove a stamp from an envelope!

ALCOHOLIC BEVERAGES: These stains will turn brown with age, so it is important to treat them as soon as possible. First, flush the area with cold water or with club soda, then sponge immediately with a cloth barely dampened with warm water and 1 or 2 drops of liquid dish soap. Rinse with cool water and dry the area with a hair dryer set on medium.

Alcohol is often invisible when it is spilled, but it can oxidize with heat and age, which makes it impossible to remove. Presoak dry alcohol stains in an enzyme solution such as Biz All Fabric Bleach™, and launder as usual.

If you spill alcohol on a dry-clean-only fabric, sponge with cold water or club soda and then take the garment to the dry cleaner as soon as possible. Make sure to point out the stain.

For beer spills, sponge with a solution of equal parts white vinegar and dishwashing liquid, then rinse in warm water.

For treating red and white wine spills, see Wine.

ANIMAL HAIR: Removing pet hair from clothes and bedding can be a challenge. Try using a damp sponge and wiping over clothes and bedding, etc. Rinse the sponge frequently to keep it clean. You can also remove hair by putting on rubber gloves and dipping them in water. Simply dip and wipe, dip and wipe. The hair will rinse off easily.

ANTIPERSPIRANTS AND DEODORANTS: Antiperspirants that contain aluminum chloride are acidic and may interact with some fabrics. If color changes have occurred, try sponging fabric with ammonia. Rinse thoroughly, and remember to dilute ammonia with equal portions of water when spotting wool or silk.

If you want to avoid yellow underarm stains and prevent color removal, take a bar of Fels-Naptha Soap® and work it into the underarm of clothes *before* you launder them for the first time, even if you see no visible stain. Work up a good lather between your thumbs and then launder as usual.

You can also try applying rubbing alcohol to the stain and covering the area with a folded paper towel dampened with alcohol. Keep it moist and let it sit for a few hours prior to laundering.

To treat yellowed areas that have become stiff, apply an enzyme-soaking product. Biz All Fabric Bleach™ is a good one to try. Make a stiff paste of the powder by mixing it with cold water. Rub it into the stained areas. Next, put the garment in a plastic bag and leave 8 hours or overnight. Wash in very hot water. If dealing with fabrics that can't withstand hot water, drape the underarm area over a sink and pour 1 quart of hot water through the fabric. Launder as usual.

Don't iron over a deodorant stain or you will never be able to remove it.

I have also had success soaking garments with underarm stains in a solution of 1 quart warm water and 3 tablespoons of Brilliant Bleach®. Soak up to several days if necessary. Brilliant Bleach® is safe for whites and colorfast garments.

Last-ditch effort: Spray the stained area heavily with heated white vinegar, work in 20 Mule Team® Borax, roll up in a plastic bag and leave overnight, then launder as usual.

BABY FORMULA: For white clothes, try applying lemon juice to the stains and laying the garment in the sun. Pretreat and launder as usual.

Unseasoned meat tenderizer is also great for removing formula and baby food stains. Make a paste of the tenderizer and cool water, rub it into the stain and let sit for an hour or so before laundering. Meat tenderizer contains an enzyme that breaks down protein stains. Just make sure to use *unseasoned* tenderizer.

Soaking colored clothes and whites in Brilliant Bleach® is also effective, although you may have to soak for several days to achieve perfect results on difficult stains. Remember, this bleach is nonchlorine, so it's totally safe for baby things.

BARBECUE SAUCE: See Tomato-based stains.

BERRIES (blueberries, cranberries, raspberries, strawberries): There are many complex ways to deal with berry stains, but I've had great success with one of the simplest, a product called Wine Away Red Wine Stain Remover™. Don't be fooled by the name, it works on red fruit stains and juices too.

Just spray Wine Away™ straight on the fabric and watch in amazement as it breaks down the stain. Follow the directions on the container carefully and launder immediately after use. Totally nontoxic, Wine Away™ is safe on all washable surfaces.

BEVERAGES: Blot beverage spills immediately until you have absorbed all you can, then sponge with clean, warm water and a little borax. (About ½ teaspoon 20 Mule Team® Borax to ½ cup of water.) Sponge and blot repeatedly and launder as usual.

Also see information under specific beverage stains.

BLOOD (fresh and dried): If you have blood all over your clothes, laundry may not be your biggest problem . . . for those little accidents try the following:

For washable fabrics, soak as soon as possible in salt water or flush with club soda. You can also make a paste of unseasoned meat tenderizer and cold water, and apply it to the stain for a few hours. Wash in cool water and detergent, by hand or machine.

Pouring 3 percent hydrogen peroxide through the stained area can be effective in many instances. The sooner you do this the more success you will have. Make sure to do this only on washable fabrics, please. Pour the peroxide through the stain, then flush with cold water, pretreat and launder as usual.

Biz All Fabric Bleach™ and Brilliant Bleach™ both work well on blood. When using Biz™, make a paste with cold water and apply to the stain, allowing it to sit for several hours. With Brilliant Bleach™, soak the garment for a significant period of time—anywhere between 1 to 24 hours. Neither of these products will harm colorfast fabrics.

For dry-clean-only fabrics, sprinkle with salt while the blood is still moist, then take to a dry cleaner as soon as possible.

Human saliva will break down fresh bloodstains, so try applying a little of your own saliva to a small spot of blood—this may do the trick.

For a quick fix for fresh bloodstains, apply cornstarch to the surface and then flush from the "wrong" side of the fabric with soapy water. Pretreat and launder as usual.

Blood on leather can be foamed away with 3 percent hydrogen peroxide. Dab on the peroxide. Let it bubble and then blot. Continue until the blood is removed. Wipe the surface with a damp cloth and dry.

BUTTER OR MARGARINE: Scrape off any solid concentration of butter with a dull edge, such as the back of a knife.

On washable fabrics, work in undiluted dishwashing liquid, wash and dry.

If the stain is old, spray it with WD-40® Lubricant to regenerate the grease, then work in undiluted dishwashing liquid and wash in the hottest water possible for that fabric type.

Sponge silks and delicate fabrics with Energine Cleaning Fluid®. Allow to air-dry. Repeat if necessary.

Do not iron the fabric until all traces of the grease have been removed. Ironing will set the stain and make it impossible to remove.

Take dry-clean-only fabrics to the dry cleaner as soon as possible. Be sure to identify the stain and its location on the garment.

CANDLE WAX: For candle wax on clothes and table linens, place the article in a plastic bag, place the bag in the freezer and let the wax freeze. Scrape off what you can with a dull, straight edge—the back of a knife or an old credit card works well. Lay a brown paper bag, with no writing facing the fabric, on the ironing board. (Grocery store bags work well. Just make sure that the writing is face down on the ironing board *away* from the fabric—otherwise you may transfer lettering to your garment.) Cover with a similar bag (again, with the writing *away* from the fabric) and press with a medium/hot iron, moving the paper bag like a blotter until you have absorbed every bit of wax you can. Be patient! Blot with Energine Cleaning Fluid® to remove the balance of the grease from the wax.

Wieman's Wax Away™ also works beautifully on any kind of wax. Follow the directions with care.

CANDY: To remove candy from fabrics, combine 1 tablespoon of liquid dish soap with 1 tablespoon of white vinegar and 1 quart of warm water. Soak the stain in it for 15 to 30 minutes, then flush with warm, clear water. Pretreat and launder as usual.

For chocolate stains, see Chocolate.

CHEWING GUM: See Gum.

CHOCOLATE: Scrape off all that you can, then soak washable fabrics for 30 minutes in an enzyme prewash solution such as Biz™. Rub detergent into any remaining stain and work well between your thumbs. Rinse the area under forcefully running cold water. If a grease spot remains, sponge the area with dry-cleaning solution such as Energine Cleaning Fluid®. Any residual stain should come out during normal washing. If the stain is still visible after washing, soak in Brilliant Bleach® or combine ½ cup of 3 percent hydrogen peroxide and 1 teaspoon of clear ammonia and soak the stain for 10 minutes at a time, checking every 10 minutes and resoaking if necessary. Remember, fabrics need to be tested for colorfastness before using peroxide.

For dry-clean-only fabrics, flush the stain with club soda to prevent setting, then sponge the area with Energine Cleaning Fluid®. If the stain persists, take it to your dry cleaner.

COFFEE AND TEA (black or with sugar): Blot up all that you can and, if the garment is washable, flush immediately with cold water. Rub detergent into the stain and work well between your thumbs before laundering as usual. If the stain is still visible and you can use hot water on the fabric, spread the stain over the sink, or stretch over a bowl and tie or rubber band in place (like a little trampoline) and sit the bowl in the sink. Cover the stain with 20 Mule Team® Borax and pour boiling water through it, circling from the outside of the stain until you have reached the center. Let soak 30 minutes to an hour and relaunder.

For more delicate fabrics, soak in Brilliant Bleach®.

For sturdy whites, such as knits and T-shirts, dissolve 2 denture-cleaning tablets in warm water and soak the stain for 30 minutes. Check the garment. If the stain is still visible, soak again and launder as usual.

Out at a restaurant? Dip your napkin in water and sprinkle with salt and blot the offending stain.

For stains from lattes and cappuccinos, see Milk.

COLA AND SOFT DRINKS: Sponge these spills as soon as possible with a solution of equal parts alcohol and water. On washable clothes, bleach out remaining stains with an equal mixture of 3 percent hydrogen peroxide and water. Saturate stain and wait 20 minutes. If the stain is gone, launder as usual. Repeat if the stain remains. You can also soak the fabric in a solution of Brilliant Bleach® as directed on the container.

Borax is also effective in soft drink/cola removal. Moisten the spot thoroughly and sprinkle with 20 Mule Team® Borax, working well between your thumbs. Flush with water and retreat if necessary.

Getting the stain out as soon as possible is important: cola and soft drinks will discolor fabrics as they oxidize.

COLLAR STAINS: This is for those women whose husbands won't share laundry duty, the women who didn't know that the wedding ring came with a ring around the collar! It's easy to remove, though. Just use some inexpensive shampoo! Shampoo dissolves body oils so it works great on that collar ring. Keep some in a bottle with a dispenser top in the laundry room. Squirt on enough to cover the offending stain and work it in well, then launder as usual.

COPIER TONER (powder): First, carefully shake off any loose powder and brush lightly with a soft brush. An old, soft toothbrush works well. Pretreat with your favorite spotter or try Zout® or Spot Shot Instant Carpet Stain Remover® and launder as usual, using the hottest water for the fabric type. Don't rub or brush with your hand. The oil in your skin will spread and set the stain.

COSMETICS (foundation, blusher, eye shadow, eyeliner, and mascara): Bar soap such as Dove®, Caress™ and other such beauty bars work well on cosmetics spots. Wet the stain and rub with the soap, working it in well. Flush with warm water and, once stain is removed, launder as usual.

Sometimes just working in laundry detergent will be all you need. For difficult cases, add some borax to the area and work well between your thumbs.

If your garment is dry clean only, try some Energine Cleaning Fluid® directly on the spot. Make sure to use a cool blow-dryer to keep a ring from forming on the fabric. You'll need to take the garment to a professional cleaner if the stain doesn't come out. (See also Makeup.)

CRAYON AND COLORED PENCIL: Place the stained area on a pad of paper towels and spray with WD-40® Lubricant. Let stand for a few minutes, then turn the fabric over and spray the other side. Let sit for a further 10 minutes before working undiluted dishwashing liquid into the stained area to remove the crayon and oil. Replace the paper-toweling pad as necessary. Wash in the hottest possible water for the fabric, along with your normal detergent and appropriate bleaching agent (depending on whether the clothes are white or colored). Wash on the longest wash cycle available, and rinse well.

Another way to remove crayon from washable fabrics, such as wool, acrylic, linen, cotton and polyester, is to lay the offending stain between two pieces of brown paper and press with a warm/medium iron. A grocery bag works well—just remember to keep any ink that may be on the bag away from the fabric. The paper works as a blotter to absorb the crayon, so keep changing it as the wax is absorbed. If any color mark remains, soak the garment in Brilliant Bleach® or flush with Energine Cleaning Fluid®.

Note: Don't panic if the crayon has also gone through the dryer. Simply spray an old rag with WD-40® Lubricant, then thoroughly wipe down the drum. Make sure the dryer is empty when you do this—no clothes, no crayons. Place a load of dry rags in the dryer and run through a drying cycle when you're through. This will remove any oily residue.

DYE (see also Hair dye): Dye stains are difficult if not impossible to remove. Try one or all of these methods.

Spread the stained area over a bowl and put a rubber band around the fabric *and* the bowl to hold the fabric taut, like a trampoline. Sit the bowl in the sink with the drain in the open position to allow the water to run freely away. Turn on the cold water faucet to a nice steady drip and let it drip through the dye spot for 3 to 6 hours. Monitor the sink to be sure the water is draining. This treatment is effective in many cases.

You can also try saturating the dye spot with a combination of equal parts 3 percent hydrogen peroxide and water. Sit the fabric in the sun, keeping it moist with the solution until the spot completely disappears. Rinse well and launder as usual. Use only on colorfast clothes.

If your dye problem is caused from fugitive color—that is, color that has run from one fabric to another during the wash cycle—all the bleaching in the world won't help. Try Synthrapol™ or Carbona Color Run Remover™ instead.

Quilters have used Synthrapol™ for years to remove color that runs in homemade quilts. Make sure to read *all* the directions on the bottle prior to using.

Carbona Color Run Remover™ is extremely effective on cotton fabrics. It is not for delicates or some blends, so do read the box with care. It may also cause damage to buttons and, in some cases, zippers. You may want to remove these prior to treating.

EGG: First scrape off any solid matter. Then, soak the fabric in a glass or plastic container with any enzyme-soaking product, such as Biz Non Chlorine Bleach™. Soak for at least 6 hours or overnight. If a stain remains, work in powder detergent, rubbing vigorously between your thumbs. Rinse and wash as usual. Check the garment carefully for any remaining stain when you remove it from the washer. Don't apply heat until all of the stain is removed or the stain will become permanent.

You can also try treating the area with cool water and unseasoned meat tenderizer. Work this into the area well, and allow it to sit for a few hours, being sure to keep the area moist. Continue treating until no stain remains.

Take nonwashables to the dry cleaner as soon as possible. Quick treatment is important. Make sure you identify the stain to your cleaner so it can be treated properly and promptly.

EYELINER AND EYE SHADOW: See Cosmetics.

FABRIC SOFTENER SPOTS: For the greasy spots that sometimes appear on clothes after drying with dryer fabric softener sheets, dampen the spot and rub with pure bar soap and relaunder.

For spots from liquid fabric softener, rub with undiluted liquid dish soap and relaunder.

FELT TIP MARKER: See Marker.

FOOD DYE: Fruit juices, gelatin desserts, fruit smoothies, and frozen fruit sticks all contain food dye that can leave a nasty stain on clothes.

Treating the stain while it is still fresh is the very best thing you can do. If you are out in public and don't have access to any cleaning supplies, wet the spot with club soda or cool water and blot, blot, blot. If you are at home, then treat the spot with 1 cup of cool water to which you have added 1 tablespoon of ammonia. Once you have flushed the spot well with this solution, grab the salt shaker and rub salt into the wound . . . I mean stain! Let this sit for an hour or so, and then brush off the salt. If the stain is still visible, retreat the same way.

You can also try stretching the fabric tight and holding it under a forceful stream of cold water. This will flush out much of the spot without spreading it. Next, rub in your favorite detergent, scrubbing vigorously between your thumbs. Rinse again in cool water. Do not apply heat to the stain until it is completely removed.

I have had great success soaking food dye spills in Brilliant Bleach® (follow the directions for hand-soaking on the container).

If you are dealing with a red, orange, or purple stain, try Wine Away Red Wine Stain Remover™, used according to directions. Don't be fooled by the name—it is great for all red-type stains. You will be amazed!

Remember, if the stain is not removed during the spotting process, it will not come out in the laundry!

FRUIT AND FRUIT JUICE (also see Berries): These stains absolutely must be removed before the fabric is washed. The combination of heat and age will set fruit stains and they will be impossible to remove, even for the Queen.

Sponge or spray the area immediately with soda water or seltzer. If these products aren't available, use cold water. *Do not use hot water.* Rinse the offending spot as soon as possible while it is still wet. Rub in your favorite detergent and scrub the area between your thumbs. *Now* rinse under hot running water—as hot as the fabric can tolerate. Pull the fabric taut and allow the full force of the water to flow through the area. The stronger the flow the better.

If the stain is still visible after this treatment, make a paste of 20 Mule Team® Borax and warm water, and work it into the stained area. Let this dry and brush off. Repeat as needed. You can also try pulling the fabric tight over a bowl, using a rubber band to secure it. Sprinkle 20 Mule Team® Borax over the stain and, using the hottest water possible for the fabric type, start at the outside edge of the stain and pour the water through the borax in circles until you are pouring through the center of the stain.

Fresh fruit stains, if treated promptly, will usually come out. Quick treatment is especially important for fruits such as peach and citrus.

Old Fruit Stains: Before you can remove the stain you must reconstitute it. You can do this by applying glycerin to the area. Rub it in well and allow to soak for 30 minutes. Treat as above.

For nonwashable fabrics, gently sponge the stain with cold water as soon as it occurs and then take to a dry cleaner as quickly as possible. Be sure to identify the stain so it can be treated properly.

If the stains are red in nature, use Wine Away Red Wine Stain Remover™ as directed in the section on berry stains.

FURNITURE POLISH: Furniture polish is usually an oil-based stain, so it must be reconstituted. Restore the oil in the polish by spraying with WD-40® Lubricant. Allow the lubricant to soak for 10 minutes, then work in undiluted dishwashing liquid. Work this in well between your thumbs to remove the grease. Flush with a forceful stream of the hottest water you can for the fabric type. Pretreat with a product such as Zout®, which is great for grease spots, and launder as usual.

You can also try cleaning the area with Energine Cleaning Fluid®, used according to can directions.

If the furniture polish has color in it, refer to the section on dye.

GLUE, ADHESIVES, MUCILAGE: Modern adhesives and glues are very hard to remove. You may have to use a special solvent. Take the garment to the dry cleaner and be sure to identify the spot.

Here's a rundown of glue types and how to remove them.

Model glue: Can usually be removed with nail polish remover containing acetone, although you may need to purchase straight acetone at the hardware store or the beauty supply. Always test the acetone in a small area first.

Plastic adhesives: For best results, treat these stains before they dry. Try washing in cool water and detergent. If the stain remains, bring 1 cup or so of white vinegar to a boil, and immerse the stain. Have more vinegar boiling as you treat the stain so that you can switch to the hot vinegar as soon as the first cup starts to cool. Continue reheating the vinegar and treating for 15 to 20 minutes.

Rubber cement: Scrape off all that you can with a dull, straight edge that you can throw away. (Don't use a credit card for this—unless it's over its limit!) Treat with Energine Cleaning Fluid® as directed.

You can also try working petroleum jelly into the glue until it pills into balls that you can then scrape from the fabric. Treat the area with undiluted liquid dish soap and launder in the hottest water the fabric will tolerate.

Miscellaneous glues: Sponge or rinse the fabric in warm water. Work in your favorite powdered detergent or liquid detergent along with some 20 Mule Team® Borax. Rub vigorously between your thumbs. Rinse and wash in the hottest water you can for the fabric type.

Remember, soap and water will remove most synthetic glue when the spot is fresh. Acetone will remove most clear, plastic cement-type glues. Make sure to test acetone in an inconspicuous area, and never use on acetate fabrics—it will dissolve them.

For old, dried glue stains, soak the fabric in a solution of boiling hot white vinegar and water. Use 2 parts white vinegar to every 10 parts of water and soak for 30 to 60 minutes. You may need to scrape off the glue as it softens. Then pretreat and launder as usual.

GRASS, FLOWERS AND FOLIAGE: There are several ways to remove grass stains from fabrics. Pick one and try it. If it doesn't completely remove the stain, try another. Don't put clothes into the dryer until the grass stain is removed.

"Who, in their infinite wisdom, decreed that Little League uniforms be white? Certainly not a mother."

—Erma Bombeck

First a word of caution: Avoid using alkalis such as ammonia, degreasers or alkaline detergents. They interact with the tannin in the grass stains and may permanently set the stain.

Okay—first, washable fabrics: Sponge on rubbing alcohol, repeating several times. If the stain persists, sponge with white vinegar and rinse. Work in your favorite laundry detergent and rinse well.

Rubbing white nongel toothpaste into grass stains will often remove them. Rub well, then rinse and wash as usual.

For jeans, apply undiluted alcohol to the area and allow to soak 15 minutes before laundering as usual.

Zout® and Spot Shot Carpet Stain Remover® also work very well on grass stains. Follow the label directions. Biz All Fabric Bleach™ made into a paste with cold water is effective in treating stubborn grass stains too.

For grass on white leather shoes, rub the grass stain with molasses and leave it on the shoe overnight. Wash the molasses off with hot soap and water, and the grass stain should be gone.

For grass on suede fabric, including shoes, rub the stain with a sponge dipped in glycerin. Then rub with a cloth dipped in undiluted white vinegar, brush the nap gently to reset, and allow to dry and brush again. Remember: test in an inconspicuous spot first.

GRAVY: With gravy you need to remove the starch used to thicken it, so you will want to soak the garment in cold water long enough to dissolve the starch. It may take several hours.

Pretreat prior to laundering with a good spotter, such as Zout®, Spot Shot Carpet Stain Remover® or Whink Wash Away Laundry Stain Remover™. Launder in the hottest possible water for the fabric type.

You can also soak the garment in Brilliant Bleach®, for days if necessary.

GREASE AND OIL (including cooking oil and salad dressing): Grease and oil must be removed thoroughly, otherwise a semitransparent stain will set and will turn dark from all the soil it attracts.

To treat a grease stain it helps to know whether it is from animal oil, vegetable oil or automotive oil.

To remove a grease stain, first remove as much of the greasy substance as possible without forcing the grease further down into the fabric fibers. Use a paper towel to blot and absorb all the grease that you can. Next, apply a drawing agent such as baking soda, cornstarch, or talcum powder. Rub it in gently and let it sit for 15 to 30 minutes to allow the agent to absorb and draw the grease out of the fabric. Brush the powder off thoroughly and check the stain. If it looks like you can absorb more grease, repeat the process.

Next, lay the fabric over a thick rag or a heavy fold of paper towels. Working from the back of the fabric, blot with Energine Cleaning Fluid®. Change the pad under the fabric as needed and repeat if necessary.

When grease stains are stubborn, we need to fall back on the idea that grease removes grease. Spray the grease spot with WD-40® Lubricant and let it soak for 10 minutes, then work in undiluted dishwashing liquid and work well between your thumbs. Flush with the hottest water you can for the fabric, pretreat and launder as usual. Do not use this method on silk or crease-resistant finishes.

Many grease stains will eventually turn yellow when set with age and heat. Treat these stains by soaking in diluted hydrogen peroxide or Brilliant Bleach®. Don't use this process unless you know that the clothes are colorfast.

Use Energine Cleaning Fluid® on dry-clean-only fabrics, or take to a professional dry cleaner.

For heavily soiled, greasy work clothes, try pouring a can of original Coca-Cola® in the washer with your detergent and launder as usual. The combination of sugar and cola syrup works wonders!

GUM: The best way to deal with gum is to harden it first. Harden any item marred by chewing gum by placing it in a plastic bag in the freezer and leaving it overnight. Immediately upon removing the bag from the freezer, scrape off any gum that you can with a dull straight edge. If all the gum is removed, treat the fabric with an equal mixture of white vinegar and liquid dish soap. You may also try treating the area with lighter fluid, although you must do this outside and use extreme care, testing the fabric first.

Sometimes rubbing the area with egg white (*not* the yolk—no joke!) will remove the remaining residue.

If gum is still trapped, try working petroleum jelly into the fibers, and scraping off the little balls that form. Be sure to follow the directions under Grease in this section to remove the grease from the petroleum jelly.

Petroleum jelly will also soften old, dry gum. You want to work the petroleum jelly into the gum and then scrape off all that you can.

For those of you who ask, yes, peanut butter will work too, but it is messier. My advice is to eat the peanut butter and use the petroleum jelly!

Carbona® makes a Stain Devil for Chewing Gum Removal. It's a great little specialty spotter.

For dry-clean-only fabrics, you may freeze the fabric and scrape off what gum you can. Take it to your dry cleaner right away.

HAIR DYE: If you didn't listen to me when I told you to dye your hair naked in the backyard, then hair-dye spots may be a major problem for you. Here's what to do:

Clothing or fabrics stained with hair dye should be washed in warm water, to which you have added white vinegar and your normal detergent. Do this in a sink or container, adding about 2 tablespoons of detergent and 2 cups of white vinegar to a gallon of warm water. Let it soak for several hours.

If the stain still remains, try our favorite bleach, Brilliant Bleach®. You can soak whites and colorfast fabrics for several days if necessary, without damage. Try to avoid the hair dye problem if you can. I suggest using the same old towel when you do your hair.

HAND CREAM: Blot off all that you can and treat with Energine Cleaning Fluid®, working from the back of the fabric. Once all of the stain is removed, launder as usual.

ICE CREAM: Yummy-yummy in the tummy—not so great on clothes! Sponge the garment as quickly as possible with cold water, club soda, or seltzer. If a stain still remains, treat it with cold water and unseasoned meat tenderizer. Let this soak on the fabric for about 30 minutes or so and then flush with cold water to see if the offending spot is gone. Pretreat with Spot Shot Carpet Stain Remover® or Zout® and launder as usual.

If a grease spot remains, treat with Energine Cleaning Fluid® working from the back of the fabric over a pad of paper towels to absorb the spot and the spotting solution.

Sometimes treating ice cream-stained fabric with a small amount of ammonia will also work. Then, of course, launder as usual.

INK: How can one little pen cause so much grief? The first line of offense is rubbing alcohol. Sponge the ink mark, or dip it into a glass of rubbing alcohol, letting it soak until the offending spot is removed. Don't be tricked into using hair spray. That may have worked in the past, but hair spray now contains a lot of oil, and that just spreads the stain.

Denatured alcohol—a much stronger version of rubbing alcohol—may be more effective. Test this first in an inconspicuous spot, as denatured alcohol may damage some fabrics.

You also can try using acetone. This too must be tested. (And remember, *never* use acetone on acetates.)

White, nongel toothpaste rubbed firmly and vigorously into the stain may work. After this method be sure to pretreat and launder as usual.

Often just soaking ink stains in milk will dissolve them.

Turpentine is effective on very challenging ink stains. Working over a pad of paper towels, tap the spot on the back of the fabric using the back of a spoon or an old toothbrush. Don't rub. Work in undiluted dishwashing liquid prior to laundering, and wash in the hottest water possible for the fabric type. Dispose of all paper, etc., saturated with turpentine immediately—outside, please.

Some inks only respond to solvents, so you may need to use Energine Cleaning Fluid®.

On leather, remove ballpoint ink by rubbing with cuticle remover or petroleum jelly. You may need to leave it on the stained area for several days to achieve success.

On vinyl, believe it or not, the best thing is for you to be so mad that you could spit! Saliva will remove ballpoint ink from vinyl—as long as you are quick. Apply generously and wipe with a soft cloth. For old stains, apply glycerin, let it soak for 30 minutes or so, and then attempt to wash the stain away with a wet soft cloth rubbed over a bar of soap.

KETCHUP: See Tomato-based stains.

KOOL-AID™: Flush the spot as quickly as possible with club soda and then hold under forceful running water. If a stained area still remains, soak in Brilliant Bleach® until the stain is removed. This may take hours or days, depending on the fabric and the stain. Soak only white or colorfast clothes in Brilliant Bleach®.

For red, grape, fruit punch, and other red Kool-Aid™ flavors, treat with Wine Away Red Wine Stain Remover™ for instantaneous stain removal.

LIPSTICK: Lipstick is actually an oily dye stain. Water, heat or wet spotters will only spread it and make the problem worse and set the stain.

Rub in vegetable oil, WD-40® Lubricant or mineral oil and let it sit on the spot for 15 to 30 minutes. Next sponge the area with a little ammonia—sudsy or clear is fine.

Now, before you launder, work in undiluted liquid dish soap to be sure you have removed all of the oil.

Another method I have had real success with is GOJO Crème Waterless Hand Cleaner®. Look for this at hardware stores and home centers. Work it into the lipstick, rubbing between your thumbs vigorously. Launder as usual. This method is great for the smear of lipstick on cloth table napkins.

In an emergency, try spraying the spot with a little hair spray. Let this sit for a few minutes and then wipe gently with a damp cloth. Test this method in an inconspicuous spot first.

You will also find that Zout®, Spot Shot Carpet Stain Remover® and Whink Wash Away Laundry Spotter™ are generally effective on lipstick.

For really stubborn, old stains, try moistening with denatured alcohol, then treat with undiluted liquid dish soap.

If you are getting dressed and you accidentally get lipstick on your clothes, try rubbing the stain with white bread. (Yes, it has to be white!)

MAKEUP (oily foundation, powder, cream blush, cover creams): Sprinkle baking soda on the makeup smudge, then brush the area with an old wet toothbrush until the makeup is removed. Nongel white toothpaste scrubbed with a toothbrush is also effective.

Liquid dish soap or shampoo will generally remove makeup stains. Work the product into the stain vigorously between your thumbs.

For stubborn makeup stains use nonoily makeup remover, pretreat and launder as usual. (See also Cosmetics.)

MARKER, WASHABLE: Rinse the stain from the fabric with cold water until no more color can be removed. Place the fabric on paper towels and saturate the back of the fabric with alcohol, using a cotton ball to blot the stain. Replace the paper towels as needed as they absorb the color. Work in Fels-Naptha Soap® until the spot is well lathered and wash in hot water with laundry detergent and fabric-appropriate bleach. Rinse in warm water.

MARKER, PERMANENT: First of all, permanent usually means permanent. But before you give up and throw in the towel—or blouse, or pants, or whatever—here are some things to try.

Fill a glass with denatured alcohol (use a size appropriate to the stain) and dip the stained area into the alcohol, allowing it to soak. If it appears that the marker is being removed, continue the process.

If the stain appears stubborn, try scrubbing the marker spot with an old toothbrush, white, nongel toothpaste, and some baking soda. Give it a really good scrubbing. Rinse. If the marker stain is almost gone, soak in a cup of warm water and 2 denture-cleaning tablets for whites, and Brilliant Bleach® for colorfast clothes. This will require some time, but the stain all comes out, so it's worth it.

If the marker is still there, scrub with Lava™ soap prior to trying the denture-cleaning tablets or bleach.

Good luck. And look out for those big black permanent markers and those Sharpies™. They're great pens, but they're murder on clothes! I can't even tell you how many times I have "accidentally" written on my clothes during a book signing with a Sharpie™ in my hand!

MAYONNAISE: See Grease.

MEAT JUICES: Once dry, meat juices are very tough to remove, so it's important to react quickly. Sponge the area immediately with cold water (not hot—it will set the stain), or with club soda. Next, apply unseasoned meat tenderizer and cold water, working the mixture in well. Let it sit for 30 to 60 minutes. Pretreat and launder as usual, but be sure to use *cool* water.

On dry-clean-only fabrics, sponge with cold water and take to a professional cleaner.

MEDICINES: It would be impossible to list all the medicines on the market. But this section should give you an idea of what to look out for, as well as what to do for each family of medicine.

Alcohol: Medicines containing alcohol stain quickly. Treat these stains as you would spilled alcohol.

Iron: Iron or medicines containing iron products should be treated as rust.

Oily Medicines: Oily medicines should be treated with a degreasing product. I have had great luck with Soapworks® At Home All-Purpose Cleaner, used undiluted. Work it in well and then rinse.

You can also treat these stains as you would an oil or grease stain.

Syrups: Cough syrup or children's medicines can usually be removed with water. Soak the fabric with cool water as soon as possible. Running cold water full force through the fabric can be helpful, and you may also want to try working in Fels-Naptha®, or soaking the stain in Biz Non Chlorine Bleach™ or Brilliant Bleach®. If the syrup is red, use Wine Away Red Wine Stain Remover™. (See, I told you not to be fooled by its name! It is murder on red stains!)

MILDEW: Mildew is a fungus that grows and flourishes in warm, humid, dark conditions, like the shower, the basement, etc. The best way to avoid mildew is to ensure that things are totally dry *before* you put them away. Invisible spores can quickly grow to huge proportions, especially on natural materials such as cotton, wool, leather, paper, wood, etc.

Air needs to circulate to keep mildew from forming, so do not crowd clothes into closets.

Store clothing only after it has been cleaned and dried thoroughly.

If you are storing things such as leather purses, belts, shoes, even suitcases, clean them well, then sit them in the sun for an hour or so. Do not store things in plastic as this caters to damp conditions.

If you smell a damp or musty smell coming from a closet, suspect mildew immediately and act quickly to dry it out. Even allowing a fan to blow in the closet overnight can make a huge difference by drying and circulating the air.

Okay—here's what to do if you already have mildew stains on fabrics. First, try working some Fels-Naptha Laundry Bar Soap® into the area and laundering. If stains remain and the fabric will tolerate chlorine bleach, soak it in 1 gallon of cold water to which you have added 2 to 3 tablespoons of chlorine bleach.

Moistening white or colorfast clothes with lemon juice, sprinkling them with salt and laying the garment in the sun may also remove mildew. If in doubt, test this method first.

Leather presents a different challenge. Take the item outside and brush off all the powdery mildew that you can with a soft brush. Wipe the leather with equal parts of rubbing alcohol and water, or try massaging cuticle remover into the area. After 10 minutes, wipe vigorously with a soft cloth.

Wash leather with a complexion bar soap such as Dove® or Caress™ and buff dry—do not rinse.

Remember: with mildew, the best defense is a good offense, so try to keep it from occurring.

MILK/CREAM/WHIPPING CREAM/HALF AND HALF: Rinse fabric under a cold, forceful stream of water from the faucet. Treat with unseasoned meat tenderizer and cool water. Allow to soak for 30 minutes, then flush with cool water again. If greasy-looking marks remain, treat with Energine Cleaning Fluid®, working from the back of the fabric over a heavy pad of paper towels. Launder as usual.

Treat washable fabrics stained from milk by flushing with cool water before working in detergent and a little ammonia. Wash in cool water and air-dry.

For dry-clean-only fabrics, take to a professional as soon as possible and identify the stain when you drop off the item.

MUD: The key word here is *dry.* Let mud dry. Never treat a wet mud stain other than lifting off any solid pieces with a dull straight edge. Once mud has dried, take the vacuum cleaner and vacuum the area with the hose attachment. You'll achieve the greatest suction that way. This may be a two-person job. One to hold the fabric, one to hold the hose.

Rub the cut side of a potato over the mud stain and launder as usual.

For stubborn stains, sponge with equal portions of rubbing alcohol and cool water. For red mud stains, treat with a rust remover. (See Rust.) Rubbing 20 Mule Team® Borax into a dampened mud stain will often remove it.

Spraying with Spot Shot Carpet Stain Remover® prior to laundering is also helpful.

MUSTARD: The word makes me shiver! This is a terrible stain to attempt (notice I said *attempt*) to remove.

The turmeric in mustard is what gives mustard its distinctive bright yellow color—it's also what would make it a darn good dye!

Remove as much of the mustard as possible, using a dull straight edge. Next, flex the fabric to break the grip of the embedded residue on the fabric fibers. Apply glycerin (hand cream section, drugstore) and let it sit at least an hour. Pretreat and launder as usual.

If the fabric is white or colorfast, soak the stain in hydrogen peroxide for 30 minutes. Again, Brilliant Bleach® may remove the stain after a lengthy soaking.

For white clothes, dissolve a denture-cleaning tablet in ½ cup of cool water and allow the stained area to soak.

Things to avoid: Ammonia and heat. They will both set the stain and you will never get it out.

Kind of makes you think that ketchup and relish are all you need on that hotdog, doesn't it!

MYSTERY STAINS: These are spots and spills that you have no idea where they came from. The unknowns. Here's what to do:

* Blot with cool water (hot water sets stains).
* Blot with a sponge or cloth dampened with water and a teaspoon or so of white vinegar (not for cotton or linen).
* Blot with a sponge or cloth dampened with water and a teaspoon or so of clear ammonia (again, not for cotton or linen).
* Blot with rubbing alcohol diluted 50/50 with cool water.
* Sponge with a solution of Brilliant Bleach® and water.

NAIL POLISH: Okay, if you had polished your nails naked in the backyard you wouldn't be reading this, would you? Stretch the fabric over a glass bowl and make a little trampoline by securing the fabric with a rubber band. Drip acetone-based polish remover through the stain with a stainless steel spoon (not silver) and tap the stain with the edge of the spoon. Continue dripping the acetone through the fabric until the polish is removed. This requires time and patience. If you run out of either, walk away and come back later. Straight acetone, purchased at the hardware store or beauty supply, may work faster, but be sure to test an area first.

If a color stain remains after the polish is removed, dilute hydrogen peroxide (50 percent peroxide, 50 percent water) apply to the stain, and sit the fabric in the sun, keeping it moist with the peroxide solution. Do this only for white or colorfast clothes.

Do not use acetone on silk or acetates, and always test the acetone on an inconspicuous area prior to beginning.

Nonwashable fabrics should be dry-cleaned.

ODORS: Eliminate odors, don't use a perfumed cover-up. I like ODORZ-OUT™ odor eliminator because it absorbs odors and removes them permanently—without leaving any telltale smells behind. It is nontoxic and safe for all surfaces, and it can be used wet or dry. It is also safe for the environment and a little goes a long way. Keep some on hand. It's great for just about any odor you're likely to come across, such as smoke, mildew, mold, feces, urine, food odors, any kind of odor. Do not use a perfumed cover-up.

OIL (also see Grease and oil): Blot up all oil quickly. Avoid rubbing or you will force the oil further into the fibers. Pretreat washable fabrics with your favorite spot remover, or use one recommended for oily stains in this book. Launder in the hottest possible water for the fabric.

Nonwashables should be dry-cleaned.

OINTMENT (A and D ointment, Desitin, zinc oxide): Anyone who has had a baby will be familiar with this problem stain. Use hot water and detergent, rubbing the fabric against itself to remove the oil. If the stain remains, treat as indicated in the section on Grease and oil.

For zinc oxide, soak the garment in white vinegar for 30 minutes after treating as above, then launder as usual.

PAINT, LATEX: Treat this stain immediately for best results. It is important to remove paint *before* it dries, so keep the stain wet if you can't work on it right away.

Flush the paint from the fabric with a forceful stream of warm water. Next, treat the stain with a solution of liquid dish soap and water, or laundry detergent and water. Work it into the stained area, soaping and rinsing until the stain is removed. Do this as many times as necessary. If the fabric is colorfast, you can also work in some automatic dishwasher detergent and let it soak on the fabric for 5 to 10 minutes before laundering as usual.

You can also try a product aptly named OOPS!™ Just follow the directions on the can closely.

On fabrics such as cotton and polyester, try spraying the garment with oven cleaner and letting it sit about 15 to 30 minutes before flushing with plenty of water. Use *extreme* care with this method and use it at your own risk. Some fabrics cannot tolerate the oven cleaner, but if the garment is ruined by the paint, it is worth a try. Also use care where you spray the oven cleaner and what you sit the fabric on afterward.

PAINT, OIL-BASED: Get busy and remove this spill ASAP. You're out of luck if it dries. If you must go to the store for products, keep the spill moist: *Do not allow oil-based paint to dry.*

Check the paint can and use the thinner recommended by the manufacturer. Sometimes thinner for correction fluid will also work. Remember to test an area first with these two methods.

I fall back on turpentine when all else fails. Work the turpentine into the spill, and once the paint is removed, work in GOJO Crème Waterless Hand Cleaner®. That will take out the oiliness from the turpentine. Remember to dispose of turpentine-soaked rags or paper towels outside, as soon as possible.

When working on a paint spill, work from the back of the fabric over a thick pad of paper towels. Tap the stained area with an old toothbrush or an old spoon as you work to force the paint out.

Now that you have removed the stain, saturate it with detergent and work in vigorously. Cover the area with the hottest water you can use for the fabric, and let it soak overnight. Scrub again, between your thumbs, and launder as usual.

PENCIL: Okay, how easy is this? Take a nice, clean, soft eraser, and gently rub the offending mark away! Just be sure the eraser is clean, or you will create a large stain. If the spot is stubborn, sponge with Energine Cleaning Fluid®.

PERFUME: Follow the directions in the section on Alcoholic beverages. A few words to the wise: The best time to put it on is right before you put on your clothes, not after. And never spray perfume directly on your clothes. This will damage them. The combination of alcohol and oil is death to fabrics.

PERSPIRATION STAINS: These stains really are the pits, so I've devoted an entire chapter to their removal. Also check out the section in this stain removal guide on Antiperspirants and deodorants.

PURPLE OR BLUISH COLOR ON SYNTHETIC FIBERS: Sometimes synthetic fibers will develop a purple tinge after repeated laundering. Remove it with Rit Color Remover™ and launder as usual.

RUST: On white fabrics, saturate with lemon juice and sprinkle with salt, then lay in the sun. (No, not you—the fabric!) If the rust is stubborn, apply the lemon juice and salt, and pour water through the stain. Use boiling water if the fabric will tolerate it; otherwise use hot. Check the care label.

You can also cover the stained area with cream of tartar, then gather up the edges of the fabric and dip the spot in hot water. Let stand 5 to 10 minutes and then launder as usual.

There are good commercial rust removers on the market. Try Whink Rust Remover®, Magica®, and Rust Magic®. Be sure to read directions carefully when using commercial rust removers. Some cannot be used on colored fabric, so check carefully.

SAP, PINE TAR: See Tar.

SCORCH MARKS: Sorry to say, but severe scorch marks cannot be removed.

Light scorch marks may be treated with a cloth dampened with 1 part 3 percent hydrogen peroxide and 3 parts of water. Lay the cloth over the scorch mark and press with a medium/hot iron. Do not iron off of the cloth or you will scorch the fabric again. Make sure to try this method first in a small, inconspicuous space.

If the scorch is still visible, moisten the spot with the diluted peroxide and lay it in the sun.

Very light scorch marks may also be removed by wetting them with water and laying the garment in the sun.

If the scorch mark has appeared on white clothes, saturate the scorched area with lemon juice and lay it in the sun. Keep it moist with the lemon juice until the stain is removed.

For white cottons, sometimes boiling in ½ cup of soap and 2 quarts of milk will remove the stain. Try this at your own risk. Some fabrics may not tolerate boiling.

For light scorches you can also rub the fabric with the cut side of a white onion (not a red onion—it will stain) and then soak the fabric in cold water for several hours. Launder as usual.

Remember: scorching weakens fibers, so use care and always relaunder the item once the scorch mark has been removed.

SHOE POLISH: Work laundry detergent into the fabric immediately and rinse. For persistent stains, sponge with alcohol. Use undiluted alcohol on white clothes, and 1 part alcohol to 2 parts water on colored fabrics. Rinse again, or try using turpentine after first testing in an inconspicuous spot.

Shoe polish has an oily base containing dye. Using the wrong things such as water, heat, or wet spotters will spread and set the stain. Work in vegetable oil or WD-40® Lubricant and let it sit for 15 minutes. Sponge on a little ammonia (not on silk, please), then work in undiluted dishwashing liquid and launder as usual.

Energine Cleaning Fluid® may also help to eliminate the final stained area.

If you have any discoloration remaining from the dye in the shoe polish, soak the fabric in Brilliant Bleach® until the stain is removed.

If the shoe polish stain is old and heavy, you may need to treat it with petroleum jelly. Cover the polish and work in the petroleum jelly, let it soak for 30 to 60 minutes, and then scrape off all that you can of the polish and the petroleum jelly. Work in undiluted dishwashing liquid and flush with a forceful stream of hot water. Pretreat and launder as usual.

Liquid shoe polish: Blot up all that you can from the fabric. Do not rub—this will spread the stain. Do not apply water. Instead, saturate with alcohol—undiluted for whites, diluted as above for colors. Continue to flush with alcohol, work in your favorite laundry detergent, then rub vigorously to remove all trace of the stain.

SILK SPOTS: Spots on silk are hard to remove and must be handled with care.

Dry-cleaning solvent may spot-clean silk, but you're likely to be left with a ring on the fabric. Make sure to use the blow-dryer on the spot to avoid that telltale ring.

For unusual or heavy stains, take to a professional. Too much rubbing can remove the color from silk.

SILLY PUTTY®: First of all, let gravity do the work for you. Lay the fabric over a bowl and let it simply drop off. You'll only have to clean up what's left!

Scrape off the balance of any Silly Putty® with a dull edge such as an old credit card or knife back. Spray with WD-40® Lubricant and let stand a few minutes. Scrape again, removing all the Silly Putty® that you can. Continue to do this, changing from the dull straight edge to cotton balls. If any stain remains, saturate a cotton ball with rubbing alcohol, blot the stain, and rinse. Work in liquid dish soap and launder as usual in the hottest water you can for the fabric type.

If you don't have WD-40® Lubricant, use petroleum jelly instead.

SOFT DRINKS: See Cola and soft drinks.

SOOT: Launder clothing in the hottest possible water for the fabric with your normal detergent, ½ cup of 20 Mule Team® Borax and ½ cup of Arm and Hammer® Washing Soda.

STICKERS: Heat white vinegar and apply it, undiluted, directly to the fabric. Allow the vinegar to soak until the sticker can be peeled back with ease.

TAR: Lift off as much solid matter as possible using a plastic (disposable) knife. Spread the stained area over a heavy pad of paper towels and apply glycerin to the fabric, tapping it with the back of an old toothbrush or plastic spoon. Change the paper towels as they absorb the tar. Finally, once you have removed all the tar you can, work in some turpentine or eucalyptus oil. Flush the stained area with alcohol, or work in undiluted liquid dish soap. Pretreat and launder as usual. Spot Shot Carpet Stain Remover® is a good spotter for this.

Dried tar: Warm the glycerin or some olive oil and spread over the area, allowing it to soak until the tar is loosened. Then proceed as above.

Nonwashables should be taken to the dry cleaner as soon as possible.

TEA: See Coffee and tea.

TOMATO-BASED STAINS (ketchup, spaghetti sauce, tomato sauce, barbecue sauce, etc.): Flush these stains well with cool water as soon as possible. Make sure you apply water to the back of the fabric. Apply white vinegar and then flush again with a forceful stream of water.

Apply Wine Away Red Wine Stain Remover™ per package directions.

URINE: Fresh urine stains are fairly easy to remove. First rinse well, flushing with lots of cool water. Presoak using an enzyme powder or Biz All Fabric Bleach™. Then launder as usual.

You may also soak urine-stained fabric in salt water, then rinse and launder as usual.

If the color of the fabric has changed due to the urine, sponge the area or spray with clear ammonia, then rinse and launder as usual.

For old urine stains: Soak in clear hot water for an hour—the hotter the better. Add detergent and wash as usual, then rinse. Use the appropriate bleach for the fabric type, or Brilliant Bleach™ if you prefer.

See also the treatment mentioned under Odors.

VOMIT: Shake off or scrape what you can over the toilet. Flush the fabric from the wrong side with cool water, using a forceful stream. Once you have removed solid matter and excess liquid, make a paste of liquid laundry soap and 20 Mule Team® Borax and vigorously scrub the fabric. Rinse with salt water, pretreat and launder as usual.

Quick treatment is important to avoid stains from foods and stomach acid.

See also the treatment mentioned for Odors.

WINE: Never serve red wine without having white wine nearby! And always tend to the stain *as soon as you can!*

For red wine spills, dilute the spot with white wine, then flush with cool water and apply salt.

If no white wine is available, sprinkle heavily with salt and flush with club soda or cool water.

Applying a paste of 20 Mule Team® Borax and water usually works.

For red wine spills and other red stains, keep Wine Away Red Wine Stain Remover™ on hand. It is totally nontoxic and works so fast on red wine and red stains that even I am still amazed. The directions are simple and easy. Blot up the spill, apply the Wine Away™ and watch the red stain disappear. Blot with a wet cloth. You'll thank me many times for this one!

YELLOW SPOTS AND STAINS: These stains are common on white clothes and linens. Denture-cleaning tablets will generally remove these stains. Fill a basin with water and add one or two tablets. Allow the tablets to dissolve and then soak the fabric until the yellow is removed.

62

Cleaning Guide for Fabric Types

In these next pages, I am going to walk you through laundry procedures for certain fabric types and unusual items.

Acetate: This is a temperamental fabric. Do not allow it to become heavily soiled and do not use an enzyme detergent when laundering. Acetate is commonly used for curtains, brocades, taffetas, and satin. (Think evening wear.) It's also a popular lining. You can machine wash acetate in cold water or you can hand wash. Be sure not to spin or wring acetate as this will set wrinkles. Rinse extremely well and press with a cool (low setting) iron on the wrong side of the fabric.

Acrylic: This fabric should be laundered frequently since it can retain perspiration odors. Acrylic is usually machine washable in cool water. Check the care label. Dry flat or hang to dry, being sure to reshape the garment while it is still damp.

Angora: This wool is made from rabbit fur or goat hair. Angora sheds a lot, although if it's blended with nylon it will shed less. Wash angora in warm or cool water using a very mild soap or a little shampoo. Do not rub, twist, or lift the garment up and down in the water as this will cause stretching. Washing in a sink is best. Let the water run out and then press the liquid out of the garment. Rinse well again, pressing the water out. Roll the garment in a towel and then reshape. Dry flat out of the sun. Do not press—instead, hold a steam iron just above the garment to remove wrinkles.

Blends: Blends, such as cotton/polyester, are made from combined fibers. To launder these fabrics, follow the guidelines for the most delicate or the most prominent fiber. The most common blends are cotton/polyester, cotton/linen, and silk/polyester.

Brocades: Use care when laundering brocades. You don't want to crush or flatten the pile design. Hand wash in cool water or dry clean according to the care label. Do not wring. Iron on the "wrong" side using a press cloth or towel between the fabric and the iron.

Canvas: A heavy, firm, very tightly woven fabric, canvas was originally made from cotton or linen, but now it comes in synthetics or blends. Machine wash canvas in cold water and tumble dry on a low setting. Test for colorfastness before washing. If it's not colorfast, have it dry-cleaned.

Cashmere: This is an expensive fiber that comes from the undercoat of cashmere goats. Treat it with respect. Dry-clean these prizes or hand wash with care in cool water and well-dissolved gentle soap. Rinse well and do not wring. Dry flat, reshaping the garment as it dries. Iron on the "wrong" side while still damp with a cool iron, if necessary.

Chiffon: This is a very thin, transparent fabric, made from silk or synthetic fibers. Hand wash as you would silk.

Chintz: Glazed cotton, and often printed. Dry-clean this fabric unless the label states that it can be washed. Follow the care label instructions carefully.

Corduroy: Take care when washing corduroy. It wears well, but care is needed to avoid crushing and distorting the pile. Turn corduroy inside out and launder using warm water. Dry at a normal setting. Remove from the dryer while still damp and smooth the seams, pockets, etc. Hang to complete drying, and iron on the "wrong" side of the fabric. Pile may be restored by brushing gently.

Cotton: This natural vegetable fiber is woven and knitted into fabrics in all weights and textures. Hand wash lightweight fabrics such as organdy and batiste and hang to air dry. Iron when damp with a hot iron.

Machine wash light-colored and white medium to heavyweight cottons in warm water. Use cold water for bright colors that may bleed. Dry on a low dryer setting. Remove from the dryer while still damp and iron with a hot iron right away.

Damask: This is a jacquard-weave fabric. It may be made of cotton, linen, silk, wool, or a blend. Hand wash lightweight fabrics and be sure to check the individual fiber listings. Dry-clean silk, wool and all heavier-weight fabrics.

Denim: If you have jeans, you know this strong fabric is prone to shrinking, streaking and fading. Machine wash denim in warm water. Blue and other deep colors bleed the first several washings, so be sure to wash separately. Washing older, faded jeans with the new ones will restore some of their original color. Dry at low settings to avoid shrinkage. Iron while damp if necessary and be aware that jeans may bleed color onto your ironing board.

Down: Down is the soft underfeather of waterfowl that is often combined with adult feathers. It is machine washable and dry-cleanable. Just be sure to follow the care label closely. Much of the treatment will depend on the fabric covering the down, so pay attention to manufacturer's directions.

Do not air-dry down. It dries too slowly and mold or mildew may form in the process. Dry in your dryer, using a large-capacity dryer if need be. Set temperatures low (under 140 degrees), fluffing and turning the item often. Make sure to dry the item thoroughly. This can take time.

Want really fluffy duvets and pillows? Putting a clean tennis shoe or tennis ball in with the item will fluff it up!

Flannel: Flannel is actually a napped fabric, and it comes in a plain or twill-type weave. Cotton and synthetics should be washed according to the care label, but when in doubt, use cool water and mild detergent. Dry at a low dryer setting and remove flannel while damp to avoid wrinkles. You may also line-dry this fabric. Wool flannel should be dry-cleaned.

Gabardine: Firm, tightly woven twill fabric, often worsted wool, but sometimes made of cotton and synthetic fibers. We are seeing a large amount of synthetic fibers sold as gabardine in trousers and blazers for men and women. Follow your label directions—many synthetics are machine washable and dryable. If the care label says dry-clean, be sure to do so.

Lace: An extremely delicate fabric, lace may be made of cotton, linen or synthetic. Wash using a mild soap or detergent intended for delicates. Avoid rubbing since it will distort the fibers. Rinse well without wringing, shape by hand, and hang to air-dry or dry flat. Delicate lace pieces may need to be reshaped and pinned down to dry. If you must iron lace, do so over a terry cloth towel. (White is best.) Never put lace in the dryer.

Leather and suede: Generally, leather and suede are not washable. Check your care label carefully. If you have washable leather items, wash them by hand and be sure to protect them with a leather spray protectant. To clean suede, rub it with another piece of suede or a suede brush (not any other kind of brush) to restore the nap and keep it looking new.

Remember, leather needs to breathe, so do not cover it with plastic or store in a tightly enclosed area. If you are looking for a dust cover for leather or suede, use cloth—an old pillowcase is ideal.

To remove spots from leather (not for suede), try using cuticle remover. Rub it into the spot, wait 10 minutes, and then massage the area with a cloth dipped in the cuticle remover. Wipe down thoroughly.

To remove spots from suede, try dabbing with white vinegar.

Linen: A tough fabric that withstands high temperatures, linen is a favorite in hot climates. It is made of natural flax fiber, and comes in light to heavyweight fabrics. Hand wash or machine wash linen in warm water (again, read your care label). If the fabric is colorfast you may remove stains and brighten the fabric with an oxygen bleach or Brilliant Bleach® from Soapworks®. Do not use chlorine bleach.

Iron while still damp, and to help prevent creasing you may treat with starch or sizing. Press heavyweight linens with a hot iron, and for lighter-weight linen and blends (linen, plus other fibers), iron with a warm iron.

Linen is also dry-cleanable.

Mohair: An oldie but a goodie! This is fiber taken from angora goats. Follow the directions for cleaning wool.

Nylon: This is a durable synthetic fiber that comes in varying weights and is often blended with other fibers. When used alone it is machine washable in warm water. It can also be cleaned.

Dry on a low setting or hang to dry using a nonmetal hanger. Do not dry in sunlight—that will cause yellowing. Nonchlorine bleach is best for nylon.

Organdy: Think party dress! Sheer and lightweight, organdy is actually a cotton fiber. Hand wash this and iron damp with a hot iron. Use starch as you iron to give it a crisp look. May also be dry-cleaned.

Polyester: This strong synthetic fiber won't stretch or shrink, which is probably why it's so popular. It comes in various weights and textures, and is often found blended with cotton and wool.

Wash polyester in warm water. Tumble dry and make sure not to let it sit in the dryer, because that will encourage wrinkles. Remove it immediately and you may not need to iron it. If ironing is necessary, make sure to use a low setting.

If the polyester is blended with another fiber, just follow the washing instructions for the more delicate fiber.

Ramie: Very similar to linen, ramie is a natural fiber made from—what else—the ramie plant! It can be used alone or blended with other fibers, such as ramie/cotton.

Machine wash in warm water, tumble dry and iron while damp with a hot iron. Avoid twisting the fibers or they will become distorted. May be dry-cleaned also.

Rayon: This is a synthetic fiber that is sometimes called "viscose." Follow the care label directions closely, but for the very best results, have this fabric dry-cleaned. Dry-cleaning not only cleans well, but it gives rayon the crisp pressing it needs to maintain its shape and good looks.

Satin: Originally made only from silk, this shiny fabric is available in acetate, cotton, nylon, and even polyester.

Dry-clean satin made out of silk and acetate. You may wash cotton, nylon and polyester satins, as long as you follow the washing instructions for those fibers.

Seersucker: You've seen this fabric in shirts, blouses and nightwear. It has puckered stripes that are woven in during the manufacturing process. Seersucker is most frequently made of cotton, but it's also available in nylon and polyester. Be guided by the fiber content for washing and drying.

Drip-dry or tumble dry and iron on low heat if necessary.

Silk: This is a natural fiber made by the silkworm. It is a delicate fabric that requires special care to avoid damage. Check the care labels, but you may be able to hand wash crepe de chine, thin, lightweight and medium-weight silk in lukewarm water with mild soap or detergent. You can also use cold water with cold water detergent.

Do not use chlorine bleach. You may use Brilliant Bleach® by Soapworks® without damaging the fibers.

Rinsing silk well is important. Rinse several times in cold water to remove all suds. Towel blot and dry flat. Do not wring or rub silk.

Iron on the "wrong" side of the fabric with a warm iron.

If your care label indicates that the garment is machine washable, follow the directions with the utmost care. Dry cleaning works best for suits, pleated silks, and silks that are not colorfast.

Do not use strong spotters or enzyme spotters on silk.

Spandex: Spandex is added to other fibers to give them stretch and elasticity. Machine wash in warm water on the delicate or gentle cycle. Do not use chlorine bleach. Do not put them in the dryer, or iron; high heat will break down spandex fibers. Line dry or dry flat, per care label.

If you have exercise clothes containing spandex, be sure to launder each time you wear them. Body oil can break down spandex fibers.

Terry cloth: A toweling-type of fabric, terry cloth has a looped pile made of cotton or cotton/polyester blend. You find it in towels, of course, and even sleepwear.

Machine wash in warm or hot water. Tumble or line dry. Add softener for a softer texture.

Velour: This is a napped fabric that is available in wool, cotton, silk and synthetics. Dry-clean unless the care label indicates it can be washed and dried.

Velvet: A beautiful soft pile fabric, velvet comes in silk, rayon or cotton. Dry-clean for best results.

To raise the pile on velvet, steam from the "wrong" side over a pot of boiling water. Hold the fabric at least 12 inches from the water, and be careful not to allow the fabric to come in contact with the water. This works well for creases in the back of dresses, etc.

Wool: This is a natural fiber made from the fleece of sheep. Hand wash sweaters and other knits in cold water with cold water detergent. Rinse several times and do not wring or twist.

Towel blot and dry flat, reshaping as needed.

Part 4

Let's Take It Outside

63

Paint by Numbers

One of the questions men ask me most frequently is how to get through the job of painting quickly and make it easier. Actually, there are things you can do to make the job go much more smoothly.

Short-Term Storage

If you need to store a paintbrush or roller in the middle of a project or between coats of paint, place it in a tightly sealed plastic bag and place in the freezer. The brush or roller will not dry out for a day or two and no cleanup is needed until you have completed the project.

Protect Hardware

When painting woodwork, cover door knobs, locks and other hardware with a generous coat of petroleum jelly. If the paint splashes where it shouldn't, it can easily be wiped up.

Splatter Removal

For easy removal of paint splatters on window panes, use a round typewriter eraser with a brush on the end—it's safer than a razor and easy, too!

Painting Screws

To make painting screws from hardware easier, stick them in a piece of foam packing material. The screw heads will all be facing up, ready to be sprayed or painted in one coat.

> Use vegetable oil to clean oil-based paints off hands. The oil is safer than paint thinner, has no fumes and is mild to the skin. After using the oil, wash well with soap.

Preventing White Paint from Yellowing

To stop white paint from yellowing with age, put several drops of black paint in for every quart of white paint. Mix very well.

Keep Cans Clean

Cover the rim of the paint can with masking tape if you are going to pour paint from the can. When you are done, remove the tape to clean the top.

Drip Realignment

If you are painting from the can, punch two or three nail holes in the small groove in the top rim of your paint can. As you wipe the paint from your brush on the rim, the paint will drip back into the can instead of collecting in the groove and spilling over and down the sides of the can.

Clean Brushes in a Second

To make a paintbrush easier to clean, wrap masking tape around the metal ferrule and about ½ inch over the bristles. Rather than drying on the bristles, paint will collect on the masking tape. To clean, remove the tape and clean the paint that remains on the brush.

When sealing the lid on a paint can, wipe a thin layer of petroleum jelly around the rim. This will allow the can to open easily the next time.

Garbage Garment

Wear a garbage bag as a cover-all when painting overhead. Cut a hole for head and arms. You can cover your head with an old shower cap. No more paint splatters on clothes and hair!

Record-Keeping

Before you store leftover paint, list the rooms you have painted with it on the can. Touch-ups are easier if you don't have to try to figure out which can of paint you used for what.

Paint-Catching Wristband

If you paint like I do and have runs of paint going down your arms every time you paint over your head, wrap an old washcloth around your wrist, secure with a rubber band and remove and throw away when you are done painting.

Dry Brushes Completely

If you soak your brush between painting sessions, be sure to drain out all of the liquid or you will have a dripping mess when you start painting again. One good way to do this is to stand the brush straight up in an empty can for a few minutes to let the fluid drip out or suspend it from a stick laid across the top of an empty can that is taller than the brush. To be absolutely sure that the brush is dry, take an old rag, wrap it around the brush and squeeze the bristles from the top downward over the can.

Where to Start

Start painting at the top of the wall and work your way down. That way, if paint drips down it can be smoothed out as you go.

When to Start

No need to get up early to paint outside. You don't want to start painting until after the morning dew has evaporated. But, remember, never paint in the direct sunlight.

I'm Siding With Washing, Not Painting

Stop! Don't reach for the paint yet. If you have dirty, dingy aluminum, vinyl or wood siding, try washing it before you paint. A yearly washing can really brighten up a house and preserve the siding too. Combine the following:

3 gallons of warm water

1 cup detergent

1 quart chlorine bleach

Wear rubber gloves, goggles and old clothes, remember you are dealing with bleach and a dirty house.

Rinse the siding down first and then starting at the bottom and working up, apply the cleaner. A long-handled car wash brush works great. Don't let the cleaner dry on the house, rinse it well, working in small sections.

64

Concrete Solutions for Cleaning Cement Driveways and Patios

One question everyone asks is how to clean cement driveways, garage floors and patios. The best time to clean cement is when the temperature is between 50 and 75 degrees and the direct sun is not shining on it. Take this into consideration when using the cleaning methods in this chapter.

Grab the Dust on Cement

To make quick work of sweeping a cement garage floor or patio, pick up some sweeping compound at either a janitorial supply store, hardware store or home center. The sweeping compound will "grab" the dust instead of spreading it in the air as you sweep. When you're done, just sweep it into a dust pan and throw out.

Kitty Litter™–a Garage Floor's Best Friend

Cat box litter, either regular clay or clumping, is wonderful for absorbing liquid spills, especially oil of any kind. Simply pour it on the spot and then—the secret to success—grind it into the spot with your foot. Leave it and allow it to absorb all of the oil that it can. Then sweep up. Repeat the process if necessary.

Old Stains on Cement

Apply a spray-and-wash product and leave it on for 5 to 10 minutes. Sprinkle with laundry detergent, scrub with a stiff brush or broom and then rinse.

Another good method is to make a paste of hot water and automatic dishwasher detergent. Scrub it into the spot and let it soak for at least one hour or overnight. Add additional water and scrub, then rinse well.

Removing the Toughest Stains

Use oven cleaner to remove the toughest spots. Spray it on, keeping your face well back. Let it stand for 15 minutes and then scrub with a stiff brush or broom and hose off. Repeat if necessary. Do not allow children or pets in the area when using this method. Rinse cement and brush with plenty of water. Do not combine other cleaning products with the oven cleaner until it is rinsed well with water.

Removing Rust from Concrete

A method that may work for you is applying ZUD Heavy Duty Cleanser®. This can be purchased at the store in the cleanser section. Make a paste with warm water and work in well with a brush. Let soak for 30 minutes and then scrub with additional hot water and rinse well.

To remove rust stains, wet the concrete and sprinkle with lemon Kool-Aid™. Cover with plastic and soak for 15 minutes. Remove plastic, scrub with a brush and rinse well.

If the rust stain is really bad, you will have to use a solution of 10 parts water to 1 part muriatic acid. Let this sit 2 to 3 hours and then scrub with a stiff (nonmetallic) brush. Use extreme caution if you use this method. Wear goggles, gloves and old clothes, and rinse, rinse, rinse! Keep children and pets away from the area while using the acid.

65

Do Away with Window Pains

To achieve professional results you need to use the same tools the professionals use. You can find all of these things at either a janitorial supply store (look in the yellow pages) or a hardware store.

Use the Right Tools

Squeegee

A good squeegee is an absolute must. Don't be fooled into thinking that a cheap plastic squeegee or a car windshield squeegee will do the job—they won't! The best size to start with is a 12- or 14-inch squeegee. This will work well on most windows, and once you have mastered this size you can move up to an 18-inch for large-paned windows and down to a 6-inch for small French panes.

Scrubber

A good scrubber is a plus. This tool looks like a squeegee wearing a fluffy coat. It is used to wet and clean the window prior to using the squeegee. If you do not want to invest in this, be sure you buy a good natural sponge.

Rag or Chamois

Use a dry rag or chamois for drying the squeegee rubber (blade) and the edges of the glass.

Scraper

Use a window scraper for removing paint, concrete and other stubborn debris. If you don't purchase this you can use a good medium- to fine-grade steel wool pad. If you use this be sure the pad and the window are soapy wet. Never use one of those scrub pads that you use on dishes; this will scratch the glass. Never use steel wool on tinted glass.

Extension Pole

If you have difficult, high, hard-to-reach windows, you might consider an extension pole made for a squeegee. This will enable you to stand on the ground and reach the high windows without a ladder.

Bucket and TSP

A bucket of water and TSP, trisodium phosphate, or dishwashing detergent (2 or 3 squirts to a bucket) added after you have filled the bucket with water.

Let's Get Started

Fill your bucket with warm water and add the TSP or dishwashing liquid.

Be sure you have all the necessary equipment laid out and ready for use.

Follow the steps listed below, in order. You'll be cleaning like a pro in no time!

Dip your scrubber or sponge into the cleaning solution and wash the window thoroughly, using a very wet steel wool pad to remove any stubborn spots, such as bug stains. You do not have to press too hard on the steel wool pad. Rewet the window so you will have time to squeegee the window before it dries. Try not to clean in the direct sunlight, as it will cause streaking and spotting.

Tilt the squeegee at an angle so that 2 inches of rubber blade touches the glass. Start at the top corner and draw the squeegee along the top edge of the window.

Wipe the squeegee blade on a sponge, start on the dry surface close to the frame and draw the squeegee down to within about 3 inches of the bottom of the glass.

Repeat this stroke until you have squeegeed all of the glass. Be sure you overlap each stroke and wipe the squeegee blade after each stroke.

Soak up excess water with a well-rinsed sponge.

Do the same thing you did in step two at the top of the glass, this time working at the bottom of the glass.

Have your rag or chamois handy to wipe the window edges if needed. If you see a streak on the window, let it dry, then use poly/cotton rag, such as an old T-shirt, to polish it out.

DON'T DO IT!

No matter what you may have heard about cleaning windows with newspaper, don't do it! It's dirty and messy and leaves newsprint all over white window trim and paint.

Spray-and-Wipe Cleaning Solutions

If you prefer to wash your windows the spray-and-wipe way, here are a couple of good cleaning solutions.

Polishing Glass or Removing Screen and Bug Stains

Make a thin paste of baking soda and water, rub onto glass, rinse well and dry with a soft cloth.

Easy Window Cleaner

Combine:

2 quarts warm water

½ cup cornstarch

Apply to window with a sponge and buff dry with paper towels or soft, lint-free rags.

Tough-Job Window Cleaner

Combine:

1 pint rubbing alcohol

2 tablespoons clear ammonia

2 tablespoons dishwashing liquid

Apply to the window using a nylon-covered sponge, rinse and buff dry. Great for hard-water spots.

Screen Savers

Most people just hose screens down to clean them. This just moves the dirt from one part of the screen to the other. Here's a better way. Just soap the screen with a sponge dipped in a pail of warm water containing 2 tablespoons of dishwashing liquid, ¼ cup of ammonia and 2 tablespoons of borax. Really suds up the screen. Now lay a rag on the ground and gently tap the screen on it. Most of the soapy water containing the dirt will come off this way. To finish, rinse the screen with the hose and stand to dry, or rag dry.

Use a dry blackboard eraser on a dry window or mirror after cleaning to banish any streaks you've left behind!

66

All Hands on Deck

A certain amount of routine maintenance is required to keep your backyard deck structurally sound, safe and looking its best.

Though other types of lumber may have been used, chances are that your deck is built of cedar, redwood or pressure-treated yellow pine. These are the most commonly used materials for decks because they are resistant to rot and insect damage. When exposed to the elements for extended periods of time, any wood will show signs of weathering. Even if the deck was originally treated with stain or a preservative, this treatment eventually needs to be renewed.

Inspect and Protect

The first thing you need to do once the weather turns nice is inspect the deck surfaces for any splintering, which you will need to sand. Pay special attention to the railing.

You'll find many stains and sealers designed for decks. Several manufacturers now offer products called deck brighteners, which actually bleach the surface to remove stains and weathering on wood surfaces. Apply these products carefully, following the instructions. Usually you will brush the product on with a stiff-bristle brush, and rinse off thoroughly prior to applying any finish coating.

Now go over the actual decking to be sure it is tight and in place, fixing whatever is required. Finally, if no repair or staining is needed, follow some of these suggestions to give the deck a good cleaning.

If there are leaves and other debris on the deck, either sweep or use a blower to remove it.

Sealers protect the deck from moisture and are available in clear or tinted varieties to act as a stain. They require periodic renewal to maintain protection.

Hose Off the Deck

With a garden hose and a strong—and preferably long-handled—brush, use the strongest spray setting on the nozzle to break up dirt on the surface. Follow this with the brush to loosen any stubborn soil. This works especially well with two people, who can take turns hosing and scrubbing.

Kill Mildew

Check the condition of the wood. Green or black areas indicate mold and mildew. To remove mold and mildew from the wood you will need either a commercial deck-cleaning product (which may be purchased at your local home center) or you can prepare your own using a mixture of 1 cup trisodium phosphate (available at janitorial supply stores and home centers), 1 gallon of oxygen-type bleach (safer to use than chlorine bleach) and 1 gallon of hot water. The bleach will kill the mildew and the TSP will thoroughly clean the wood surface. You can apply this with a garden sprayer or mop it on.

First wet down the deck with the hose and then apply the cleaning solution. Spread the solution evenly and scrub with the brush you used earlier. Let the solution sit for about 15 minutes and then hose off. Repeat the wetting, bleaching and rinsing process as necessary until the entire deck is clean. Make sure you do stairs, handrails and any other deck parts.

After you have done the entire deck, I recommend that you hose down the grass and any plants surrounding it to remove any solution that has dripped on them. No damage should be done to plants, but rinsing is a good precaution. If you have used a garden sprayer, be sure to wash it out well and rinse the brush before storing.

> To give the deck a quick cleaning during the use season, mix up a gallon of hot water and ¼ cup of any good-quality household cleaner, or 1 gallon of hot water, 1 tablespoon of dishwashing liquid and ¼ cup of borax. Mop the deck down with one of these solutions and rinse well. Again, be sure to rinse plants and grass down.

Removing Sap from an Unfinished Wood Deck

Tree sap can be a problem on wood decks. To remove it, apply mineral spirits with an old rag, rub and wash off with dishwashing liquid and water (1 teaspoon of dishwashing liquid to 1 quart of hot water). Rinse well.

67

Everything Under the Sun for Patio Furniture

No matter what part of the country you live in, at some time you have to clean the outdoor furniture. Follow this advice to make the job go faster.

Furniture Cushions

There are several ways to clean outdoor furniture cushions. You can use Spot Shot Upholstery Stain Remover® or Spot Shot Instant Carpet Stain Remover®. Follow the directions on the can. Or, mix your own solution. In a spray bottle combine 1 teaspoon of dishwashing liquid and 1 teaspoon of borax per quart of warm water. Spray this on the cushion on both sides and let it sit for about 15 minutes. Then take out the hose and, using a strong spray, rinse the solution and the dirt off the cushions. Put them back on the chairs and set them out of the direct sun to dry. Once they have dried to just damp, apply a good coating of Scotchgard™ Fabric Protector® (available at grocery stores and home centers) to protect the cushions and make cleaning easier the next time. Vacuum the cushions as needed to remove dust between cleanings.

Aluminum

Although it doesn't rust, aluminum can become dull and pitted when left outdoors. To clean and restore the shine, scrub the frames with a plastic scrubber soaked in detergent or a soap-filled steel wool pad, then rinse and dry.

Aluminum with Baked-Enamel Finish

Use a sponge soaked in detergent and wash well, rinse and dry. To protect, apply a coat of good-quality car wax. This will make cleaning easier and maintain the shine. It can be used on tables with a baked-enamel finish, too.

Canvas

Soiled canvas seats and chair backs are usually machine washable, but be sure to put them back on the furniture when they are still damp to maintain their shape. To clean canvas that you cannot put in the washing machine, such as large seats, backs or awnings, run a scrub brush back and forth across a bar of Fels-Naptha Soap®. Rub this back and forth across the canvas and then rinse well. This will even remove bird droppings and, many times, the staining, too.

To maintain the shine on plastic, resin and metal furniture, apply a good-quality paste car wax just as you would when waxing a car.

Plastic

Wash with good all-purpose cleaner and water, then rinse with water and dry. An alternative for white furniture is automatic dishwasher detergent and warm water (1 gallon warm water to 3 tablespoons automatic dishwasher detergent). Wash and let solution sit on the furniture for 15 minutes or so and then rinse and dry.

68

The Grill Drill

Let's talk about ways to make cooking on the grill easier and more fun.

Cleaning the Grill

To clean the grill surface when it is heavily caked with baked-on food, follow this procedure. Simply wrap the rack in a piece of heavy-duty aluminum foil, dull side facing out. Heat the barbecue to high heat and place the rack over the coals or flame for approximately 10 to 12 minutes. When you remove the foil after it has cooled, all the burned-on grease and food drippings will fall off and your rack will be spotless and ready to grill again.

Immediately After Cooking

Make a ball of aluminum foil and "scrub" the warm grill rack surface with it, taking care not to burn your fingers.

The Bathtub Method and a Less-Messy Version

Many people recommend putting the grill rack in the bathtub filled with hot water, detergent and ammonia. I find this a particularly messy way to do it because you have to clean the tub when you're done. If you do use this method, be sure to lay old rags or a garbage bag in the tub to prevent scratching the tub surface with the grill rack.

I suggest you try this method instead. Lay some paper towels moistened with undiluted ammonia on both sides of the rack. Put it in an appropriate-size plastic bag and seal. Leave it overnight and the next day open the bag, away from your face—it stinks. Wipe down with the paper towels in the bag, wash with soapy water and rinse.

Keeping Pan Bottoms Clean

Before setting a pan on the grill rack to warm barbecue sauce or cook additional foods, rub the pan bottom with bar soap and it will be easier to clean the soot off when you are done.

Cleaning Permanent Briquettes

Flip the briquettes occasionally and ignite the grill with the cover closed. Allow it to burn at a high setting for about 15 minutes.

Grease Splatters

For cement or wood patios, keep a container of salt nearby when barbecuing. Should grease spatter or drip, immediately cover with salt. Sweep up and reapply until grease is absorbed. Scrub with dishwashing liquid and rinse.

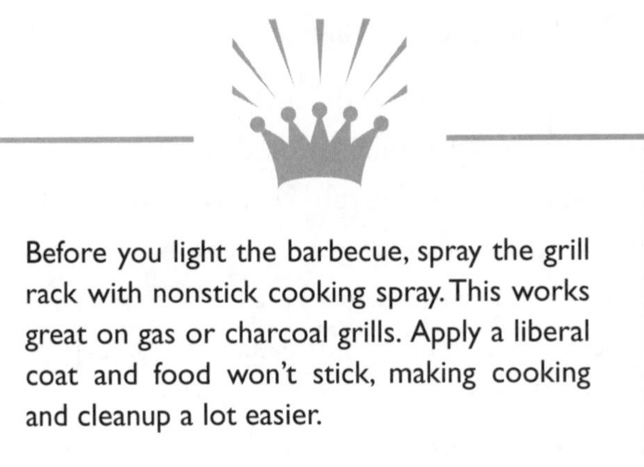

Before you light the barbecue, spray the grill rack with nonstick cooking spray. This works great on gas or charcoal grills. Apply a liberal coat and food won't stick, making cooking and cleanup a lot easier.

Keeping the Outside of the Grill Clean

This is such a fast, easy way to clean the outside of the grill. It works well on charcoal and gas grills and will make them look almost like new. Take some GOJO Crème Waterless Hand Cleaner® (available at grocery stores, hardware stores and home centers) and rub it on the outside of a cool grill with an old rag or paper towel. Work it into the metal well, paying special attention to any grease or barbecue sauce spots. Do not rinse; instead, take paper towels and buff the grill surface and watch as the dirt is replaced by a great shine.

Keeping the Glass Grill Window Clean

Many gas grills have glass windows in them. Of course, once you use the grill a few times you can no longer see through the window! To clean this, spray the inside of the glass with oven cleaner. Wait a few minutes and then scrub and rinse well. On the outside of the glass use GOJO Crème Waterless Hand Cleaner® and buff well.

69

Bug Out—User-Friendly Pest Control

Are the bugs bugging you? Are the pests pestering you? You can control bugs without chemicals, the safe, environmentally friendly way. When planting flowers or controlling insects inside the house, keep this guide handy.

A wonderful substitute for insect repellent is white vinegar. Apply it liberally to the skin with a cotton ball. Bugs hate the way you taste and the smell of the vinegar disappears once it dries. Great for kids!

Insect Repellent

When using insect sprays, especially those containing DEET, try spraying clothes instead of skin—it's much safer, especially for children.

Aphids

Mix nonfat dry milk with water according to the directions on the box, then put in a spray bottle and apply it to the leaves of your plants. As the milk dries, the aphids get stuck in the milky residue and die. You can rinse the plants from time to time with the hose. This will not harm your plants and offers an inexpensive solution to a big problem.

Aphids and Spiders

Wash off the plant with a mild solution of dishwashing liquid and water. Try a ratio of ½ teaspoon dishwashing liquid to 1 quart water. Flush leaves, including undersides, with the solution. Do not rinse off.

Aphids and Whiteflies

These bugs are attracted to bright yellow and can be trapped by placing a yellow board or other yellow objects, such as yellow poster board, oleo lids, or sticks painted yellow, coated with heavy motor oil, petroleum jelly or Tack Trap® near susceptible plants. Recoat when the traps dry out.

Aphids on Roses

Use 1 ½ teaspoons of baking soda per pint of water and apply every seven days. This method is user-, earth- and child-friendly.

Grasshoppers

To deter grasshoppers, plant basil around the flower bed borders. Grasshoppers will eat the basil and leave the plants alone.

Ants

For ants on the counter, wipe the counter down with undiluted white vinegar.

To prevent ants from coming in the house, or getting into cupboards, sprinkle dried mint or red pepper where they are entering the house and in the cupboards.

To get rid of anthills, pour 3 gallons of boiling water down them. This is best done when the ants are active and near the surface. Do not do this close to flowers or they will die, too.

Another way to kill ants is to mix a combination of 50 percent borax and 50 percent confectioner's sugar. Place this on cardboard or a piece of board near the ant hill. The ants are attracted by the sugar and carry the fatal borax/sugar combination back to the nest to feed the queen and other ants. Soon all are dead. A note of caution: Do not place this where children or pets may ingest this mixture. Borax is sold in the laundry aisle at the grocery store as a laundry additive, not as a pesticide.

Cockroaches

To keep cockroaches out of the cupboards, place some bay leaves on the shelves.

Kill cockroaches with a mixture of ⅓ borax, ⅓ cornmeal, ⅓ flour and a dash of powdered sugar. Sprinkle this in crevices under sinks and vanities where cockroaches love to hide. Remember, keep this away from children and animals.

"A garden is a thing of beauty and a job forever."

—Anonymous

You can also try this formula for cockroaches: Mix powdered boric acid with sugar and powdered nondairy creamer. I use a mixture of 50 percent boric acid to 25 percent each sugar and creamer. This is inexpensive and relatively safe, but it should be kept away from children and pets. Sprinkle the mixture in all the dark, warm places that cockroaches love—under sinks and stoves, behind refrigerators, in cabinets and closets, and so on. The roaches will walk through the powder and then clean themselves, much the way a cat preens. Once they ingest the powder they die.

70 Flower Power

Making Fresh Flowers Last Longer

To make fresh flowers from your garden or floral arrangements from the florist last longer, use the following recipe. Remove any foliage below the waterline, trim the stem ends periodically and keep the solution fresh and your flowers will live longer.

Combine:

1 quart of water

2 tablespoons of lemon juice

1 tablespoon sugar

½ teaspoon liquid bleach

Add the solution to the flower container and enjoy. If you have an arrangement from the florist, add this solution each time you add water.

If you don't have the above ingredients on hand, add 2 ounces of Listerine™ mouthwash per gallon of water.

To make cut flowers last longer without shedding, spray with hair spray. Hold the spray can about a foot away from the flowers and spray in an upward direction to prevent the flowers from drooping.

Transporting Fresh Flowers

If you are taking fresh flowers from your garden as a gift, or to the office, fill a balloon with water, put the stems in and secure the neck of the balloon to the stems with a rubber band, twist tie or ribbon. Poking the stems through a paper doily will also hold the stems in place and make an attractive presentation. Your flowers will arrive fresh-looking at their destination with no spilled water to worry about!

The Dirt on Flower Pots

When planting flowers in a pot with a drainage hole in the bottom, line the bottom of the pot with enough coffee filters to cover it. Add a few pebbles and then add the soil. When you water the plant the dirt won't run out the bottom.

Flower Filler

When planting shallow-rooted flowers in a large pot, line the bottom with coffee filters and pebbles, fill the pot ⅓ full of packing peanuts and then fill with soil. The pot will be much lighter to move and you won't require as much soil to fill the pot.

Healthful Water

When you boil eggs, save the water to water your plants. It is full of minerals.

Cold coffee or tea combined with water provides an acidic drink for your plants. (Be sure it doesn't run out on the carpet.)

Water from an aquarium provides excellent fertilizer for plants.

Club soda that has lost its fizz is good for plants.

To easily clean a flower vase, fill with warm water and add one or two denture-cleaning tablets, depending on the size of the vase. Let it soak at least an hour or overnight. Wash, rinse and dry well. If you don't have any denture-cleaning tablets, throw in a handful of dry rice and some white vinegar and shake, shake, shake. Let soak with vinegar and warm water if necessary. Wash and rinse the vase well.

Going on vacation? Stand plants in the sink or bathtub, depending on the number you have. Be sure they are in pots with a hole in the bottom. Add a few inches of water to the tub and plants will be automatically watered while you are gone. To preserve the tub finish, lay an old towel in the bottom to set plants on.

Unbugged

If bugs are a problem on indoor plants, spray the soil with insect spray and immediately cover the plant with a plastic bag. Leave in place for a couple of days and then uncover.

Let Them Shine

To shine indoor plant leaves, wipe gently with glycerin. Another great way to add shine is by wiping leaves with a mixture of half milk and half water. Do not use oil on plant leaves, as it attracts dust and dirt.

Window Boxes and Patio Flower Pots

These are easy to keep clean. After you plant the flowers in the pots, put a layer of gravel or marbles on top. When you water or it rains, the dirt won't splash all over the plants, pots, patio or porch.

Hanging Plants

To water hanging plants with ease and without the mess of water running all over, use ice cubes. The cubes melt slowly and won't allow water to run out onto the floor or patio.

Weed Prevention

To kill weeds growing in sidewalk cracks, pour boiling salt water on them. Use a mixture of ¼ cup salt to 2 quarts water.

To prevent the weeds from growing in the cracks, sprinkle salt into the cracks.

Cleaning Artificial Flowers

To really clean and remove soil from artificial flowers, dried silk or polyester, place them in a bag with table salt. Add salt in proportion to the size of the flowers. Close the bag and shake the flowers in the salt for several minutes, or longer if the flowers are heavily soiled. Shake gently to remove the salt. The salt won't look dirty when you are done, but if you run water into it, you will be surprised how much dirt is removed from the flowers.

You can also place silk flowers in a pillowcase, tie a knot in it and put it in the clothes dryer on "air fluff" or "air only" for about 15 to 20 minutes.

Spray polyester flowers with acrylic spray from the craft store and they will resist soiling. If they get very dusty, wash under a mild stream of running water, shake and stand up to dry.

Part 5

And You Thought I Forgot . . .

71

Fly the Flag Proudly

Many people have asked me about caring for flags. I'm honored to provide you with this information.

American flags should never be thrown in the washing machine or washed by hand. They need to be dry-cleaned. You'll need to call around, but in my experience, most dry cleaners will perform the service for free.

To repair rips and holes, iron-on patches come in handy. Match the fabric and colors of your flag. Pretty much all you'll need to do is follow the directions on the package. Many flag shops also carry repair kits.

Flags that are beyond repair should be burned completely in a "modest, but blazing fire. This should be done in a simple manner with dignity and respect." Make sure the flag is burned completely to ashes and that there are no recognizable swatches left behind.

72

Taking Charge of Electronic Equipment

Television Screens

Denatured alcohol (available at hardware stores) makes a great cleaner for many pieces of electronic equipment. To clean the TV screen, turn off the power to the TV. Apply alcohol to a rag or paper towel and wipe the screen thoroughly, then buff.

Stop Dust from Settling

Apply antistatic product to a rag and wipe the screen and cabinet, or mix 1 part liquid fabric softener to 4 parts water and apply with a soft cloth and buff.

A special reminder: Never clean any electronic equipment without unplugging it first!

Radios

These need to be dusted often. Clean them occasionally with denatured alcohol applied with a cotton ball. Do not use alcohol on wood.

"I only know two tunes. One of them is 'Yankee Doodle' and the other isn't."

—Ulysses S. Grant

Cameras

Cameras should always be stored in their cases when not in use. This prevents them from becoming dusty. Except for wiping off the outside of the lens with a cotton ball and a little alcohol, leave cleaning to the professionals.

Videocassette Recorders

These need to be kept free of dust to stay in good working order. It is best to cover them with a plastic cover when not in use. If the room is damp, keep silica packets (available from florists or many times found in new leather shoes or purses) on top of the VCR (keep these packets away from children). Clean the VCR occasionally using a cleaning tape to ensure good-quality pictures on playback. Store videotapes in cardboard or plastic cases to keep them clean and in good condition for playback or recording.

Answering Machines

These need to be dusted with a lambswool duster, particularly inside the machine. You can use an aerosol cleaner, but make sure that the machine is dry before you replace the cassette.

Fax Machines

These also need to be kept dusted and occasionally wiped with denatured alcohol.

Computers

To avoid costly problems with computers, it is important that they be kept dust-free. Dust between the keys of your keyboard with a cotton swab, or vacuum with the duster-brush on your vacuum or with a special computer vacuum that helps you get between the keys.

Mix 1 part water and 1 part alcohol and apply to the keys with a cotton swab. Don't overwet. Undiluted denatured alcohol may also be used in the same manner.

Dust the screen and spray with an antistatic product.

Make sure that computers are situated out of direct sunlight, which can cause overheating. Sunlight also makes it difficult for the user to see the computer screen clearly.

To keep your compact discs clean, mix 2 tablespoons of baking soda and 1 pint of water in a spray bottle. Shake well to mix and spray on the disc, wiping with a soft cloth. Do not wipe in a circular motion; wipe from the center hole in the disc out to the outside edge.

73

The Care and Hanging of Pictures and Paintings

Pictures and paintings are part of the personal touches that make a house a home. Here are some ideas for hanging and cleaning pictures and oil and acrylic paintings.

Finding the Stud the Easy Way

When you are ready to hang a picture, especially a heavy one, it is a good idea to find a stud to hang it from. Take an electric razor and run it across the wall. You will notice a distinct difference in the sound of the razor going over a hollow wall and the sound when it hits a stud. Use this whenever you need to find the stud to hang anything around the house.

Keeping Cockeyed Pictures Straight

Wind some adhesive tape around the center of the picture wire. The wire will be less likely to slip on the hanger.

Place masking tape on the back four corners of your picture and press against the wall. Wrap masking tape, sticky side out, around the middle of a round toothpick and place a few near the bottom, backside of the frame.

Preventing Experimental Holes

Cut a paper pattern of each picture or mirror that you plan to hang and pin to the wall. After you've found the correct positions for the hangers, perforate the paper with a sharp pencil to mark the wall.

When you want to avoid nail holes in the walls, hang pictures with a sewing machine needle. They hold up to 30 pounds and leave almost no marks on the wall.

Staining Unfinished Picture Frames

Stain them beautifully with ordinary liquid shoe polish. Apply one coat and let dry. Follow with another coat, then wax with a good paste wax. Brown shoe polish gives the wood a walnut glow and oxblood emulates a mahogany or cherry color. Tan polish will look like a light maple. This hides scratches, too.

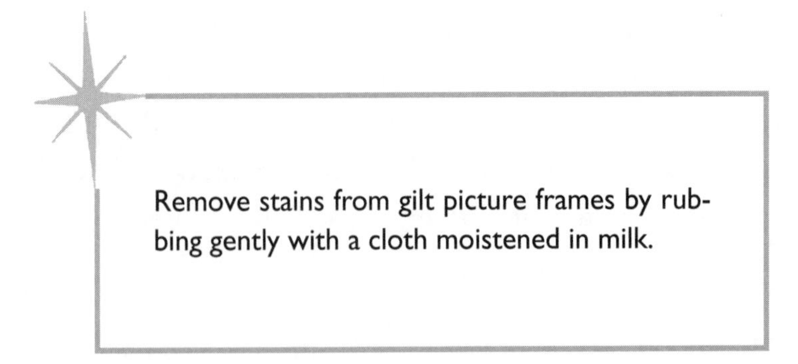

Remove stains from gilt picture frames by rubbing gently with a cloth moistened in milk.

Cleaning Glass-Covered Pictures

Never spray any cleaner directly on the glass; it may seep under and onto the picture. Spray a paper towel with window cleaner, wipe and polish with a dry towel.

Polish glass with a used fabric softener sheet to shine and deter dust.

Cleaning Oil and Acrylic Paintings

Give them an occasional dusting with a clean, lint-free cloth or a soft brush. Spot-clean if necessary with a barely damp rag or piece of white bread. If the painting is worth a lot of money or has sentimental value, take it to a professional. Even a soft dust cloth can snag and cause a chip.

Photo Emergency

If you have a picture that is stuck to the glass, immerse the glass and the photo in a pan of room-temperature water and keep testing until the photo pulls free. Don't try to rush it! Let the photo air-dry. Since most photo prints get a water bath during processing, there shouldn't be any damage, though this is not a 100 percent guarantee.

74

The Fireplace Fandango

What could be nicer than sitting by a warm, cozy fireplace on a cold winter's night perhaps watching the snow fall outside and listening to the wind blow? (This of course is on a weekend when you don't have to drive to work the next day.) If you take care of your fireplace properly and keep it clean and use it properly it can be an asset to your mood and your heating system.

Cleaning chimneys: Wood-burning chimneys should be swept twice a year. Residual resin from the wood may catch fire.

Metal parts: To clean metal on fireplaces use blacking or a commercial cleaner. If you are using blacking wear gloves and apply on a piece of fine-grade (0000) steel wool. Polish with an old soft cloth that you can throw out. It is a good idea to have a plastic trash bag nearby as you are working to drop the soiled rags and steel wool and gloves in.

Clearing grates: Wood ashes do not need to be cleaned out of the grate frequently. They act as a good base for the fire all winter long. When they pile up, cover them with wet newspaper to keep the dust down and remove with a shovel into a trash bag. You must be sure that the ashes are cool first. Remember, hot ashes can lie dormant a long time, so use care and consideration.

Removing soot from the fireplace surrounds: Before you apply water to the soot that collects on the brick, stone or tile around a fireplace, you need to "erase" it away with a Soot and Dirt Removal Sponge. These look like large brick erasers and are sold at hardware stores and home centers. Using the sponge dry, you erase the soot from the surround area. If you apply water first you will "set" the greasy soot stain and will have a difficult time removing it or you may even end up sealing and painting the area.

For brick surrounds, after using the Soot and Dirt Removal Sponge, scrub well with a stiff scrub brush and clean water. A handful of trisodium phosphate added to the water will help. Purchase this at hardware stores and home centers. Rinse when you are done.

For ceramic tile surrounds, use the removal sponge and then wash with a solution of dishwashing liquid or household detergent, and rinse.

For marble, use the removal sponge and then sponge with a soap flake solution or a mild all-purpose cleaner such as At Home All Purpose Cleaner™, by Soapworks®. Then rinse it well and dry it with an old towel.

Important: **Never dispose of hot embers in anything but a metal container that you keep for that purpose. Allow the embers to cool in the container for 24 hours before putting in a trash bag or trash can.**

On ceramic tile and marble, I suggest a coat of Clean Shield® made by the Unelko Corporation. Clean Shield® will put a protective coating on the tile and marble turning it into something easy to clean, like nonstick cookware.

Stains and dirt can be easily removed with water. When the water quits beading, it is time for another coat.

Now Some Fireplace Efficiency Tips and Cheap Tricks

- Consider buying a heat exchanger to make your fireplace more efficient. This device reclaims much of the heat that would normally go up your chimney and out of the house.
- Never burn green wood. It is a total waste of energy and because of the creosote content, also dangerous. It is the creosote buildup in chimneys that causes serious chimney fires.
- For an inexpensive and safe fire starter, use the lint you gather from your dryer lint filter. The soft balls of lint ignite quickly to get the kindling blazing.

Allow your wood to age at least one season prior to burning.

- Looking for inexpensive kindling? Gather a supply of waxed cardboard boxes that are used to ship fresh fruit and vegetables to your supermarket. Cut them into convenient strips (about 3 x 4 inches) with a utility knife and use three or four to ignite small logs. As with everything, don't overdue these strips or you could create such a quick hot fire that it could trigger a chimney fire.
- To create a wonderful aroma in your house, throw pieces of dried citrus peel (orange, lemon, lime) into your fire. You can also use one or two pinecones if they are prevalent in your area.

Last Things to Remember

* Lower the thermostat for the rest of the house to about 55 degrees.
* Close all doors and warm-air ducts entering the room with the fireplace.
* Open a window near the fireplace about 1 inch or less if possible. This will allow the fire to get its oxygen from outside the house, instead of drawing the air from the rest of the house.
* Remember to install a glass screen or radiant grate to stifle the flow of warm air through the chimney.

75

Turning Down the Heat on Fire Damage

I honestly hope that you never have any reason to do anything more than just glance through this chapter, but if you ever have a fire in your home, remember it's here. I spent 15 years as the owner of a disaster restoration company in Michigan and I can tell you that in those first hours after a fire it's all you can do to remember your name.

The fire truck has just left and there you stand amid what once was your home and is now a smelly, wet, black mess that you hardly recognize. You want to sit down and have a good cry, but there isn't any place clean to sit. What do you do now? Is everything ruined? This chapter will help you deal with the emotional turmoil and give you sound information about what you, as the homeowner, need to do.

Get on the Phone

After the fire is out, call your insurance agent or the 800 number that is often provided on your policy to report claims.

First, as soon as you are done reading this, put your homeowner's policy, along with your agent's name and phone number, in a fireproof box or bank safety deposit box. This enables you to easily find them and protects them from being destroyed in the fire. Make notes from this chapter and put them with your insurance information.

Call immediately. It may seem like the damage couldn't be worse, but it could. After a fire there can be ongoing damage from acid soot residue. Fire produces two main pollutants—nitrous oxide (from burning wood, food, etc.) and sulfur dioxide (from burning plastics and petroleum by-products, etc.). When these pollutants combine with moisture and humidity, they form acid! Within hours this can cause substantial and continuing damage. Prompt attention from your local disaster restoration firm will eliminate the problem and prevent further damage to valuables. Disaster restoration companies are listed in your phone directory and are available 24 hours a day for emergencies. They will preserve, protect and secure surfaces that may be subject to continuing damage, and will work with your insurance adjuster to estimate the damage.

What Is an Insurance Adjuster?

The insurance adjuster works for the insurance company. He is an expert in smoke damage, such as chimney fires, furnace backups and actual fire damage. He will help you decide what can be saved and what can't. He will require a written estimate from a disaster restoration company and any contractors or dry cleaners who will participate in the cleanup. Sometimes more than one estimate will be requested.

During this time you will be receiving all kinds of comments and advice from friends, relatives and even strangers. Ignore it! Your insurance adjuster is a professional and knows the best way to handle smoke damage. The adjuster may even be able to give you advice on a company that they have dealt with before if you are unsure who to call.

Disaster Restoration Companies

Disaster restoration companies (i.e. cleaning companies) do two types of cleaning: structural and contents cleaning. Structural cleaning is wall-washing, carpet cleaning, cupboards—the things you can't remove from the house when you move. Contents cleaning is the upholstery, hard furniture, dishes, clothes, etc.—things you take with you when you move. They will provide a complete estimate to the insurance company and a copy to you.

Once coverage is confirmed and appropriate authorizations are secured, the cleaning and repairs will take place as quickly as possible. This will include dry cleaning, laundry and deodorization, also covered in this chapter.

Payment

After completion of all the cleaning and restoration, the insurance company will generally issue a check in your name and in the name of the firm that did the work. Once the work is satisfactory, you sign over the checks.

Deodorization

Deodorization is one of the most important parts of any smoke damage cleanup. Everything smells—even your clothes.

First, the initial odor must be brought under control immediately to make the house habitable, if you are able to live in it during the restoration.

During any reconstruction, exposed interior wall sections will be deodorized and any singed wood will be sealed to prevent odor. In serious fires, deodorization will take place after cleaning, too.

All clothing will have to be deodorized during laundry and dry cleaning, and in serious cases will be put in an ozone room that opens the oxygen molecules and releases odor.

Ozone machines are also used for deodorizing the home, resulting in a smell much like the air after a thunderstorm.

The best deodorization technique I have ever known is recreating the conditions causing the odor. In the case of smoke damage a deodorant "smoke" is produced, which allows the deodorization process to penetrate in exactly the same manner the smoke odor did.

Additional odor control is done with duct sealing and deodorization.

Additionally, all walls that are washed and painted should be sealed first with a special sealer to eliminate residue "bleed through" from the oily smoke film. Then the walls are painted in the normal manner. This process is one that your disaster restoration firm and adjuster will be familiar with.

With light smoke damage, many times the wall washing is necessary, but not painting. Deodorization is generally always advised.

What If You Don't Have Insurance?

The best advice I can give you is to carry insurance. If you live in an apartment or condominium, buy renter's insurance. If smoke damage occurs, you'll be glad you did.

But, if you don't have insurance, here's some helpful advice:

Go to a janitorial supply store and ask their advice on which cleaning chemicals to use. They can provide you with a professional-quality deodorant to wash clothes, linens and hard surfaces. You will put this deodorant in the water that you clean with or wash clothes with.

Call a disaster restoration firm and try to rent an ozone machine to deodorize the structure and your contents, bearing in mind that prolonged ozone use will yellow plastics.

Buy a soot and dirt removal sponge to clean walls. This is somewhat like a blackboard eraser that removes oily smoke film, so that when you begin to wash the walls the sooty film won't smear.

Rent a carpet cleaning machine with an upholstery attachment to clean carpet and all upholstery that can be cleaned with water.

Wash hard furniture with oil soap and dry, then use furniture polish if you want a brighter shine.

Wash Everything

Wash everything thoroughly—this means walls, cupboards, collectibles, dishes, clothes, etc., otherwise the odor will remain.

Start in one room and do it completely except for carpet cleaning (you'll track during the cleaning process and spread soot on the carpet). Clean the carpet in all rooms last.

If you still have odor, do a final deodorization with an ozone machine, or if you can, hire a firm to come in and do it for you.

76

Taking the Cough Out of Your Air Ducts

Picture yourself in this situation: You have had smoke damage in your home. All the cleaning and repainting is done and now you are ready to turn on the furnace. You go to the thermostat and turn it up. You hear the furnace spring to life. The central blower is activated . . . and, suddenly, you run screaming from the house. What's wrong? All the odor that collected in the duct system during the smoke damage has just been blown full force from the duct system and into the house. It smells like the house is on fire again. As if the smell isn't enough, you now see black soot residue blowing out in a dark cloud and settling all over the newly cleaned walls, carpet and furniture. How could this happen? Nobody thought to clean the duct system prior to cleaning the house and turning on the furnace.

Duct cleaning and deodorizing is not just for houses that have had fire or smoke damage. It is very beneficial in older homes where dust and allergy-causing bacteria have accumulated in the duct work and are blown through the home each time the furnace runs. Duct cleaning can be very beneficial for people who have allergy problems, too.

What Is Duct Cleaning?

Duct cleaning consists of removing register covers and vacuuming out all the duct work that leads to the furnace. After some elaborate preparatory vacuuming and cleaning procedures, which include cleaning all the register covers, a duct sealer is introduced into the system in the form of a fine mist. This sealer is a plastic-like resin. The chemical itself actually neutralizes odor and seals onto the interior walls of the system the loose soot, dust and dirt that remain after vacuuming. During this process all odor is eliminated and minor residues remaining in unseen or unreachable areas are permanently sealed onto the interior surface of the ducts.

This process gives you a dirt-, dust- and pollen-free environment. If allergies run in your family you will immediately notice the difference. This is particularly good in older homes that, naturally, have the original duct systems in place.

When you have this procedure done it is a good idea to have your furnace cleaned at the same time. Many furnace companies clean duct work, too, as do many disaster restoration or cleaning companies.

77

The Big Drip—Water Damage

What a shock! When you left the house everything was fine.

You come home and unlock the door; you walk in and hear the sound of running water. As you step in, water comes up to your ankles. Now you find water running across the carpet and floors and lapping at the legs of furniture as the sofa and chairs try to soak it up. Here's what you need to do immediately.

> Remember: **BE SURE THE ELECTRICAL POWER SOURCE IS OFF BEFORE YOU WALK IN STANDING WATER.**

Turn It Off

First, know where your water shut-off is and use it. Turn off the water and look for the source of the leak. The leak could be from a toilet, the washing machine hoses, or a broken pipe.

How quickly you react will have impact on what can be saved in your home.

Call the Professionals

Now that you have shut off the water and located the problem, call your insurance agent. Your agent will act quickly to help you, because by the time an adjuster receives the information it is often too late to reverse some of the damage that has taken place.

Wet carpet and pad are restorable if it is taken care of as soon as possible after the damage has occurred.

A professional company that deals in water damage of all kinds can stop further damage from occurring and also save the carpet and pad.

To find a water damage expert, look in the yellow pages under "water damage" or under "cleaning companies" or "disaster restoration firms." Be sure to get a company that specializes in this problem.

Dry Out

First they will extract water from the pad and the carpet and treat both with an EPA-registered disinfectant. They will then install drying equipment, which consists of high-powered carpet blowers that are slipped between the carpet and the pad. They also will install dehumidification equipment to facilitate drying. They will advise you to keep your home's interior temperature at 70 degrees or warmer for ideal drying conditions. This drying equipment will also facilitate drying of upholstered furniture and walls as it dries the carpet.

Upholstered furniture will need to have water extracted from it and be treated with an EPA-registered disinfectant, too. Wood furniture will be wiped down and allowed to dry.

The water damage restoration firm will check, usually every 24 hours, to see how the drying process is coming and to move equipment to continue the drying process.

What Is an Antimicrobial?

Many water damage restoration firms have a wonderful antimicrobial product available that not only disinfects, but also inhibits the growth of mold, mildew and bacterial spores. This is applied to the carpet after extraction takes place and has certainly saved many a carpet.

After all the carpet and contents of your home are dry, the upholstery and carpet will be cleaned and again treated with a disinfectant product or antimicrobial. Hard furniture will be washed and polished and hard floors will be given a final cleaning. If your carpet or upholstery had a protective coating on it, this will be reapplied.

Walls will be washed as needed and your home will be returned to normal once again.

Answers to Your Sea of Worries

The Pad Will Dissolve!

Not so! Most pads are made of non-water-sensitive foam bonded with a dry solvent-soluble adhesive.

The Seams Will Separate!

Now that is logical. Wet carpet naturally means shrinkage, right? WRONG! Non-water-soluble adhesives are used on seams. Regardless of what happens, seams can be repaired.

The Carpet Shrank Off the Wall!

Only poorly installed carpet will come loose from the wall and this is easily restretched.

The Carpet Will Fall Apart!

This is not likely. During the manufacturing process carpet manufacturers actually immerse carpet in water many times during the dyeing and rinsing process. Synthetic fibers, the primary backings, and latex adhesives are virtually unaffected by water for at least 48 hours.

Sewer Backups

If your water damage is due to a sewer backup, these restoration firms are trained to deal with it. Stay out of the water and waste. Let the trained experts deal with the water and bacterial problems; that's their job and they know what can be saved and what can't.

78

Stop the Science Experiment—Mold and Mildew

Left unchecked, dampness in a home or basement can rot wood, peel paint and promote rust and mildew.

Find the Source

Here is a simple test to determine if dampness is caused by seepage or excessive humidity:

Cut several 12-inch squares of aluminum foil. Tape them in various spots on the floor and walls; seal the edges tightly. If moisture collects between the foil and the surface after several days, waterproof the interior walls. If moisture forms on the foil's surface, take the following steps:

Close windows on humid days.

Install a window exhaust fan.

Vent your clothes dryer to the outside.

Use a dehumidifier, especially during summer months.

Treat walls with epoxy-based waterproofing paint or masonry sealer. (To clean walls in preparation for paint, look for special mildew cleaners in home centers.)

Make Your Own Treatment

You can also make your own mildew treatment by mixing a quart of chlorine bleach and a tablespoon of powdered nonammoniated laundry detergent with 3 quarts of warm water. Scrub the mildew-stained surface with the solution and allow it to work until the discoloration vanishes, rinse thoroughly and allow to dry.

> Caution: **Be sure to wear goggles, rubber gloves and protective clothing when using this solution. Never allow it to come in contact with carpet or fabrics, and clean the shoes you wear before walking on carpets. Do this in a well-ventilated area.**

Resource Guide

ACETONE: A great spotter, but be careful. It is exceedingly strong and can damage fibers. Look for this at hardware stores, home centers and beauty supply stores.

ACT NATURAL® MICROFIBER CLOTHS: See Euronet USA.

ART GUM ERASER: You remember the little brownish-tan rectangular eraser that you used in school, the one that crumbled as you erased? That's the one!

AT HOME ALL-PURPOSE CLEANER®: See Soapworks®.

BAKING POWDER: If you bake, you already have this in the cupboard. If not, look in the baking section near the baking soda. Baking powder and baking soda are not the same thing, so don't even go there!

BEESWAX: Is usually found in drugstores, hardware stores and natural product stores. If you don't see it, ask!

BITTER APPLE: This keeps pets from dining on your plants, etc. It is not harmful to them, but tastes terrible so it discourages them entirely. Look for it at pet supply stores.

BIZ® ACTIVATED NON CHLORINE BLEACH: A great all-purpose powdered bleach. Look for it in the laundry aisle at grocery stores and discount stores.

BORAX: Better known as 20 Mule Team® Borax, this laundry additive can be found in the detergent aisle.

BRILLIANT BLEACH®: See Soapworks®.

BRUCE FLOOR CARE PRODUCTS: Look for these products at hardware stores, home centers and wherever wood flooring is sold.

CALGON WATER SOFTENER®: Look for it with the laundry additives at the grocery store.

CARBONA® COLOR RUN REMOVER: Removes fugitive color from fabrics. Available in grocery and discount stores.

CARBONA® STAIN DEVILS: A great series of spotters that target specific stains, like gum, blood, milk, etc.

CHAMOIS: Found in hardware stores and home centers.

CHARCOAL: This is the type made for fish tanks and is available at pet supply stores.

CLEAN SHIELD® SURFACE TREATMENT (formerly Invisible Shield®): This is such a wonderful product—just the name gives me goose bumps! It turns all of those hard-to-clean surfaces in your home (the exterior of the washing machine and dryer, shower doors, stovetops, windows, any surface that is not wood or painted) into nonstick surfaces that can be cleaned with water and a soft cloth. No more soap scum or hard-water deposits! It never builds up so it won't make surfaces slipperier, and it's nontoxic too! Call 1-800-528-3149 for a supplier near you.

CLEAR AMMONIA: There are two types of ammonia, clear and sudsy (sometimes called "cloudy"). Clear contains no soap and should be used where suggested for that reason.

COLD CREAM: Plain old Ponds that your grandma used on her face, or the store brand.

CUSTOM CLEANER®: Try this if you're looking for a do-it-yourself dry-cleaning kit to freshen and spot-clean clothes. I love it. Custom Cleaner® works on all kinds of spots and has a very pleasant, clean scent. Look for this at grocery stores and discount stores.

CUTICLE REMOVER: The gel you apply to your cuticles to soften them. Let's be clear, it is cuticle remover, NOT nail polish remover.

DENATURED ALCOHOL: This is an industrial alcohol reserved for heavy-duty cleaning. Don't use it near open flame and dispose of any rags that were used to apply it outside the home. Launder or clean anything that you treat with it as soon as possible. Look for this in cans at hardware stores and home centers. Remember the Queen's rule: always test in an inconspicuous place before treating a large area with this product.

DE-SOLV-IT CITRUS SOLUTION™: Available in home centers, hardware stores, etc., De-Solv-It Citrus Solution™ has a multitude of uses both inside and out. Great for laundry.

ENERGINE CLEANING FLUID®: A great spotter. Look for this at the hardware store, the home center and even in some grocery stores (usually on the top shelf with the laundry additives).

EPSOM SALTS: Usually used for medicinal purposes, but handy for laundry and household uses too. Look for this in the drugstore.

EURONET USA: Makers of the ACT Natural® Microfiber Cloths and mops. They clean and disinfect without chemicals using only water. They have been scientifically proven to kill germs and bacteria and even come with a warranty. They are easy to use, great for people with allergies, and can be cleaned and sanitized in the washer (this is particularly important with the mop). Use them in the kitchen, bathroom, to spot carpet, on windows, mirrors, hard furniture, in the car, virtually anywhere you clean. Call 1-888-638-2882 or visit www.euronetusa.com. They are a wonderful investment. My mop is almost two years old and is still doing the job.

FELS-NAPTHA HEAVY-DUTY LAUNDRY BAR SOAP®: What a wonderful laundry spotter and cleaner this is. You'll find it in the bar soap section of the grocery store. It's usually on the bottom shelf in a small stack and always has dust on it, because nobody knows what to use it for! Call 1-800-45PUREX.

FINE DRYWALL SANDPAPER: This sandpaper looks like window screen. Make sure you buy a package marked "fine grade."

FINE STEEL WOOL: Look for the symbol "0000" and the word "fine." And don't try soap-filled steel wool pads. They are not acceptable substitutes.

FRESH BREEZE LAUNDRY POWDER®: See Soapworks®.

GLYCERIN: Look for glycerin in drugstores in the hand cream section. Always purchase plain glycerin, not the type containing rose water.

GOJO CRÈME WATERLESS HAND CLEANER®: People with greasy hands have used this product for years. It's a hand cleaner and so much more. Look for it at home centers and hardware stores.

HYDROGEN PEROXIDE: Choose the type that you use on cuts and to gargle with—not the type used to bleach hair. That will remove color from carpet or fabric.

LEMON OR ORANGE EXTRACT: These are found in the spice area of the grocery store where vanilla extract is sold.

LINSEED OIL: You'll find this at the hardware store, usually in the paint and staining section. It is combustible, so use care in disposing of rags or paper towels used to apply it. Keep it in the garage or basement away from open flame.

MEAT TENDERIZER: Use the unseasoned variety please, or you will have a whole new stain to deal with. Store brands work fine.

NAIL POLISH REMOVER: I caution you to use nonacetone polish remover, which is much less aggressive than acetone polish remover. (Straight acetone is exceedingly strong.) Use only where recommended and with great care. Look for this product at beauty supply stores.

NATURAL SPONGE: A natural sponge is the best sponge you will ever use. It has hundreds of natural "scrubbing fingers" that make any wall-washing job speed by. Look for these at home centers and hardware stores and choose a nice size to fit your hand. Wash them in lukewarm water with gentle suds. You can put them in the washing machine if you avoid combining them with fabrics that have lint.

NATURE'S MIRACLE®: An enzyme-based odor removal product for urine-based pet accidents. Available at pet supply stores across the country.

NONGEL TOOTHPASTE: This is just a fancy name for old-fashioned plain white toothpaste. Gels just don't work, so don't even try.

ODORZOUT™: A fabulous, dry, 100 percent natural deodorizer. It's non-toxic, so you can use it any place you have a smell or a stink. It is especially effective on pet urine odors, and since it is used dry it is simple to apply. Call 1-800-88STINK, or visit their website at www.88stink.com.

OIL OF CLOVES: Widely available at health food stores, vitamin stores and natural food stores.

OUTRIGHT PET ODOR ELIMINATOR®: An enzyme odor removal product for urine-based pet accidents. Available at pet supply stores across the country.

POWDERED ALUM: This old-fashioned product was once used in pickling. Look for it at drugstores and if you can't find it, ask the pharmacist.

PREPARATION H®: Sold in drugstores. An ointment intended for hemorrhoids.

PUREX® LAUNDRY DETERGENT: Available wherever detergents are sold or call 1-800-45PUREX for a location near you.

RED ERASE®: Made by the same people who make Wine Away Red Wine Stain Remover™, Red Erase® is for red stains such as red pop, grape juice, grape jelly, etc. Look for it at Linens 'n Things, or call 1-888-WINEAWAY for a store location near you.

RETAYNE®: Used *before* you launder colored clothes for the first time, it will help retain color. Available wherever quilting supplies are sold.

ROTTENSTONE: This is mild pumice. Look for it at hardware stores and home centers.

RUST REMOVER: These are serious products, so follow the directions carefully. Look for products like Whink® and Rust Magic® at hardware stores and home centers.

SADDLE SOAP: You will find this in the hardware store, or in the shoe polish section at most any store.

SHAVING CREAM: The cheaper brands work fine, and shaving cream works better than gel.

SOAPWORKS®: Manufacturer of wonderful nontoxic, user- and earth-friendly cleaning, laundry and personal care products. Try their At Home All-Purpose Cleaner® and Fresh Breeze Laundry Power®, originally designed for allergy and asthma sufferers. Also try their Brilliant Bleach®. Believe me, it *is* brilliant! Soapworks® products are very effective, and they are economical, so everyone can use them. Call 1-800-699-9917 or visit their website at www.soapworks.com.

SOOT AND DIRT REMOVAL SPONGE: These are used to clean walls, wallpaper, lampshades and even soot. They also remove pet hair from upholstery. These big brick erasers are available at home centers and hardware stores, usually near the wallpaper supplies. Clean them by washing in a pail of warm water and liquid dish soap, rinse well and allow to dry before using again.

SPOT SHOT INSTANT CARPET STAIN REMOVER®: My all-time favorite carpet spotter and I have tried them all! Try SPOT SHOT UPHOLSTERY STAIN REMOVER® too. Available most everywhere, or call 1-800-848-4389.

SQUEEGEE: When buying a squeegee for washing windows, look for a good-quality one with a replaceable rubber blade. Always be sure that the rubber blade is soft and flexible for best results. Look for these at hardware stores, home centers and janitorial supply companies. They come in different widths, so be sure to think about the size windows, etc., that you are going to use it for. A 12-inch blade is a good starting point.

SYNTHRAPOL®: Great for removing fugitive color. Available wherever quilting supplies are sold.

TACK-TRAP®: Bugs are drawn to the color of this sticky sheet. Sold in garden supply stores and some hardware stores.

TANG™ BREAKFAST DRINK: Yes, this is the product that the astronauts took to the moon! It is also a great cleaner. (Store brands work just as well.)

TRISODIUM PHOSPHATE (TSP): Cleaning professionals have used this product for years. It is wonderful for washing walls and garage floors and for any tough cleaning job. Look for it at hardware stores, home centers and janitorial supply stores. Wear rubber gloves when using it.

TYPEWRITER ERASER: A thing of the past, but still available at office supply stores. Shaped like a pencil with a little brush where the pencil eraser would be, they can be sharpened like a pencil and will last for years.

UN-DU™: Removes sticky residue from fabric and hard surfaces. Look for it at office supply stores, home centers and hardware stores.

WASHING SODA: I like Arm and Hammer® Washing Soda, which can be found in the detergent aisle at the grocery store along with other laundry additives. No, you cannot substitute baking soda, it is a different product!

WAX CRAYONS: These are sold in hardware stores and home centers and come in various wood colors for concealing scratches in wood surfaces. Don't be fooled by the color name; try to take along a sample of what you need to patch to get the best possible match.

WD-40® LUBRICANT: I bet you will find a can in your garage or basement. Fine spray oil for lubricating all kinds of things, it's a wonderful product for regenerating grease so that it can be removed from clothes. Look for WD-40® at the hardware store, home center and even the grocery store.

WHITING: Look for this at the hardware store, usually near the paint.

WIEMAN'S WAX AWAY™: Removes candle wax from fabrics and hard surfaces. Look for it at grocery and discount stores.

WINDOW SCRUBBER: This looks like a squeegee wearing a coat. Look for it at janitorial supply stores and home centers.

WINE AWAY RED WINE STAIN REMOVER®: This unbelievable product can remove red stains, such as red wine, red pop, cranberry juice, red food coloring, grape juice, etc., from carpet and fabric. It is totally nontoxic and made from fruit and vegetable extracts. I just can't believe how well it works! Look for it where liquor is sold or call 1-888-WINEAWAY for a store location near you.

WINTERGREEN OIL: Widely available at health food stores, natural food stores and some linen stores.

WITCH HAZEL: An astringent toning product sold at drugstores.

ZOUT® STAIN REMOVER: A very versatile laundry prespotter, Zout® is thicker than most laundry spotters, so you can target the spot. It really works! Look for it in grocery stores and places like Kmart, etc.

ZUD HEAVY DUTY CLEANSER®: This is a wonderful cleanser for really tough jobs. It works great on rust on hard surfaces too. Find it at hardware stores, home centers and grocery stores. Well worth keeping on hand.

Index

A

Q

R

T

Y

Z

Your Personal Tips and Hints

The humble (but clean!) beginnings of a Queen.

ABOUT THE QUEEN

LINDA COBB first shared her cleaning tips with readers in a weekly newspaper column in Michigan, where she owned a cleaning and disaster-restoration business dealing with the aftermath of fires and floods. After moving to Phoenix, she appeared weekly as a guest on *Good Morning Arizona;* since then she has shared her housekeeping tips on radio and television shows across the country, and in three *New York Times* bestsellers, *Talking Dirty with the Queen of Clean*®, *Talking Dirty Laundry with the Queen of Clean*®, and *A Queen for All Seasons.* Linda Cobb lives in Phoenix with her husband. Visit her popular Web site: *www.queenofclean.com.*